Fighting Invisibility

Fighting Invisibility

Asian Americans in the Midwest

MONICA MONG TRIEU

Rutgers University Press
New Brunswick, Camden, and Newark, New Jersey
London and Oxford, UK

Rutgers University Press is a department of Rutgers, The State University of New Jersey, one of the leading public research universities in the nation. By publishing worldwide, it furthers the University's mission of dedication to excellence in teaching, scholarship, research, and clinical care.

Library of Congress Cataloging-in-Publication Data
Names: Trieu, Monica M., 1978- author.
Title: Fighting invisibility: Asian Americans in the Midwest / Monica Mong Trieu.
Description: New Brunswick: Rutgers University Press, [2023] | Includes bibliographical
    references and index.
Identifiers: LCCN 2022018549 | ISBN 9781978834286 (paperback) | ISBN 9781978834293
    (hardback) | ISBN 9781978834309 (epub) | ISBN 9781978834316 (pdf)
Subjects: LCSH: Asian Americans—Race identity—Middle West. | Asian Americans—Middle
    West—Social conditions—20th century. | Asian Americans—Middle West—Social conditions—
    21st century. | Middle West—Race relations. | Group identity—Middle West.
Classification: LCC F358.2.A75 T75 2023 | DDC 305.895/073077—dc23/eng/20220427
LC record available at https://lccn.loc.gov/2022018549

A British Cataloging-in-Publication record for this book is available from the British Library.

References to internet websites (URLs) were accurate at the time of writing. Neither the author nor Rutgers University Press is responsible for URLs that may have expired or changed since the manuscript was prepared.

♾ The paper used in this publication meets the requirements of the American National Standard for Information Sciences—Permanence of Paper for Printed Library Materials, ANSI Z39.48-1992.

rutgersuniversitypress.org

For my study participants, with deepest gratitude

Contents

Illustrations

Figures

Tables

Fighting Invisibility

Introduction

Asian America in
America's Heartland

Chung was ten months old when he took a long plane ride from Taiwan to the United States in 1972 with his mother and older brother.[1] In the United States, they were reunited with Chung's father, who had arrived the year before to complete his medical residency in the Midwestern state of Michigan.[2] The family subsequently moved to a suburb of Chicago, where Chung spent most of his youth and teenage years. In describing what it was like to come of age in the Midwest in the 1970s and 1980s, Chung stated: "In retrospect, looking back, . . . as a Taiwanese and an Asian American kid, it was very isolating and critical to how I see, today, Asian American identity and the importance of community building. So, if I had to put it simply, I would say it pretty much sucked growing up in the primarily White suburban area of Chicago."[3] When asked why, he said:

> Just because, I think, the fact that at that time when I was in grade school, I would be the one of the two Asian kids, maybe, in my class, and that felt like that was the way it was for most of my grade-school years. . . . So, if someone ever pointed out your ethnicity, or the fact that you are different, then you really felt like, wow, I'm actually really—I feel really different, I have no one to ally with. And you kind of have to just deal with it, or just kind of brush it off basically. It was definitely character-forming.

Chung's response underscores the overwhelming sense of isolation that emerged from being "different" and not having an "ally" while growing up in a "primarily White" spatial context and having limited interactions with other Asians outside of his family. In this space, he had to "just deal" with his racialized visibility, which he defined as "definitely character-forming."

Experiencing isolation and invisibility along racial lines in America's heartland is not a new phenomenon for Asian Americans. The historian William Wei emphasizes this point in his assessment of the dynamics among regional Asian American activists during the 1960s and 1970s: "While East Coast Asian American activists felt misunderstood by those on the West Coast, the ones in the Midwest felt ignored by both. As the Rice Paper Collective (a progressive Asian American student organization at the University of Wisconsin–Madison) put it, 'Our invisibility is so total that Asian Americans are not thought to exist in this 'vast banana wasteland.'"[4] Wei's use of a 1974 statement about the "vast banana wasteland" by the Rice Paper Collective highlights Midwestern Asian Americans' long-standing feeling of being ignored and rendered invisible despite being visibly racialized. The visually, and arguably pejorative, racialized descriptive label "banana" (suggesting that they are "yellow," or Asian, on the outside and White on the inside) suggests that Midwestern Asian Americans are perceived as being fully acculturated into White American culture and living away from their communities and Asian co-ethnics.[5] Also evident in the statement is that Midwestern Asian Americans view their experiences as different from those of their non-Midwestern counterparts.

This last point is further substantiated by Chung, in his description of walking among West Coast Asian Americans for the first time and how, ironically, that felt like a foreign experience. His visit to California made him feel different in a way that was "hard to describe":

> My only impression of what "Asian American" was like on the West Coast was really through a couple of early Asian American magazines. . . . They would sometimes do articles about the rising tide of Asians in Orange County or the new Little Taipei, or the Little Saigon areas and such. So, I'd read about that. That was my only impression of [how] those . . . communities were forming. But I knew there were many Asian Americans out there. So when I actually got out there [to California] to take Asian American studies courses, it was actually a little of a shock walking around [the University of California, Los Angeles] campus. So, walking through campus, suddenly, wow, there was a lot of folks who look like me, but they act very much not like me. You know what I mean? They are very—if there was any term of "Americanism," that was it. There was no sense that as you are walking by, you are a stranger that people look at. There, it was just a norm to be Asian. So that was a definite contrast, I guess. This is so hard to describe. I didn't feel like I belonged there either because always my experience has been: I should be the minority. But suddenly,

I was walking around in a minority-majority. Does that make sense? Suddenly you feel different for another reason. You feel like, oh, I feel like I am comfortable because there are many Asians, but yet I don't feel comfortable because it is not what I am used to.

Chung's statement highlights the salience of spatial context in his racial self-identity and his sense of belonging within that space. On the West Coast, an unfamiliar geographical location, he felt discomfort in the visually familiar, but culturally different, Asian faces he encountered.

I open with Chung's story because it features the central themes and questions explored in this book on the intersection of race, space, differential racialization, and Asian American identity. What are the experiences of children of the post-1950s Asian immigrants and refugees who come of age within the Midwest spatial context? What are their stories, and how do those stories contribute to the national discourse on race and Asian America? What is the role of spatial dimensions in the (differential) racialization of Midwestern Asian America? I argue that the role of the space must be considered if we are to more fully understand the racialization of Asian Americans.

While Chung's experience is singular, it highlights a gap in the literature on the experiences of children of post-1950s Asian immigrants. Over the past three decades, many studies have examined the adaptation of children of post-1960s Asian immigrants and refugees. However, most existing empirical scholarship on immigration has primarily documented the experiences of those living in larger U.S. cities.[6] This glaring omission has been acknowledged in the field of Asian American studies. In 2009, the *Journal of Asian American Studies* published a special issue on the Midwest, which specifically addressed the invisibility of Asian Americans living in the so-called heartland and calling for more research on their experiences.[7] The contributing scholars noted that while previous research had shied away from the region as a site of study because of its relatively small Asian population, the recognition of Asian Americans' experiences in such areas can reveal a lot about contemporary processes of adaptation, racialized experiences, and outcomes.[8]

Aside from these writings on Midwestern Asian and Asian American experiences—as well as a discrete number of in-depth historical accounts of Asian communities in the Midwest in the second half of the nineteenth and the early twentieth centuries[9] and numerous memoirs about growing up as Midwestern Asian Americans[10]—there have been few studies about Asian American lives in "new destination" cities or areas with relatively smaller concentrations of Asian co-ethnics.[11] Many of the existing studies primarily focused on specific subgroups of Asians. For example, Stacey Lee's seminal ethnographic study of Hmong American youths in Wisconsin provided one of the first in-depth examinations of the central role of whiteness on Midwestern Asian American identity and experience in the educational context.[12] One of the central find-ings of Lee's study is that Hmong Americans are largely invisible to White America because they are not perceived as good students or as meeting White, middle-class cultural norms. In another example, Nancy Abelmann investi-gated the impact of race and segregation on Korean American college stu-dents in Illinois. Her examination provides an in-depth look into Midwestern Korean Americans in various contexts, including their families and religious groups and the colleges they attended.[13] Finally, Kim Park Nelson examined transracial Korean adoptees from Minnesota, the Pacific Northwest, and South Korea. Although her study informants were not limited to the Midwest, she offered findings specific to Korean adoptees from Minnesota. From her work on this subgroup, she identified themes that are also central to the findings in this book: themes of "racial and social isolation," hypervisibility, and invisibil-ity.[14] In addressing the paradox of being both invisible and hypervisible, Nel-son argues that it is only through understanding these two "linked" forms of racism "as two sides of a single oppressive ideology that it becomes possible to see that neither is necessarily a good choice."[15] How can we understand this paradox in the lives of other Asian Americans, especially when considered alongside the role of space and differential racialization?

Fighting Invisibility was written as a direct response to the call for more empirical research on Asian Americans living in the Midwest. It is an inter-disciplinary project that puts race, space, racialization, and the post-1950s Midwestern Asian American community at the center of its analysis. Merging theoretical discussion from the disciplines of Asian American studies, the soci-ology of race and migration, American studies, ethnic studies, and Midwest-ern studies, this book expands on previous scholarship on race and space,[16] differential racialization in Asian American lives[17] and racial positionality within the U.S. racial paradigm,[18] and Asian American history. Specifically, I chronicle how 1.5- and second-generation Midwestern Asian Americans navi-gate issues of identity, belonging, racism, and discrimination in various settings (such as their families, schools, and co-ethnic communities) to create a pan-ethnic cultural community as racialized subjects within racialized spaces.

Adding a spatial dimension to the racialization lens acknowledges that Asians in the Midwest are subject to a distinct type of racialization, one charac-terized by examples such as Anna, a twenty-six-year-old study participant who was born in South Korea and adopted by a White family in Minnesota when she was four months old. About growing up in the Midwest, she said: "I identify . . . growing up here [in Minnesota] as being a part of the American, particularly Midwest, culture. I like hot dish[es] and I bring Jell-O salads to places. All of that is part of who I am. So when people use 'White' and 'American' interchangeably, I feel invalidated."

Anna's strong identity as a Midwesterner is contested and "invalidated" by other Midwesterners who use the terms "White" and "American" interchangeably. This use—which embraces whiteness as the dominant and normative narrative—works to erase Anna's identity and physical presence as a Midwestern Asian American. Moreover, it reveals the instrumental role of exclusion in the process of defining who is part of America's heartland.

In considering these distinct experiences, I build on previous scholarship to argue that to fully understand the nuances of the racialization of Asian America, we must use the theoretical lens of differential racialization, with an emphasis on space,[19] to examine other pockets of underexplored Asian America. One such Asian American population resides in the Midwest. In applying this spatial and relational lens to race relations, I demonstrate how Midwestern Asian Americans are subjected to racialization in ways that are both similar to and different from the ways it is applied to Asian Americans outside the Midwest. In other words, Midwestern Asian Americans are racialized similarly to their non-Midwest counterparts because they are also subjected to the national racial framing of Asian Americans (e.g., the stereotypes of the model minority and the perpetual foreigner) and consequent forms of individual and structural anti-Asian racism.[20] As a result, Asian Americans who grew up in rural spaces, irrespective of region, have similar experiences. However, Midwestern Asian Americans also must contend with what it means to be Asian as defined by non-Asian Midwesterners within their Midwestern spaces. These individual-level interactions impact Midwestern Asian Americans' perceptions of identity and belonging not only within U.S. history, but also within Asian American history. Thus, applying the lens of differential racialization, with an emphasis on space, provides a more nuanced portrait of how Asian America is racialized.

In shifting the primary focus to Midwestern Asian American narratives, one of the central goals of this book is to confront the issue of who is centered and privileged in both U.S. and Asian American history. I build upon the critical, but limited, contributions of previous studies on the Midwest by theorizing, more broadly, the missing Midwestern Asian American presence within national panethnic Asian American race discourse. I confront the questions of representation by asking who has historically represented Asian America, and who gets to represent Asian America? While there have been representations of Asian Americans in the Midwest, the emphasis has been on specific Asian ethnic groups. The experiences of Midwestern Asian Americans highlight the necessity to expand the scope of Asian American history telling and knowledge production.

In the pages that follow, I demonstrate how three recurring themes—spatially defined isolation, invisibility, and racialized visibility—reflect the differential racialization of Midwestern Asian Americans, as well as how these themes produce outcomes both external (e.g., institutional barriers) and internal (e.g., internalized racism). However, the story does not end there. In the face of all these challenges, I find strong evidence of negotiation of and resistance to invisibility and erasure within America's heartland. These actions include forming connections with co-ethnics, educating themselves about their panethnic history, and creating cultural productions to sustain collective Asian American memory. The experiences of Midwestern Asian Americans reflect both the multiplicity of common patterns in their collective Midwestern voice and the distinctions among the complex Asian American lives scattered throughout the Midwest. Asian American racial positionality in America's heartland reveals how race and racialization are subject to potential variability and negotiation within the existing spatially influenced racial system.

The Midwest: Whose Racialized Space and Place?

Who represents the Midwest, also known as America's heartland? Where do Midwestern Asian Americans fit in the dominant framing of who is perceived to represent the Midwest? To answer the question of representation, it is important first to examine how the heartland is depicted within the national narrative. John Mellencamp, one of the Midwest's most famous White musicians (he hails from Seymour, Indiana), built his career singing about small-town America. He is a prominent figure associated with the heartland rock genre, and his songs (e.g., "Jack and Diane," "Small Town," and "The Great Midwest") frequently draw on his own Midwestern experience to evoke a sense of nostalgia for growing up in small-town middle America.

In "The Great Midwest," Mellencamp's description of the heartland includes references to church, cornfields, time warps, and the conjuring up of bygone years.[21] These themes mirror Kristin Hoganson's account of recurring depictions associated with the heartland: "References to the heartland tend to depict it as buffered and all-American: white, rural, and rooted, full of aging churchgoers, conservative voters, corn, and pigs. . . . This pastoral heartland is a place of nostalgic yearnings. . . . Flyover jokes deride it as a provincial wasteland. Out of touch, out of date, out of style—the heartland is the place that makes isolationism seem possible, the place where people think it desirable. It is the mythic past that white ethnonationalists wish to return to, the place that animates their calls to the barricades."[22]

While Whites remain implicitly dominant in Mellencamp's rendering of America's heartland, Hoganson's account explicitly highlights the prevailing depiction of this space as one that embodies White conservatism and xenophobia. The reaching for a "mythic past"—which likely harks back to days of blatant institutional White supremacy and de jure segregation—clashes with the changing demographics of the present-day United States. Consequently, as

Hoganson notes, this has given rise to a mobilized, xenophobic, White-supremacist agenda of building social and physical barricades.

A similar reference to the Midwest's barren physical, social, and racial terrain can be found in a 2017 article in the *New York Times* about "America's Heartland."[23] The authors quote the historian William Cronon, who claims that America's heartland is "much more a state of mind than an actual place[.] It describes a deep set of beliefs about places that somehow authentically stand for America." Cronon further complicates notions of authenticity by asking, "Who's authentically from the middle? Who's from implicitly the heart? Who represents the core? There's a slippage here." Later in the article, the historian Toby Higbie responds to these questions in racial terms, positioning the "slippages" in defining who represents the Midwest in terms of the national imaginary. He claims that "stock images of heartland America tend to turn up few faces of color, whether on the farm or in nostalgic manufacturing. When people use the term . . . they're often envisioning a white version of the Midwest without its most diverse pockets, circumscribing Detroit, Chicago and St. Louis, and its Native American reservations."

Notably, both Hoganson's and Higbie's statements reveal the instrumental role of exclusion in the process of defining America's heartland. Their descriptions of the Midwest provide an insight into who is left out of "authentic" representations of the Midwest: nonwhites. Again, the Midwest is popularly imagined as a conservative, White, rural space that reflects the nostalgic values of yesteryear. If Whites within this vast space of flatlands are perceived as the only ones who "authentically stand for America," where does that leave those who are missing from the dominant national representations of America's heartland?

These dominant representations omit the vast histories of Midwestern communities of color and their extensive contributions to the region's social, political, and economic history. A small glimpse of these broadly overlooked histories include the diverse Indigenous communities whose members lived in the region centuries before the arrival of White European colonial settlers in the sixteenth century;[24] the African American people who, via the Great Migration, became a large part of the labor force in the urban Midwest;[25] and the Mexican nationals who arrived in the nineteenth century as students, merchants, guides, and laborers.[26] Also largely missing from this retelling is the long transnational history of Asians in the Midwest that began in the mid-nineteenth century with hundreds of them migrating to urban Midwestern regions in search of economic opportunities or, to a lesser extent, as students. Some of these early migration narratives include those about Chinese miners, merchants, and factory workers in St. Louis and Chicago in the mid-1800s;[27] Filipinx students in early twentieth-century Chicago who arrived as students under the 1903 Pensionado Act and stayed for work (e.g., as train porters);[28] and Japanese Americans who moved from the West Coast to the Midwest—mainly because of employment opportunities—during and after their incarceration in World War II.[29] Some more contemporary narratives include 1950s Korean adoptees in Minnesota;[30] South and East Asian university students all over the United States (including the Midwest), who were influenced by the National Defense Education Act of 1958;[31] and Southeast Asian refugees, especially Hmong refugees in Minnesota and Wisconsin, in the 1970s.[32]

The Midwest has also played a pivotal role in the history of Asian American activism. Rich histories of Asian American community organizing and social movements can be found in the flatlands. Some examples include student activism during the 1960s and 1970s at numerous Midwestern college campuses,[33] the 1980s social movements for racial justice following the murder of Vincent Chin,[34] and the life and work of the activist Grace Lee Boggs, which spanned seven decades.[35] In short, critical Asian American movements and people have existed in the Midwest. The dominant representation of the Midwest that associates its people and history with whiteness erases the voices and stories of communities of color that have thrived in the region.

Fighting Invisibility documents these Midwestern Asian American narratives for their survival in both the national and Asian American panethnic collective memories. The stories need to be told. Otherwise, Midwestern Asian American lives will be silenced and made invisible. Cathy Park Hong, in her brilliant but somber rendering of the horrific rape and murder of Theresa Hak Kyung Cha, a Korean American novelist and artist, argues that one of the most detrimental consequences of "silence" is erasure, manifested through forms of "forgetting": "The problem with silence is that it can't speak up and say why it's silent. And so silence collects, becomes amplified, takes on a life outside our intentions, in that silence can get misread as indifference, or avoidance, or even shame, and eventually this silence passes over into forgetting."[36]

This book pushes back against the silencing that too often surrounds the history of marginalized communities in the United States. Michelle Caswell uses the term "symbolic annihilation" to capture the way members of marginalized communities feel about how they are misrepresented and/or made invisible in the existing archival collection process and, indeed, in archives.[37] This book fights against the symbolic annihilation of an extensive and nuanced history of individuals of Asian ancestry in the United States.

On Race: Asian American Racial Positioning and Differential Racialization

The racialization of individuals of Asian ancestry in the United States is situated in a long history of their social and legislative exclusion. The broad history of their racialization as the perpetual foreigner and model minority has been well documented in academic literature and print media.[38] The first label can be traced back to the mid-1800s, when large numbers of Chinese laborers entered the United States to work in mining and agriculture and on the railroad.[39] This categorization of Asian Americans included many negative stereotypes, including seeing the Chinese immigrants as the so-called yellow peril—posing political and economic threats to the United States.[40] The notion of the perpetual foreigner was later broadly applied to other Asians.[41]

In contrast, the model minority is a more contemporary term that aims to valorize all Asian Americans for achieving success through cultural means.[42] The term was first used as a Cold War strategy to support the image of the United States as a democratic nation, and it was later used as a divisive racial tool during the social and political unrest of the 1960s.[43] This valorizing label is damaging because it hides the socioeconomic diversity among Asian Americans[44] while also fueling divisive racial politics among racial minorities.[45]

The historical legacy of racialization remains stubbornly persistent and plays a major role in shaping racial discourses in the United States and transnationally.[46] In particular, the framing of racial discourses about Asian Americans has led to various social and institutional forms of anti-Asian racism, including exclusionary laws and other legal barriers to land ownership,[47] limited access to and mobility in the labor market, limited access to education, and the use of denigrating and gendered portrayals in visual culture.[48] Evidence of the continuation of anti-Asian violence is exemplified by the proliferation of anti-Asian hate crimes during the COVID-19 pandemic.[49]

An example of problematic racialized portrayals in visual culture can be seen in *Drop Dead Gorgeous*, a 1999 Hollywood dark comedy. The film is set in the Midwest (specifically, in the fictional town of Mount Rose, Minnesota) and centers on a beauty pageant gone awry. Made as a mockumentary, the film exaggeratedly embraces the traditional Midwestern themes of church, cornfields, and heartland nostalgia throughout. It includes a subplot that centers on a Japanese couple, the Howards, and their two teenage daughters—one of whom (Molly) is adopted and White. The audience is left to assume that the family anglicized their last name to Howard in an effort to acculturate. The plot of an Asian family adopting a White child is a parody and a nod to the existing inverse reality in Minnesota. In fact, a large number of White Minnesota families adopted Korean children in the aftermath of the Korean War.[50] Interestingly, the family in the film is a Japanese, not a Korean, family. Whether this change is intentional or not, the message is clear: all Asians are interchangeable in the Midwest and, by extension, in the United States.

The audience is introduced to the family in a scene in which Mr. and Mrs. Howard sit on the couch with Molly. Mr. Howard, who has a heavy Japanese accent, begins by explaining why they adopted Molly: "So we adopt

Molly three year ago, when we come to America, to help acclimate us to American." Molly quickly corrects him by noting, "To America, Dad." Mrs. Howard then adds, "She all-American girl. She our American Teen Princess girl." At this point, their biological daughter, Seiko, enters the frame behind them and speaks in Japanese: "Excuse me, Father, Mother, when are we moving back to Tokyo? I can't stand this place anymore. They put butter on everything." Mr. Howard immediately reprimands her, angrily shouting, "English! English, you stupid little [ableist slur]. We America now, Tina!" In response, Seiko corrects her dad by telling him that her name is not "Tina." In a later scene that reflects the high-achieving model minority trope, Seiko lists her impressive musical and educational accomplishments for her parents. Her dad responds by shutting her down through verbally abusive language.

There is a lot to unpack from these scenes and the representation of this Asian family in the Midwest. Some of the themes include the racialization of Asian Americans as both foreign and model minorities, the dynamics of intergenerational Asian family relationships, the role of transracial adoption in the Midwest, and the presence of ableism. One of the more glaring themes is the portrayal of the foreign Asian parents as strongly desiring whiteness and acceptance in the predominantly White American society. This is exemplified through their adoption and subsequent veneration of their White child (representative of the United States), coupled with the constant denigration of their Japanese child (representative of Japan or Asia). What does it mean for a parody of the Midwest to include such a representation of an Asian family? Is this a reflection of how Asians are viewed (when they are seen at all) by most Whites in the Midwest and, more broadly, in the United States?

Relevant to this discussion is the understanding of Asian American racial positionality in the United States. While Asian Americans are racialized as perpetual foreigners, however, the category of Asian American includes an extensive number of generations: the first documented settlement of Asian Americans in the United States dates back to the 1840s, in Louisiana.[51] In the U.S. race-relations narrative, Asian Americans, along with other racial minorities, historically have been wedged either in the middle of the Black-White binary or placed on its periphery. Asian American experiences are consistently studied and dissected for their relative proximity to whiteness.[52] Richard Delgado argues that operating under a strictly Black-White racial binary sets up a "trap of exceptionalism," which results in groups' becoming self-interested in their narrow focus on excelling and seeking whiteness and/or White approval.[53] He writes: "Narrow binary thinking—regardless of the group that engages in it—weakens solidarity, reduces opportunities for coalition, deprives one group of the benefits of the others' experiences, makes one overly dependent on the approval of the white establishment, and sets one up for ultimate disappointment."[54]

In a foundational article on Asian American racial positioning, Claire Jean Kim argues that a more relational approach is needed for the U.S. race discourse to move "beyond Black and white."[55] Kim contends that the two existing approaches are limiting. According to her, the "different trajectory approach" argues that racialization has occurred differently for different racial groups but does not account for overlapping experiences.[56] By comparison, the "racial hierarchy approach" organizes racial groups on a "single scale of status and privilege" and does not account for other ways of measuring status. Instead, Kim proposes examining racial dynamics as existing within a "field of racial positions." This approach accounts for any number of measurable definitional axes while also acknowledging that the racialization process is relational. Kim posits that there are at least two different axes worth acknowledging in the field of racial positions: the superior-inferior and the insider-foreigner axes. The underlying objective of this alternative approach to understanding racial dynamics is to promote the idea that racial groups are subject to "differential racialization."[57]

Differential racialization is based on the premise that different racial and ethnic groups have distinct experiences with racialization and racism. For example, Kim contends that the positions of Asian Americans have been "racially triangulated" in relation to those of Blacks and Whites.[58] In particular, Asian Americans are subjected to both "relative valorization" (e.g., as model minorities) and "civic ostracism" (e.g., as foreigners) relative to other racial groups. In other words, Asian Americans are relatively valorized as superior to Black Americans but inferior to White ones. At the same time, they are civically ostracized as foreign relative to both White and Black Americans.

In her work on interracial coalitions of third-world radical activists in Los Angeles in the 1960s and 1970s, Laura Pulido expands on differential racialization by highlighting the important role of spatial dimension—specifically, regions. She writes: "I emphasize regions because although all of the United States is informed by a national racial narrative, class structure and racial divisions of labor take shape and racial hierarchies are experienced at the regional and local levels. Because the United States is so large and diverse, it is primarily at the regional level that nuanced and meaningful comparison must take place."[59] Racial minorities are not only subject to a racialization process at the national level, which is promoted and sustained by racial projects. They also are subjected to differential forms of racialization within different regions, which has structural consequences such as impacts on local labor markets and economies.

On Space: Midwest Asian Americans as Racialized Interstitial Subjects

Central to the scope of my research are the roles of race and space. It is important to highlight the fact that space plays an active role in influencing and reflecting existing unequal power relations, including those of race.[60] In this book, space is conceptualized in two ways: as a physical geographical location and as a symbolic spatial metaphor. In conceptualizing space, scholars have argued that spaces are much more than geographical locations. According to Dorsey Massey, spaces are not neutral since they include social relations, which are "inherently dynamic."[61] Consequently, spaces reflect the "ever-shifting social geometry of power and signification."[62]

Similarly, George Lipsitz defines a "social space" as a "dynamic place" deeply embedded within history and thus subject to change.[63] He has long argued for disassembling "the fatal links that connect race, place, and power" by acknowledging both the spatialized dimension of race and the racialized dimension of space.[64] He contends that "the racial projects of American society have always been spatial projects as well."[65] Adding to this characterization of the dynamism of space, Brooke Neely and Michelle Samura argue that it is important to examine the connections between race and space because our racial identities reflect and alter the spaces we occupy, and vice versa: "Racial interactions and processes (e.g., identities, inequalities, conflicts and so on) are also about how we collectively make and remake, over time and through ongoing contestation, the spaces we inhabit. In turn, the making and remaking of space is also about the making and remaking of race."[66] Hence, to fully comprehend the history of communities of color in the United States requires an understanding of the role of space in this history. This is because spaces—physical geographical locations—are not ideologically blank and impartial places. History, power, and consequences are embedded within spaces. The spaces where people live matter because their exposures to the interactions of race and space have social, political, and material consequences.

The second conceptualization of space, as a symbolic spatial metaphor, serves as a lens to understand Asian American racial positioning as existing in the interstitial realm, or occupying the intervening liminal space.[67] This metaphor allows us to delve into and ultimately move beyond the discussion of Asian Americans as perpetually wedged between the dominant Black and White Midwestern or U.S. racial discourse. In his writings on culture, Homi Bhabha introduced the notion of people who exist in the world of the "beyond" or in "the interstices."[68] He defines this area as a "liminal," "in-between" space in which the concepts of nation, community, and culture are negotiated.[69] According to Bhabha, it "provide[s] the terrain for elaborating strategies of selfhood—singular or communal—that initiate new signs of identity, and innovative sites of collaboration, and contestation, in the act of defining the idea of society itself."[70] Hence, people occupying this area have the ability (indeed, the great potential) to intervene in the "here and now" via practices of "cultural hybridity," or the creation of new cultural forms.[71]

Elaine Kim has described Asian Americans as people "seeking a third space as 'both/and' instead of 'either/or.'"[72] In her work on Asian American visual arts, she uses this theoretical lens to argue that Asian American artists occupy a space at the convergence of multiple identities (ethnic, racial, and national) and thus are positioned as interstitial subjects.[73] In this space, Asian Americans have created art that has served as "a site for new cultural conversations."[74] Thus, viewing Asian Americans through the analytical lens of racial interstices makes it possible to move beyond seeing them as simply wedged between Blacks and Whites. Instead, Asian Americans can be viewed as people occupying spaces where human agency thrives and change is possible.

Leslie Bow's research further contributes to this body of work by applying "racial interstitiality" as a "conceptual lens" to understand how Asians in the U.S. Deep South are defined as "the third race"—that is, subjects who "are made within the space between abjection and normative invisibility" in numerous realms of social life.[75] In arguing for the theoretical significance of examining interstitial areas, Bow writes: "To focus on the interstitial is to focus on the space between normative structures of power—but also . . . its incompletion and irresolution. That is, what anomaly reveals is not merely a more nuanced account of racialization, but the counter-narratives that interrupt the work of the dominant, the partial stories that characterize the unevenly oppressed."[76]

Bow contends that it is critical to study interstitial sites (and the people who occupy them) to understand how White supremacy is upheld, negotiated, and contested. Furthermore, her description of Asian Americans as the "unevenly oppressed" aptly designates their racial positionality. It serves as a useful lens to increase our understanding of the differential racialization of Asian Americans. On the one hand, it acknowledges the fact that there are moments when Asian Americans benefit from the White-supremacist system because of their "proximity to whiteness" status, and some engage in work that furthers White supremacy.[77] On the other hand, it also acknowledges that Asian Americans are subjected to social and political denigration, regulation, and oppression.[78]

Bow's argument about Asian American racial positioning in the Deep South is also applicable to Asian American experiences in the Midwest. In work on Japanese Americans, Charlotte Brooks refers to Eugene Uyeki's research on the nisei generation in 1950s Chicago to point out that Japanese Americans viewed themselves as situated in between Blacks and Whites.[79] Quoting from Uyeki's work, Brooks writes: "As one [Japanese American] resettler noted, the Chicago [Japanese American] resettlers occupied 'a position in the twilight zone between the blacks and the whites.' When it came to Chicago race relations, another Nisei said, 'we are placed sort of in-between.'"[80]

In this book, I argue that we need to understand and engage with the role of differential racialization and space to move beyond the Black-White paradigm. This work is necessary if we are to understand how the White-supremacist social structure continues to function and sustain itself. Delving into Asian American lives across different spatial contexts enables us to further examine the role and power of racialization. Furthermore, doing this work requires not only exploring the "counter-narratives that interrupt the work of the dominant," as Bow writes:[81] it also requires examining narratives among the Asian American community that similarly advance a White-supremacist agenda. Only when we have done this work can we begin to understand how to dismantle White supremacy as a structure. It is important to interrogate the interplay between racial and spatial dimensions because doing so highlights the dynamism of both and, ultimately, the potential for change. Indeed, one of the central motivations for this research on Midwestern Asian Americans is the potential for change—that is, the potential for the eradication of the racialized space and spatialized race terrains that currently uphold White supremacy (which are deeply ingrained in historical memory and institutions) and to move toward more inclusive and equitable spaces and social processes.

Methods

Data for this book are drawn from multiple sources, including the U.S. Census Bureau data sets, interviews, and material culture productions. The two data sets include: (1) a merged 2008–2018 Integrated Public Use Microdata Sample-Current Population Survey (IPUMS-CPS)[82] and (2) 2019 American Community Survey (ACS). [83] These two different data sets are used to illustrate existing demographic patterns among Asian Americans in the Midwest and nationally. The sample was selected for this project because it is a national data set that makes it possible to calculate generational differences (e.g., between native- and foreign-born people), thus providing invaluable descriptive generational information on the population.

Additionally, to understand the lives behind the numbers, from 2011 to 2012 I conducted fifty-two in-depth interviews with 1.5- and second-generation Asian Americans who grew up in the Midwest.[84] I define members of the 1.5 generation as people who entered the United States before the age of twelve. This definition is loosely based on Rubén G. Rumbaut's definition of the generation as those who entered between the ages of five and twelve.[85] I define members of the second generation as those who were born in the United States of foreign-born parents. Asian Americans constitute an extremely heterogeneous category that includes everyone from the "Far East, Southeast Asia, or the Indian subcontinent" living in the United States.[86] My participants came from ten different Asian ethnicities and from various racial backgrounds, including Cambodian, Chinese, Filipino, Hmong, Japanese, Korean, Laotian, South Asian, Taiwanese, Vietnamese, and various mixed-race backgrounds. They grew up in the following Midwest states: Ohio (eighteen), Illinois (fifteen), Minnesota (nine), Wisconsin (three), Indiana (two), Iowa (two), Michigan (two), and Nebraska (one). At the time of the interviews, the participants were all adults who had earned either an associate's degree, were currently enrolled in college, or had earned at least a bachelor's degree.

I interviewed thirty-three females and nineteen males, with an average age of twenty-five. The participants were initially recruited based on convenience sampling. This began via word-of-mouth and through email advertising sent to individuals, student clubs, and organizations in the Ohio and Indiana areas. The research advertisement flier was circulated via social media networks such as Facebook and Tumblr. I received email replies from potential participants from all over the Midwest. After the initial convenience sampling, I used snowball sampling. I began recruiting participants from the overall group who would constitute an ideal sample in terms of equal representation across all Asian ethnic groups, immigration statuses and histories, genders, and other markers of differences. However, my final sample represents individuals who were generous enough to respond to my flier, donate their time, and trust me with their personal stories. As a result, the study sample does not represent the full diversity of Asian America. For example, in some instances, only one individual represents an entire category (e.g., transracial Korean adoptee). While I could have simply dropped these participants from the study, I chose not to because I strongly believe that their stories are equally important regardless of the sample size for their individual subgroup. Their stories also have equal importance as a part of Midwestern Asian American history.

All interviews (conducted using an interview instrument) were audio-recorded, transcribed, and analyzed using Dedoose, qualitative web-based software. I omitted personal identifiers and assigned all participants a pseudonym to maintain their anonymity. Interviews were conducted by one of three methods: face to face, Skype video chat, or telephone. The interviews were 1.5–3.0 hours long. The interview instrument covered nine broad topics: immigration background, family and culture, neighborhood context, ethnic identity, education, relationship status, civic participation, employment, and organizational membership, and discrimination. I began the analysis with broad-themed coding based on the interview instrument categories (e.g., family history, ethnic identity, and education). I then used an inductive approach by employing initial open coding (via line-by-line coding) to identify emerging themes.[87] After I identified key themes, I switched to more focused coding to identify key patterns among the numerous emergent codes discovered.[88]

I also used Midwestern Asian American cultural productions to further understand the interviewees' lives. These included documentary films, poetry, and music produced primarily by and about Midwestern Asian Americans. These sources help explicate the issues pertinent to this population at particular moments in time. They include materials from individuals who were not my informants.

Finally, previous scholars have viewed the 1960s as a turning point in immigration to the United States because of the Hart-Celler Act of 1965 and thus have focused on studying the post-1960s children of immigrants.[89] However, although the 1960s constitute a useful point in contemporary immigration to the United States writ large, starting from that decade does not fully capture the contemporary Asian migration to the United States. Thus, I argue that it is important to move the turning point back to the 1950s. The post-1950s experiences of Asian Americans include, for example, discussions of the Korean War, the subsequent migration of Koreans (including military brides and transracial adoptees) to the United States, and immigration policies that impacted the making of Asian America, especially in the Midwest.[90]

A Map of the Book: Invisibility in Racialized Spaces

For Asian Americans who grew up scattered throughout the U.S. heartland, the Midwest represents a space whose inhabitants are subjected to differential racialization processes and that reflects different arenas of negotiations. Their experiences with differential racialization are largely framed by themes of isolation, invisibility, and racialized visibility. This book is organized around the Midwest as a region of racialized spaces that reflect narratives of coming of age, discrimination and racism, and protest and resistance.

In chapter 1, I first draw from U.S. census data to provide a broad and descriptive demographic portrait of Midwestern Asian America. This is followed by an examination of the participants' family histories, to highlight the role of structural factors in the participants' transnational movements. The questions addressed are: How did these Asian families end up in the Midwest? What immigration policies initiated or supported the families' transnational movements? This chapter illustrates the critical impact of immigration policies passed between the 1950s and the early 2000s. The participants' families' reasons for immigrating to the United States fall into one of four categories: for political refugee resettlement, education, employment, and family. This chapter connects the lives and transnational movements of individuals and families with larger structural factors to highlight the diversity in transnational Asian American experiences.

Chapter 2 focuses on empirically examining how Asian Americans perceived and experienced their community, culture, and identity while growing up in the Midwest. Drawing on the interviews, this chapter is organized around the question: What is the role of physical, spatial context in how Asian Americans perceive and experience their co-ethnic community and culture and their panethnic identity as they come of age in the Midwest? The findings reveal variations in how Midwestern Asian Americans experience their ethnic community and culture that move beyond the problematic view of the Midwest as a "vast banana wasteland."[91] These experiences highlight the importance of acknowledging and examining differential racialization in different spaces.

Chapter 3 explores the consequence and legacy of Midwestern Asian American experiences related to racialized visibility and racism, as well as their impact on ethnic and panethnic identity. Specifically, the chapter further unpacks the linkages between the spatial (both physical and symbolic), racism, racialization, and internalized racism to explore the United States and the Midwest as racialized spaces that are responsible for Asian American narratives of racism and discrimination and, consequently, the manifestation of internalized racism from these experiences. The beginning of the chapter draws on historical, psychological, sociological, and cultural studies to interrogate racism, racialization, and internalized racism in the lives of Asian Americans. Following this is an analysis of the role of internalized racism in the lives of specific Midwestern Asian Americans—my interviewees. This second portion focuses on the following question: What is the Midwestern Asian American experience with internalized racism? The findings show that spatial isolation and racialized invisibility at both local and national levels result in differential racialization's playing a crucial role in how Midwestern Asian Americans perceive themselves and their co-ethnics.

Chapter 4 builds on the previous chapter to examine how Midwestern Asian Americans respond artistically to their experiences with differential racialization. The chapter focuses on two questions: What roles do space, race, and art play in Midwestern Asian American identity making? What stories are conveyed through these Asian Americans' cultural productions? To answer these questions, I draw primarily on the in-depth interviews and secondarily on original cultural materials produced by Midwestern Asian American artists (specifically, filmmakers, musicians, and poets). Central to this chapter is the conceptual lens of understanding Asian Americans as racial interstitial people, existing in a metaphorically in-between space. Taking this perspective allows us to see the role of agency (for those existing in the "world of the beyond") in both cultural intervention or change and the emergence of cultural hybridity.[92] It also reveals the influence of structural forces (in particular, differential racialization) that regulate and oppress.[93] Midwestern Asian American cultural productions simultaneously reflect and resist their racialized subordinate subjectivity. These works are influenced by, and serve as, examples of fighting invisibility, isolation, and racialized visibility, and engaging in identity-making and resistance.

The conclusion reviews the central arguments of the preceding chapters and provides evidence of the key role of differential racialization and space in the lives of Midwestern Asian Americans of the post-1950s 1.5 and second generations. I show how their experiences emphasize the need for further study of the roles of space, place, and differential racialization to reveal the pockets of embedded inequality among racially marginalized communities outside of larger metropolitan spaces. I conclude with suggestions for directions of future research and a commentary on the future of Asian America.

Finally, it is important to note that this book does not attempt to portray a monolithic experience for Midwestern Asian Americans, as they constitute an extremely heterogeneous population. As shown in Chung's and Anna's statements at the beginning of this introduction, the negotiation of racial identity and sense of belonging is a complex process that is heavily influenced by experiences with different communities within racialized spatial contexts. While I had initially thought that I would be sharing stories of Midwestern Asian Americans that were quite distinct from those of non-Midwesterners, the research findings reveal both similarities and differences. The narratives shared throughout this book will show Midwestern experiences that are eerily similar to those of Asian Americans living outside of the heartland (e.g., experiences of racism, struggles about racial and ethnic identities, and intergenerational family conflicts). However, as I delved deeper into the lives of my study participants, experiences emerged that were unique to their spatial context: for example, their levels of exposure to co-ethnics or ethnic enclaves and of exposure to distinct racial rhetorics. This book aims to reveal the multiplicity of Midwestern Asian Americans' experiences that stem from understanding the spatial dimensions of differential racialization. Ultimately, *Fighting Invisibility* provides a more in-depth understanding and interrogation of the intersection of race, space, and spatialized differential racialization in the lives and identity of children of contemporary Asian immigrants and refugees.

1

Who Is Midwestern Asian America?

A Demographic Overview and Personal Histories of Post-1950s Midwestern Asian Americans

From whatever I've been told, it was very difficult. My mother—when she arrived at O'Hare Airport, there was no one to meet us there. There wasn't anybody there to give her any directions; she didn't speak any English. People who tried to communicate with her didn't speak any Vietnamese, so it was very frightening. She had all these children with her. She had to get from there to where she needed to go, which was actually Argyle Street. That's the Vietnamese community today, and it's in Uptown Chicago. And she got hit pretty hard. She was kind of shell-shocked.
—Adam, a thirty-three-year-old "Vietnamese; Asian American"[1]

> I do know my dad, the first day he came
> to the States, he went to a McDonald's
> and he went to a Pink Floyd concert . . .
> he had kind of been a fan at first from
> India when he was in college. And then
> he came, and that was the first thing
> he did.
> —Ashwin, a twenty-year-old, "South
> Asian American"

Who are the post-1950s Asian Americans living in the Midwest? How did they end up there? The two quotations above provide a glimpse into the diversity of Midwestern Asian Americans' experiences—more specifically, their experiences of the first day in the United States or Midwest. Adam's mom and his five siblings escaped from Vietnam in the late 1970s and ended up in a refugee camp in Thailand, where Adam was born. He and his family arrived in the Midwest (Chicago) as refugees in 1980 under the sponsorship of a Chicago charity organization. A few years later, the family relocated to Wisconsin for employment opportunities. In contrast, Ashwin's father—who had grown up in Sri Lanka but attended college in India—initially made the journey to the United States alone in the 1980s, to attend a PhD program at the University of Chicago. Ashwin's mom joined his father after six months. Years later, the family moved to Milwaukee, Wisconsin, where Ashwin was born. They moved to central Ohio during his early teen years.

Adam's politics-driven and Ashwin's education-driven family histories indicate two of the four primary explanations for how the families represented in this study ended up in the Midwest. The four main reasons for the fifty-two families were: for political refugee resettlement (17), education (16), employment (9), and family (10) (see Figure 1.1). Their reasons reflect the geopolitical relations and colonial linkages between the United States and the so-called sending countries, as well as U.S. immigration laws passed from the 1950s to the early 2000s.[2] Yen Le Espiritu argues that to fully understand Asian American history, it is important to take a transnational approach that "stresses the global structures of inequality," since "the history of U.S. imperialism in Asia suggests that Asian American 'racial formation' has never been exclusively shaped by events in the United States but has also been influenced by U.S. colonialism, neocolonialism, and militarism in Asia."[3] Taking a transnational approach enables us to see the structural and global factors that define Asian and Asian American migration.[4] Such an approach also troubles the notion of a nation-centered Asian American identity and

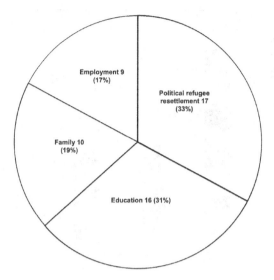

Employment 9
(17%)

Political refugee
resettlement 17
(33%)

Family 10
(19%)

Education 16 (31%)

FIGURE 1.1 What Brought Families to the Midwest? (Source: fifty-two in-depth interviews.)

defines that identity instead as one that neither begins nor ends in the United States.

Figure 1.2 provides an overview of the families' current socioeconomic status by the reasons that brought them to the Midwest. It is not surprising to see that a larger portion of those who came to the Midwest seeking education are faring better economically than those who arrived as political refugees. The categories reveal complex individual lives, representing a range of experiences that reflect both triumphs and tragedies. These individual histories show a diversity of experiences in keeping with Leslie Bow's description of Asian Americans as "unevenly oppressed."[5] For example, even Asian Americans who possess high socioeconomic status are not free from institutional racism. Racialized groups are subject to systems of oppression in much more complex ways than other groups are at the micro and macro levels (a subject further explored in chapter 3). The central goals of this chapter are to connect individuals and families and their transnational movements with larger structural factors and to illuminate the diversity in transnational Asian American experiences.

Demographic Overview: Asian Americans in the Midwest

In 2019, approximately 42 percent of all Asian Americans were residing in two states: California and New York. In terms of region, the West is home

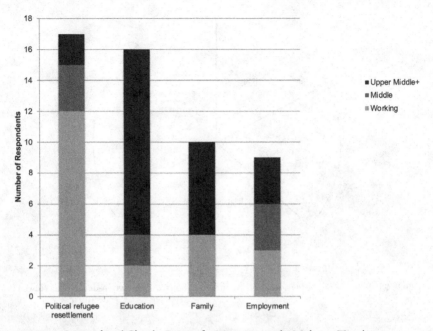

FIGURE 1.2 Respondents' Class by Reason for Migrating to the Midwest. The plus sign includes those who are upper-middle class and beyond. (Source: fifty-two in-depth interviews.)

to the largest share of Asian Americans (44 percent), followed by the South, the Northeast, and finally the Midwest (see Table 1.1). The finding that the South is home to the second largest Asian American population is not surprising, as scholars have previously identified a recent population boom in the region among Asian Americans—especially Asian Indians.[6] According to Arthur Sakamoto and colleagues, this movement of Asian Americans to the South has been driven by a "less discriminatory labor market than was characteristic of the pre-Civil Rights era," which has led them to take advantage of employment opportunities and a lower cost of living than in the rest of the country.[7] Across the United States, the Chinese, Asian Indian, and Filipinx populations combined make up the majority (64 percent) of Asian Americans (see Table 1.1). Not surprisingly, the West is home to the largest Filipinx (2.7 million) and Chinese (2.0 million) populations, while the South is home to the largest Asian Indian (1.5 million) population.

The Midwestern Asian American population has experienced a sizable boom in the past four decades. In 1990, Asian Americans made up only 1.3 percent of the total Midwestern population.[8] In 2019, the share was

Table 1.1

Top 11 Asian Ethnic Populations in the United States and by Region in 2019

West*	Number	%	South*	Number	%	Northeast	Number	%	Midwest	Number	%	United States	Number	%
All	9,932,951	44.0	All	5,398,967	24.0	All	4,260,133	19.0	All	2,779,632	12	All	22,371,683	10.00
Filipinx	2,677,101	27.0	Asian Indian	1,471,736	27.0	Chinese	1,354,468	32.0	Asian Indian	711,110	26	Chinese	5,398,763	24.0
Chinese	2,048,509	21.0	Chinese	904,632	17.0	Asian Indian	1,199,363	28.0	Chinese	499,871	18	Asian Indian	4,605,550	21.0
Asian Indian	1,223,341	12.0	Filipinx	764,023	14.0	Filipinx	397,265	9.0	Filipinx	373,051	13	Filipinx	4,211,440	19.0
Vietnamese	1,040,873	10.0	Vietnamese	764,009	14.0	Korean	365,612	9.0	Korean	239,875	9.0	Vietnamese	2,182,735	10.0
Japanese	994,219	10.0	Korean	463,647	9.0	Vietnamese	181,502	4.0	Vietnamese	196,351	7.0	Korean	1,908,053	9.0
Korean	838,919	8.0	Japanese	229,443	4.2	Pakistani	162,226	3.8	Hmong	163,955	6.0	Japanese	1,484,186	7.0
Cambodian	160,819	1.6	Pakistani	205,938	3.8	Japanese	124,774	2.9	Japanese	135,750	5.0	Pakistani	554,202	2.5
Thai	144,866	1.5	Thai	101,712	1.9	Bangladeshi	115,889	2.7	Pakistani	91,588	3.3	Thai	342,917	1.5
Hmong	122,575	1.2	Nepalese	72,700	1.3	Cambodian	70,315	1.7	Burmese	72,003	2.6	Cambodian	338,637	1.5
Laotian	113,758	1.1	Laotian	71,435	1.3	NA	NA	NA	NA	NA	NA	Hmong	326,843	1.5
Pakistani	94,450	1.0	Cambodian	70,562	1.3	NA	NA	NA	NA	NA	NA	Laotian	254,304	1.1

SOURCE: U.S. Census Bureau, American Community Survey 2019. "American Community Survey 1-Year Estimates Selected Population Profiles." https://www.census.gov/acs/www/data/data-tables-and-tools/data-profiles/2019/.

NA is not available. *There are also sizable populations of Indonesians in the West (68,184) and of the following ethnic groups in the South: Bangladeshis (208,200), Nepalese (197,880), Burmese (189,108), and Indonesians (129,329).

Table 1.2

Total and Asian American Population Nationally and in the Midwestern States, 2010 and 2019

	2010			2019		
	Total population	Asian population	Asians as % of total population	Total population	Asian population	Asians as % of total population
United States	308,745,538	17,289,750	5.6	328,239,523	22,371,683	6.8
All Midwestern states	66,927,001	2,005,333	3.0	68,329,004	2,764,852	4.0
Illinois	12,830,632	657,616	5.1	12,671,821	834,455	6.6
Michigan	9,883,640	281,914	2.9	9,986,857	394,895	4.0
Minnesota	5,303,925	242,411	4.6	5,639,632	333,624	5.9
Ohio	11,536,504	230,198	2.0	11,689,100	348,025	3.0
Wisconsin	5,686,986	148,596	2.6	5,822,434	201,512	3.5
Indiana	6,483,802	122,982	1.9	6,732,219	206,288	3.1
Missouri	5,988,927	119,483	2.0	6,137,428	162,980	2.7
Kansas	2,853,118	81,193	2.8	2,913,314	108,624	3.7
Iowa	3,046,355	62,999	2.1	3,155,070	95,994	3.0
Nebraska	1,826,341	39,353	2.2	1,934,408	52,230	2.7
South Dakota	814,180	9,753	1.2	884,659	13,270	1.5
North Dakota	672,591	8,835	1.3	762,062	12,955	1.7

SOURCE: U.S. Census Bureau, American Community Survey 2019. "American Community Survey 1-Year Estimates Selected Population Profiles." https://www.census.gov/acs/www/data/data-tables-and-tools/data-profiles/2019/

4.0 percent (2.8 million) of the total Midwestern population (see Table 1.2). The data from Table 1.2 show a fairly large increase in Asian population in the Midwest between 2010 and 2019 when this timeframe's "Asian only" category increased by 38 percent. Additionally, in 2018, 71 percent of all Midwestern Asian Americans resided in four states: Illinois, Michigan, Minnesota, and Ohio (see Table 1.3). North and South Dakota had the smallest percentages of Asians in the Midwest, collectively making up less than 1 percent of the total Midwestern Asian American population. In Michigan, the two largest groups of Asian Americans were Asian Indian and Chinese. In Minnesota, the largest group was that of Cambodians, Hmong, and Laotians; the second-largest group was "other Asians." It is important to note that the largest concentration of Hmong Americans in the United States reside in the Midwest (see Table 1.1), specifically in Minnesota's Twin Cities (St. Paul and Minneapolis). This finding suggests that Asians living outside of these four Midwestern states may experience greater isolation from their co-ethnic community.

Table 1.3

Asian Ethnic Groups by States in the Midwest, 2008–2018

	Filipinx	Chinese	Asian Indian	Vietnamese	Korean	Japanese	Cambodian, Hmong, and Laotian	All other Asians	Non-Asians	Total	All Asians	All Midwestern Asians (% of total population in the Midwest)
Illinois	138,465	102,827	214,118	37,273	69,533	21,374	8,125	107,368	11,997,946	12,697,029	699,083	33
Michigan	35,642	60,432	140,738	13,807	28,374	20,138	8,252	49,815	9,466,277	9,823,475	357,198	17
Minnesota	14,581	20,210	44,369	24,173	23,751	3,796	63,259	62,270	5,084,194	5,340,603	256,409	12
Ohio	26,274	39,933	52,082	7,945	9,916	12,837	18,868	24,928	11,206,625	11,399,408	192,783	9
Missouri	20,658	22,082	16,498	26,477	10,851	11,216	2,544	21,684	5,794,576	5,926,586	132,010	6
Wisconsin	15,124	25,274	16,835	8,977	11,858	8,338	30,591	11,289	5,521,186	5,649,472	128,286	6
Indiana	14,619	13,718	35,526	9,589	7,611	9,256	1,678	21,925	6,329,306	6,443,228	113,922	5
Kansas	10,855	16,281	13,082	9,144	6,687	4,674	9,036	18,714	2,724,868	2,813,341	88,473	4
Iowa	8,804	14,258	14,067	20,289	6,361	4,625	4,796	13,956	2,948,409	3,035,565	87,156	4
Nebraska	6,338	4,874	4,578	10,219	2,269	1,562	1,968	7,751	1,787,637	1,827,196	39,559	2
North Dakota	3,135	1,698	487	630	855	1,095	226	2,280	679,033	689,439	10,406	0.5
South Dakota	1,350	1,098	653	493	728	917	764	2,148	813,805	821,956	8,151	0.4
Total Midwest	295,845	322,685	553,033	169,016	178,794	99,828	150,107	344,128	64,353,862	66,467,298	2,113,436	100

SOURCE: Data represent weighted sample sizes from the merged 2008–2018 Integrated Public Use Microdata Sample-Current Population Survey Data. IPUMS-CPS, 2008–2018. University of Minnesota, www.ipums.org

Table 1.4

Social and Economic Characteristics of Asian Americans and Others in the Midwest and Other U.S. Regions

	Filipinx		Chinese		Asian Indian	
	Midwest	Other regions	Midwest	Other regions	Midwest	Other regions
Nativity and citizenship (%)						
U.S.-born	39	39	28	31	28	28
Foreign-born	61	61	72	69	72	72
U.S. citizen	82	82	63	71	62	62
Generation (%)						
1.0	44	42	50	50	55	56
1.5	17	19	21	18	16	15
2.0	19	24	22	26	27	27
2.5+	20	15	7	6	2	2
Education (%)						
High school dropout	10	10	10	17	8	9
High school graduate	12	17	13	18	9	9
Some college	21	30	18	15	12	10
College graduate	45	36	20	27	34	34
Advanced degree	11	7	39	23	37	40
College+	56	43	59	50	71	74
Employment, income, and home ownership (%)						
Unemployed	4	6	3	4	4	4
Below the poverty line	15	12	15	13	12	14
In the labor force	75	68	70	60	68	69
White-collar worker	29	25	40	28	35	36
Blue-collar worker	11	9	5	5	6	5
Own home	76	69	70	69	74	69
Average number of people in household	3.58	3.73	2.95	3.11	3.57	3.44

SOURCE: Data represent weighted sample sizes from the merged 2008–2018 Integrated Public Use Microdata Sample-Current Population Survey Data. IPUMS-CPS, 2008–2018. University of Minnesota, www.ipums.org. 2.5+ represents those who are 2.5-generation (one immigrant-born and one native-born parent) and later.

Table 1.4 shows that Midwestern Asian Americans possess diverse socioeconomic characteristics, which is consistent with previous findings about Asian Americans in the United States as a whole.[9] Two main findings emerge from the data. The first is that Asian Indians, Chinese, Japanese, and Filipinxs in the Midwest are highly educated. Specifically, in the Midwest Asian Indians are the most likely to have either a bachelor's degree or an advanced degree (represented by "College+" on Table 1.4) (71 percent), followed by Chinese (59 percent), Filipinxs (56 percent), and Japanese (47 percent). The second is that

Vietnamese		Korean		Japanese		Cambodian, Hmong, and Laotian		Non-Asians	
Midwest	Other regions	Midwest	Other regions	Midwest	Other regions	Midwest	Other regions	Midwest	Other regions
34	35	33	31	37	48	46	48	94	87
66	65	67	69	63	52	54	52	6	13
79	84	77	72	71	79	83	86	97	93
46	42	37	43	32	27	33	32	3	8
20	23	30	26	30	25	21	20	2	5
24	28	14	20	8	15	38	43	3	7
10	7	20	11	30	33	8	6	91	80
24	24	12	11	8	9	33	31	15	18
31	28	16	19	22	22	30	33	31	28
19	24	27	21	24	27	24	23	29	27
20	19	27	33	29	29	12	13	17	17
7	8	19	16	18	14	2	3	9	9
27	27	46	49	47	43	14	16	26	26
4	6	7	5	5	4	11	9	7	7
13	13	11	13	12	13	20	14	13	14
68	65	58	62	69	59	67	64	66	63
14	17	26	29	32	27	9	13	20	20
20	14	7	7	11	6	32	22	16	13
74	69	73	71	69	70	66	72	71	69
3.41	3.81	3.06	3.09	2.81	2.81	4.46	4.65	3.14	3.23

Midwestern Southeast Asians have a dire educational story in keeping with broader cultural narratives about their lower educational achievements in comparison to other Asian groups: Cambodians, Hmong, and Laotians are the group of Asian Americans least likely to have either a bachelor's degree or an advanced degree in the Midwest (14 percent) and all other U.S. regions (16 percent). This is coupled with an alarming high school dropout rate (33 percent) among the Cambodian, Hmong, and Laotian populations in the Midwest. The disparity is glaring when compared to Asian Indians' high school dropout rate in the Midwest (8 percent). Underscoring the dire circumstances indicated by these findings is the high percentage of the Cambodian, Hmong, and Laotian population who are unemployed (11 percent) and living in poverty (20 percent) in the Midwest. However, the data suggest that the narratives go beyond a dualistic picture of successful and unsuccessful Asian ethnic groups. For example, Vietnamese Americans display a bimodal educational outcome within group. In other words, the share of the Midwestern Vietnamese American population who are high school dropouts (24 percent) is comparable to the share with at least either a bachelor's degree or an advanced degree (27 percent). However, compared to other highly educated Asian American groups (Asian Indians, Chinese, Filipinxs, and Japanese), Vietnamese Americans have a much lower rate of employment in white-collar work: just 14 percent in the Midwest and 17 percent in other U.S. regions. Like their Southeast Asian counterparts, Vietnamese Americans in the Midwest are more likely than other Midwestern Asian American groups to be employed in blue-collar jobs (20 percent).

While these numbers reveal a lot about Asian Americans in the Midwest, they are still only part of the narrative. The following section provides an in-depth look into the four primary reasons why the families represented in this study came to reside in the Midwest.

Political Refugee Resettlement

For Emily, a twenty-one-year-old "Vietnamese American" who was born and raised in Illinois, the retelling of her family's history—which is intertwined with the Vietnam War—reflects the trauma that her parents experienced. Her parents, who met each other in Chicago, were a part of the boat people movement that fled Vietnam via boat at the end of the war:

> [My dad] only tells me things when he's drinking or when he has something to drink because I guess it's something they don't want to talk about, especially my mom. She's really quiet about it. But from what I know, my dad just claimed that being on that boat was hell, pretty much. Because they were cramped inside with a lot of people, there was barely any food, there was barely any water, [and] there were fears of pirates taking over their ships. There's just a lot of things. He commented on how my mom came and if they weren't rescued by—I believe it was some military men, but if they weren't rescued, then the people in the ship would have died because there was barely anything to eat. And my dad said that once someone did pass away, they would just throw the body in the water and move on. So I guess it was one of those things where it's just not pleasant to talk about.

Emily's family history is similar to that of a third of my participants, who either came themselves to the Midwest as political refugees or whose parents did. All seventeen participants in this category are of Southeast Asian ancestry. While they all fall into the broad categories of Vietnamese, Cambodian, or Laotian, their ethnic identities include Chinese Vietnamese, Hmong, and Khmer. Their family histories contain stories of fleeing political persecution in Vietnam and Laos after the fall of Saigon; fleeing genocide in Cambodia during and after the Khmer Rouge era; and living for years in refugee camps in Thailand, Hong Kong, or the Philippines while awaiting sponsorship from families and/or charity organizations throughout the United States. Vietnam and Cambodia were under French colonial rule from 1887 to 1954, and Laos was colonized by France in 1893. Throughout the Cold War era, these Southeast Asian countries were the sites of U.S. proxy wars against communism.[10]

For families from Vietnam, like Emily's, the end of the Vietnam War in April 1975 triggered a mass flight from the country for political, social, and economic reasons. The new communist-backed Vietnamese regime confiscated many businesses and created new economic policies (such as nationalizing trade, setting new currency exchange rates, and forcing many of its citizens into "New Economic Zones"[11]) during the post-1975 era.[12] These policies proved problematic for members of the bourgeois and petit bourgeois classes, including many ethnic Chinese. Furthermore, during late 1977 and early 1978 Vietnam clashed with China over economic, political, and land disputes, resulting in the Sino-Vietnamese War of 1979. Prior to and following the war, the Vietnamese government actively pushed the ethnic Chinese living in Vietnam to leave the country.[13] While the first wave of emigrants fled Vietnam in 1975, primarily due to their affiliation with the U.S. military, people in the second wave (known as the boat people) fled Vietnam by bribing officials and chartering small fishing boats through commercial channels. Those who survived the treacherous journey ended up in refugee processing camps in Thailand, Singapore, Malaysia, Indonesia, the Philippines, and Hong Kong. There, the refugees awaited word of sponsorship for further migration from family members, other individuals, and volunteer organizations overseas.

The mid-1970s also marked the beginning of mass migration for Cambodians, after Pol Pot's savage Khmer Rouge regime came to power at the end of the Cambodian Civil War (1968–1975). The war was between the Khmer Republic, led by Lon Nol (who was supported and funded by the United States), and the Khmer Rouge, led by King Norodom Sihanouk[14] (who had formed a coalition with the radical communist Pol Pot (born Saloth Sar).[15] Between 1969 and 1973, President Richard Nixon ordered the secret bombing of Cambodia, which ended up killing approximately 150,000 civilians.[16] Following the end of the Cambodian Civil War in April 1975, Pol Pot's victorious Khmer Rouge began a reign of terror that rippled throughout the country. Designed to "transform every aspect of Cambodian society," the Khmer Rouge's genocidal campaign imprisoned and executed members of ethnic minority groups in the country, shut down anything the Khmer Rouge deemed representative of "western modernity" (including schools, banks, and hospitals), and created a mass slave-labor camp.[17] As Sucheng Chan writes, the Khmer Rouge's intentions were "to create a 'pure' peasant society cleansed of all Western and modern 'contamination.'"[18] By the end of its genocidal campaign in January 1979, approximately 1.5–1.7 million people (out of a total population of approximately 7.9 million) had died at the hands of the Khmer Rouge.[19] People fled the country by plane or foot, heading north into Thailand. The United States accepted a total of 157,518 Cambodian refugees and their sponsored families between 1975 and 1994.[20]

This devastating history coincides with the family history of Chenda, a 1.5-generation "Cambodian American." Her family was one of the sponsored refugee families. Their migration story began when Chenda's mother escaped from Cambodia in 1979 by walking into Thailand. For a little over a decade after that, the family survived in two different Thailand refugee camps. Chenda was born during their time in the second refugee camp, where she spent the first ten years of her life. In the early 1990s, her family arrived in Minnesota under the sponsorship of her uncle and with the assistance of Catholic charities.

Many other participants had a similar family history, including Kia, a nineteen-year-old "Hmong American" who grew up in Minnesota's Twin Cities. Kia's family escaped from Laos after the end of the Vietnam War and arrived as refugees in the United States in 1979. The movement of refugees leaving Laos also began in 1975, and the initial people emigrating from the country were ethnic Hmong refugees. The Hmong people are an ethnic minority group whose ancestral roots can be traced back to China; they have lived in the mountains of Laos since the early nineteenth century.[21] The United States played a heavy military role in Laos as well as in Vietnam and Cambodia. In 1961, the Central Intelligence Agency recruited Hmong soldiers to fight alongside U.S. troops against communist North Vietnam. This collaboration became known as the secret war. During the late 1960s and early 1970s, approximately 2.5–5.0 million tons of bombs were dropped by the United States in Laos.[22] By the end of the secret war, approximately 50,000 Hmong were injured or killed due to the war.[23] As a consequence of their involvement as soldiers in the secret war, many Hmong fled when Saigon fell. Among those who fled persecution were members of other ethnic minority groups from Laos (such as the Mien and Yao) who had fought alongside U.S.-backed guerrilla forces.

Southeast Asian refugees from Cambodia, Laos, and Vietnam initially entered the United States under the Indochina Migration and Refugee

Assistance Act of 1975. This act provided emergency admission for Southeast Asian refugees and funding for their resettlement in the United States. In addition, the United States established the Indochinese Refugee Assistance Program. The program provided states with federal funds to support refugees with social welfare (e.g., medical care) and integration programs (e.g., classes in English as a second language).[24] By October 1975, Minnesota had received the largest number of refugees in the Midwest.[25] In 1977, Congress extended the Indochina Migration and Refugee Assistance Act to allow refugees who had physically resided in the United States for at least two years and who had initially been given parole status to receive permanent resident status. After five years, the refugees were allowed to apply for U.S. citizenship. In theory, this act provided the refugees with a clear pathway to citizenship.[26]

In 1980, in response to the growing number of Vietnamese refugees arriving in the United States, Congress passed the Refugee Act of 1980. This act established the first systematic process for admitting refugees and was one of the most comprehensive laws dealing with refugee admissions into the United States.[27] Previously, refugee status had been restricted to people fleeing from communist countries or the Middle East.[28] Modeled on the definition in the 1967 United Nations' Convention and Protocol Relating to the Status of Refugees, the law redefined a refugee as a person fleeing from the fear of racial, religious, national, or political persecution.[29] Additionally, the act established the Office of Refugee Resettlement.[30] Between 1975 and 1980, approximately 433,000 refugees from Vietnam, Laos, or Cambodia entered the United States.[31]

For my informants in the political refugee category, while their initial reason for going to the Midwest were political, the most common reasons for remaining there were the region's co-ethnic community, extended family support, and/or sponsorship from charities. It was the presence of all three, as well as the sponsorship of her uncle, that brought Chenda and her family to the Midwest. Chenda's retrospective description of her move and transition in that period is filled with bittersweet memories:

> I was really excited to come to United States. It was a really great decision that my mom decided to come, and it was a great opportunity, but there was a lot of struggles. Within a couple months my mom decided to leave my father [due to physical abuse]. And then finding our own place and [her] being a single mom, that was difficult. Learning about America and the transition between two cultures was really difficult for me. Also, the language barrier—I was fortunate that I was taking English in Thailand. But still, people making fun of the way you speak, and your grammar is off, and the accent and things like that. So that was difficult.

Chenda grew up in a working-class household, and she recalls hardly seeing her mother, who worked all the time. Over the years, her mother's employment included medical assembly work and working as a cook. Chenda began working at the age of fourteen because she and her sister were expected to contribute to the household financially. Growing up in Minnesota, she was surrounded by a relatively large "good Cambodian community." Via cultural events and activities, the community served to sustain her ethnic identity and pride. For example, she describes going to a summer "leadership camp" sponsored by a large Cambodian association in Minnesota, which was led by a relative: "When I came, I had leadership camp. They [would] take Cambodian youth out in the wild for three days or a week. And we would learn how to cook the old-fashioned way, and we would learn leadership skills building. We would learn many different fields, and hiking, and things like that. That was a big part of our summer when we were growing up."

Today, Chenda identifies herself as "Cambodian American" but acknowledges that this was an "evolution" from identifying as just Cambodian. While she confesses to becoming "Americanized" over the years, she says that she would never identify herself simply as "American" because she "values the Cambodian side." Chenda strongly values her Cambodian culture and traditions and hopes to pass them on to her future children. She bluntly describes identifying herself solely as "American" as an act that would be equivalent to "cutting my arms off." Her statement suggests that she would not feel whole without her Cambodian identity.

Kia relates a similar story about the presence of a large co-ethnic community where she grew up. Initially her family lived in several places on the East Coast, and then they moved to Fresno, California. They eventually settled in the Twin Cities to be close to the larger Hmong community there. In describing that community, Kia states: "East Side, St. Paul, and Minneapolis has a lot of Hmong. It is the largest [concentration] in America." However, she was the "only Hmong person" at her small and private liberal arts college in Indiana, and this taught her to better "appreciate" being Hmong. She confesses that "when I'm back in the Twin Cities, I'm like, 'Oh, there's so many Hmong people here!' You know? I don't know how to explain it! I can't articulate it! It's just like, when there's too many, you just feel like the appreciation is lost." Regardless of these feelings, being exposed to a co-ethnic community in the region has impacted her overall self-identification. She notes: "I feel like I've always identified [as Hmong] because I think, especially in the Twin Cities, there aren't as many other [Asians], or at least it's not as prevalent, so to say. You don't really see other Asians around, yeah, especially in the Twin Cities, because it's mostly Hmong. Like when you see Korean Americans, Chinese Americans, Vietnamese—like I never really had that Asian American, that API [Asian Pacific Islander] consciousness until I got to college, because I've always just really saw [sic] myself as Hmong American, not Asian American." The emergence in college of Kia's racial identity as Asian American highlights the role of spatial context in identity. Key to this is the role of exposure to a collective panethnic history—or, as Kia puts it, "API consciousness." (This topic of Asian American consciousness is further explored in chapter 3.)

The presence of a preexisting extended family in the Midwest was also a critical component that drew many political refugees to the region. This was the case for Emily's family, as discussed at the opening of this section of the chapter. Her parents' primary reason for settling in Chicago was that they had family members (an aunt and an uncle) who had previously settled there. These were the relatives her parents stayed with when they first arrived in the United States, and who introduced her parents to one another. Vanly, a twenty-four-year-old "Laotian American" born and raised in Minneapolis, reported similar circumstances. Both of her parents fled Laos for Thailand during the Vietnam War, afraid of political persecution. In the early 1980s, an uncle living in Minneapolis sponsored her parents' migration to the United States. Vanly explains that this was the primary reason why her parents decided to settle in the Midwest:

> It was because my uncle was there. My uncle was sponsored by the church, and because he was there, it was a sure thing. I should clarify that they did have options. I think they had a church sponsor in Massachusetts—the Lutheran Church. I know they had options. It was either the East Coast or the Midwest. I think I'd remember my sister would ask, "Why Minnesota?" And just like, it's really cold here, and it's really homogenous [sic], and we're too far away from everything. But they're like, no, it's because we had family here. What else are we supposed to think because we're scared and confused and can't speak English? Of course, we're going to go where the family is. He's [the uncle] been here for two years, which is true. That was at least what they've communicated the main reason was: they had family here already.

The final factor influencing refugee settlement in the Midwest for participants' families was church sponsorship in that area. This was a major part of the family narrative for Alice, a twenty-eight-year-old "Vietnamese" who grew up in Kansas and Nebraska, and whose family came to the United States as part of the post-1975 Vietnamese refugee movement. When South Vietnam fell in 1975, her father, who had served in the Republic of Vietnam Navy, immediately fled with the assistance of the U.S. government. He left a wife and toddler son behind in Vietnam. Alice describes the process her father went through at Fort Chaffee, Arkansas, when he first arrived in the United States and the organization that sponsored his eventual relocation: "[The U.S. government] trained them with a little bit of English. They actually had papers submitted to different agencies, and one of them was Catholic Charities, because my dad's

Catholic—we're all Catholic—and so they found a sponsor, and the sponsor was in Great Bend, Kansas. So my dad was relocated there, and they gave him some vocational training and some technical training. He went to a two-year college, and then he was able to sponsor my mom over. And then they sponsored all my aunts and uncles over, too."

Alice's mother and brother were not able to escape from Vietnam until the early 1980s. After two attempts, her mother finally succeeded in escaping from Vietnam via boat through the South China Sea. Alice's parents were reunited in Kansas in 1981. Alice was born in the mid-1980s and was the third of five children. When she was twelve years old, her family relocated to Nebraska because of better employment opportunities there. Her father eventually found maintenance work, and her mother secured a job in the meatpacking industry.

Phong, a twenty-two-year-old "Asian American, Chinese-Vietnamese" born and raised in Iowa, shared a similar story about the role of church sponsorship in bringing his family to the Midwest. Phong's mother also fled via boat after the Vietnam War. His mother is ethnic Chinese from Vietnam, and his father is ethnic Chinese from Cambodia; both were living in South Vietnam. Of his family's difficult escape out of Vietnam, Phong said:

Yeah, it was pretty rough. It was definitely by boat. So I remember my parents telling me stories where they would say like one of my aunts, my mom's sisters, would try to jump on a boat—you would need to get all the paperwork forged, just to get out, and if you don't get out and they catch you for having fraud papers, you'd just get thrown in jail. I think my aunt went to jail a couple of times, and—I mean, eventually she'd just get out and try again. This was over the course of so many years.

Phong's family was eventually successful in escaping from Vietnam. His parents met each other at a refugee camp in the Philippines, but they were sponsored through different means:

They spent some time in the Philippines—about a year, a year and a half—and then my mom came over first with a few of her brothers. That was like in '86, '87. They came to Iowa through a church in Perry, that was like a Methodist church kind of sponsored them, and so the church kind of helped us a little bit. My dad came over later to his older brother's restaurant in Oklahoma, sponsored somehow. So my dad spent the first few years in Oklahoma, and my mom was in Iowa. . . . [Eventually,] Dad went up north to Iowa, and they got married. They stayed in Iowa because my mom had brothers and sisters to . . . take care of and stuff, and my dad had older brothers that were doing fine in Oklahoma.

According to Phong, his family eventually stayed in Iowa to help "take care of" the maternal side of his family. Thus, while his mother first came to Iowa because of church sponsorship, the family stayed to be near and assist members of their extended family.

Education

Another reason for Asian Americans' settlement in the Midwest was education. Historically, the United States has long made an exception in providing temporary student visas within its (at times, highly restrictive) immigration policy.[32] The Chinese Exclusion Act of 1882 was enacted explicitly to bar the entry of "Chinese laborers," defined by the act as those "both skilled and unskilled laborers and Chinese employed in mining."[33] Interestingly, one section of the act specifically notes that "every Chinese person other than a laborer who may be entitled by said treaty and this act to come within the United States, and who shall be about to come to the United States, shall be identified as so entitled by the Chinese Government in each case." In other words, non-laborer Chinese migrants who had documents issued by the Chinese government would be considered for entry into the United States. Thus, Chinese students were still admitted to the United States during the exclusionary period.[34]

The United States increased migration of Filipinx students via the Pensionado Act of 1903. The law's passage was motivated by the aftermath of the Spanish-American War (1898) and the Philippines-American War (1899–1902), in which the United States claimed the Philippines as a territory. As newly minted U.S. nationals under U.S. imperial rule, Filipinxs were perceived as inferior wards of the American empire who required education for their own betterment.[35] After initially sending approximately six hundred teachers to the Philippines to meet the Kipling-esque White man's burden of educating its subjects, the United States reversed the direction of transnational educational migration by passing the Pensionado Act. This law established a government-sponsored program for Filipinx students to study in U.S. high schools and universities. In 1903, approximately 104 Filipinx students entered the United States under this act. By the end of the program in the late 1920s, thousands of Filipinx students had returned to the Philippines with degrees to work as professionals (e.g., teachers and doctors) and government officials. According to Barbara Posadas, this number included Pensionado students who attended elite universities scattered throughout the Midwest, including in Chicago.[36]

According to the Institute of International Education, in 1920 its president, Stephen Duggan, convinced the U.S. government to classify international students as nonimmigrant and begin issuing "nonimmigrant student visas" to them.[37] International students were thus unaffected by the restrictive national quotas set by the Emergency Quota Act (also known as the Immigration Act of 1921) and the Immigration Act of 1924.[38] International students also were explicitly mentioned in several key U.S. policies of the 1950s. Key legislation related to the migration of Asian and other international students began with the 1952 McCarran-Walter Immigration Act, which abolished the anti-Asian immigration restrictions of previous years and allowed people of Asian ancestry to legally immigrate to the United States.[39] The act seemed to have ended the exclusion of Asian immigrants to the United States at the start of the Cold War. However, Asian immigration was still restricted by highly limited quotas.[40] Nonetheless, a small number of Asian immigrants entered the United States in the 1950s via family reunification provisions (discussed below in this chapter). Important for an understanding of the international student movement is realizing that the McCarran-Walter Immigration Act also made the U.S. State Department and what was then known as the Immigration and Naturalization Service responsible for overseeing the issuing of visas.[41]

Today, there are three types of nonimmigrant visas for study in the United States: the F-1 visa, for full-time students; M visa, for students attending vocational school; and J visa, for cultural exchange–type purposes (e.g., the Fulbright Program).[42] The F-1 visa is the most common among international students who attend school in the United States full-time. Since the beginning of the Great Recession, the number of international students with F-1 visas[43] has more than doubled, from approximately 179,000 in 2008 to 364,000 in 2016.[44] The rise in international students enrolled at public U.S. colleges and universities has been especially noticeable. The Pew Research Center has identified an intention among public institutions to "rely more heavily on tuition from foreign students" to offset "budget cuts during the Great Recession."[45]

The educational avenue through student visas was how the parents of sixteen of my study participants came to the United States. They came to attend graduate school in fields such as medicine, biology, and types of engineering (aerospace, mechanical, and so on). They completed degrees at prestigious institutions throughout the Midwest, including the University of Chicago, Indiana University, Ohio State University, and the University of Michigan. One such parent was the father of Eric, a nineteen-year-old "Indian American" who was born and raised in southwestern Ohio. Eric's father came to the United States from India on a student visa to attend medical school. However, unlike the parents of other participants, he already had family (a sister and a brother-in-law) in the Ohio area, where he attended school. He eventually sponsored Eric's mother, who is also a physician, as an immigrant to the United States. Although Eric did not know the specific visa types his parents had, it is highly probable that his father was admitted on an F-1 visa and that his mother was sponsored on an F-2 visa, which allows the spouse of someone with an F-1 visa to come to the United States. They both stayed in the United States after securing employment, and both still work in medicine. Interestingly, Eric's statement highlights the role of the discrimination his family has faced in that field:

> As far as some of the discrimination they faced coming here, I think one of the reasons my dad is a pathologist [is because . . .] I think for a lot of immigrant doctors, maybe just in [Ohio] or maybe in the entire country at that time, there were certain positions in medicine that probably you would not be able to attain. I think that my dad, from what my sister told me, really wanted to become a radiologist, but those positions are usually reserved for American-born doctors, or at least White doctors, so I think that's one of the reasons maybe why my family seems to have a lot of people who are pathologists.

Stories like that of Eric's family show the nuances present even in the experiences of highly skilled Asian immigrants. In this instance, being a racialized subject and experiencing discrimination clearly played a critical role in altering career trajectories in the Midwest.

It is important to note that while international student policy (i.e., the F-1 visa) plays a crucial role in determining whether foreign students can be admitted to the United States, the policies of the sending country's government are equally important. Movements of people all over the world are triggered by events in their home countries and rooted in legislative policies. For Bob, a twenty-three-year-old "Chinese, Chinese American" who was born in Michigan and grew up in Iowa, the Chinese government played an important role in allowing for the movement of members of the Chinese diaspora during the post-Mao era, which is when his father migrated to the United States. The establishment of Mao Tse-tung's People's Republic of China had essentially closed the door to Chinese emigration from 1949 to 1978. However, in 1978, Deng Xiaoping transformed the country's policies, including (most importantly for this narrative) its emigration policy.[46] The changes allowed Chinese students to study abroad. As a result, the early 1980s marked a period of increased Chinese migration to the United States for the purpose of education.

Bob's father was part of this Chinese study-abroad movement. He eventually obtained a PhD in one of the science, technology, engineering, and math (STEM) fields from a Midwestern university. Bob's mother was sponsored by her husband after they were married. Her journey to the United States followed a remarkably different path from that of Bob's father, adhering more closely to what Bob describes as "what you call a stereotypical immigrant life." While Bob's mother, like his father, was college-educated (in engineering), she spent her first several years in the United States working in the service industry. According to Bob, she "cleaned houses for people, so she was a housecleaner a few times a week for some people. She worked in a Chinese restaurant . . . as a waitress. She worked in the university cafeteria as a cashier." It was not until years later, after the family had relocated to another part of the Midwest because of Bob's father's employment in higher education, that his mother was able to secure a position (also in higher education) commensurate with her education.

Mina, a twenty-seven-year-old who grew up in Minnesota and identifies herself as "Asian American," also told a student-visa family migration story. In the early 1980s, Mina's parents migrated to the Midwest so her father could obtain a graduate degree in engineering. Born in South Korea, Mina was left there with her grandmother for several years while her parents adjusted to life in the United States. Her parents sent for her when she was three years old. Mina had this to say about her father's motivation for migrating to the United States:

> The cues that I've gathered is [sic] that he grew up in a pretty poor family, and
> I think he experienced a lot of classism while he was living in Korea. And so he
> still very much had this idea—he still, to this day, very much believes in the
> "American dream." So the U.S. is much, much better than Korea is in terms of it
> [sic] being a meritocracy, you know? . . . I don't think he ever regretted the
> decision [to emigrate]. He didn't think that he would ever be able to get as far in
> terms of the social ladder in Korea if he had stayed because of his family and class
> background. So I think that's one of the reasons he decided to come to the U.S.

Her father's belief in the "American dream" and meritocracy came true, as he eventually secured a faculty position at a Midwestern university. In contrast, Mina's mother came to the United States on an F-2 visa, as the spouse of the holder of a nonimmigrant visa. Mina described her mother's experience:

> Because they were on student visas, [my mother] wasn't able to work legally. She
> was on dependent student visa, but she got really bored because I wasn't here in
> the U.S. She couldn't work, my dad was in grad school. and, you know, never
> even told my mom when he was defending [his dissertation]. It was that kind of
> relationship, where he kept his school totally separate. My mom didn't really
> know, so she didn't ask and didn't really care. But she eventually told me stories
> about how she went kind of door-to-door trying to find jobs, and there was this
> [fast-food place] in their neighborhood. They lived in graduate student
> housing, and there's this [fast-food place] that was owned by a Korean family,
> and so she got a job there illegally working at the [fast-food place] and trying
> to support my dad. Because at that time, the tuition waiver system wasn't in
> place. So they still needed to pay tuition even if he did have an RA [research
> assistantship]. There were expenses that they were trying to meet.

Her mother's life during this period was simultaneously defined by challenges, perseverance, and an assertion of agency for economic survival (e.g., circumventing the law).

Employment

Nina—a twenty-four-year-old who identifies herself as "Taiwanese American; Asian American"—said that her family's migration history began in the East Coast but ended in the Midwest. Her father arrived in Boston in the late 1970s for graduate school. Her mother came shortly afterward and also attended graduate school in the Boston area. The family ended up in Illinois after Nina's father earned his PhD in a STEM field and landed a university faculty position. Nina's family story—of migration to the Midwest for employment—put her in the smallest group of participants (nine). Half of the families in this category ended up in the Midwest due to secondary migration from elsewhere in the United States, and the other half migrated straight to the Midwest by way of an H-1B visa. The journey of immigrants to the United States via occupational paths had been paved initially by the passing of the Hart-Celler Immigration Act of 1965.[47] This act was a crucial catalyst for contemporary immigration to the United States. It eradicated the national-origin quota system of the immigration acts of 1924 and 1952, replaced it with hemisphere quotas and a limit of 20,000 immigrants per country per year, and established a seven-category preference system that favored immigrants who sought to reunite their families or could provide highly skilled labor needed in the United States. Specifically, the act created the H-1B nonimmigrant visa for skilled workers in "specialty occupations."[48] Some holders of H-1B visas who have the proper connections can use the visa as a pathway to permanent U.S. residency.

In 1990, Congress amended the Immigration Act of 1965 to expand legal immigration to the United States (accepting 700,000 immigrants annually for the years 1990–1995 and 675,000 per year thereafter) and established three preference categories: family-sponsored, employment-based, and so-called diversity immigrants. Out of the 675,000 visas issued, 480,000 were to be set aside for family-sponsored applicants, 140,000 for employment-based applicants, and 55,000 for diversity applicants. The diversity visas were intended to allow immigration from countries whose citizens had not benefited from the Immigration Act of 1965. However, those eligible for diversity visas had to have at least a high-school diploma and two years of work experience. As a result of the Immigration act of 1990 amendments, the number of issued visas tripled, allowing greater numbers of educated and skilled individuals to immigrate to the United States.[49] In the end, immigration from these other countries achieved the goal of diversifying the population of the United States—that is, its educated and skilled population. These changes have advantaged highly skilled Asian immigrants seeking employment in the United States.[50] More than half of the H-1B visas issued between 2001 and 2015 went to individuals from India (50.5 percent), while people from other Asian countries received fewer visas: for example, 9.7 percent of the visas went to people from China, 3.0 percent to those from the Philippines, and 2.8 percent to South Koreans.[51] Approximately 64 percent of the requests for H-1B visas in 2011 were for employment in STEM-related fields.

According to Ajit, a twenty-nine-year-old who self-identifies as "Indian American," his family's journey from southeastern India to the United States was made possible by an H-1B visa. The family's history in the United States began in the late 1970s, when his father arrived for "residency in New York at [a hospital on] the Upper East Side in Manhattan." Ajit explained that his father considered structural factors (India's politics and potential work opportunities both there and in the United States) in deciding to stay in the United States:

> The way my dad tells the story is he feels he's an "accidental immigrant" because what he wanted to do was go to the U.S. for training and then go back and practice in Tamil Nadu. Probably near home, quite frankly. Then, he says, the politically connected Tamil people—whose children were doctors but were getting this supposedly lower-quality education in India—wanted to consolidate their power in running hospitals, so they pressured the government at the time to create a law where the only education that would be recognized for medicine would be education that resulted in a degree being granted. And as we all know, a residency in the U.S.—you don't get a degree, so his formal training would never have been acknowledged in India. So there's this sort of dilemma of "do I go back to India and kind of have a crappy job, or do I stay in the U.S. where I can have access to a better career, essentially?"

Years later, Ajit's father was able to open his own practice as a physician, with the assistance of relatives who also practice medicine, in Ohio. The father's use of the term "accidental immigrant" and the reasons that influenced his decision to stay in the United States are noteworthy because they provide a glimpse into some of the complex decisions that migrants have to make. Not all migrants arrive in the United States with the intention of permanent resettlement. A critical factor in this narrative is that Ajit's father had access to a pathway to permanent U.S. residency. Individual life choices are often influenced by larger structural factors.

The case of Todd, a twenty-one-year-old who identified himself as "Filipino American" and was born and raised in Illinois, differs from many of the family narratives of migration mentioned above. His mother came to the United States in the early 1980s via an H-1B visa to work in the health care industry: "My mom was in nursing school, and I don't think any of our immediate family had any intentions of coming here at that time. I know that she stayed current with looking at newspapers and stuff, and she saw that Illinois was actively recruiting nurses. This was during the eighties, so she decided to come here, and at this time she was dating my dad. I don't think they were married quite yet, so then she applied to come here. She came here by herself first, and then she got a work visa."

Todd's mother's journey to the United States is an example of a common narrative for the Filipinx American community. According to Espiritu, the history of Filipinx migration to the United States begins in gendered terms with men in the Filipino navy who were essentially recruited by the United States via its "94-year military presence in the Philippines" that began at the end of Spanish-American War in 1898.[52] They were followed by Filipinx health care professionals, many of whom were women registered nurses. The historical background for this gendered migration was "one of the important outcome[s] of U.S. colonialism in the Philippines." Beginning in the 1960s, Filipinx health professionals were recruited to offset health care labor shortages in the United States.[53] Todd describes the important role of spatial context and the preexisting Filipinx community on his mother's adjustment to life in a new country:

> Yeah, there was a very strong Filipino presence in Rockford, Illinois, that made my parents feel more at home. Because I remember [this] from when I talked to their family friends [or people at] the nursing home or hospital that recruited Filipino nurses. They would pick you up from the airport. They would take you to the area. . . . And then whenever they got to the nursing home, like they had Filipino food there already. And there was just a very good sense of community that—at least [for] my mom, when she first came here—was at least something she was familiar with. I think that helped eased the transition because they are really good family friends right now. The community there considers my parents extended family. I think that's really important in the sense that my mom was able to identify with something that was familiar when she came here, so that was good for her.

His mother's experience points to the important role of spatial context, as well as that of having an accessible co-ethnic community. Todd's mother was eventually able to sponsor his father as an immigrant.

Family

The last category consists of immigrants who settled in the Midwest through a family visa. This category includes everyone who came for any reason related to family. For the ten participants in this category, the dominant themes were that they settled in the Midwest via family reunification and marriage. In one case, the reason for migration was an international transracial adoption. These participants' stories clearly show the role of the U.S. military's presence in South Korea during the Korean War and its aftermath. In this section, I highlight two of the most dominant narratives tied to the Midwestern spatial context: those of children of Korean military brides and those of transracial Korean adoptees. The stories of people in these two categories underline two important points. The first point is that both narratives are vestiges of the Korean War, the legacy of which remains in the lives that were impacted[54] (the United States maintains a military presence in South Korea today). The second point is that we need to shift our perception of the 1960s as a turning point in contemporary Asian immigration and go back to the 1950s instead. Otherwise, the historical origins of the narratives of an entire generation of Korean Americans, especially in the Midwest, are rendered invisible. Their life stories contribute to the making of Asian American history, especially of the Midwest's Asian American history.

Both marriage and family reunification served as the basis for the family migration history of Jae, a twenty-two-year-old who identifies himself as "Korean American." Jae was born on a U.S. Air Force base in Maine but grew up in northern Ohio. His White American father was stationed in South Korea in the early 1980s when he met Jae's mother, a Korean national, at a U.S. military camptown (see below for explanation) there. The U.S. military's occupation of South Korea began in 1945, the year when Japan was ousted from Korea after thirty-five years of colonial rule. However, an independent Korea did not last long: it was almost immediately split into North Korea (backed by the Soviet Union and China) and South Korea (backed by the United States). This split resulted in a war that lasted until 1953. According to scholars, Korea served as another site for the encroachment of "expanding U.S. power" to further its "Cold War policy of containment" against communism.[55] Ji-Yeoh Yuh writes that the contemporary era of Korean migration (that is, migration since the 1950s) "can be traced to the war and its consequences."[56] Specifically, two of the most notable groups of immigrants from Korea since the 1950s consist of military brides and adoptees.[57] It has been estimated that "more than 100,000 Korean military brides" have come to the United States since the 1950s.[58] While some Korean military brides entered the United States through amendments to the War Brides Act of 1945, which allowed U.S. servicemen to bring their international spouses home, the majority of Korean military brides gained entry to the United States through the McCarran-Walter Immigration Act mentioned above, via the family reunification provisions.

While the civil war in Korea ended in 1953, the U.S. military's presence in South Korea remains salient. Drawing from his own research, Jae describes the country's "camptowns":

So in South Korea around the military cities, there's like these prostitution industries that cropped up. Korean women, most of them are normally—like they could be orphans or come from bad families, be raised by a single mother, you know, just very underprivileged members of society and they feel like they have no other means to bring money home to the family or make their own money. I mean that's one reason. Other reasons are women get tricked into it [prostitution], literally kidnapped, and then sold to a pimp at a camptown bar, and then he keeps her in there by saying, "You owe us this debt now." There's violence, obviously, that force[s] the girls to stay within that system, but pretty much they're just prostitution industries that cropped up around American military bases. And actually the Korean government did a lot to make sure that those industries stayed there to appease the U.S. soldiers because it was viewed as a very essential part of U.S.-Korean relations in keeping those soldiers happy.

According to Jae, his dad does not believe that his mom was a "camptown woman," but Jae has his doubts:

My dad said he doesn't think she was a camptown woman because she was different than all the other women. For one, she was educated and whatnot, but then there's this story of when they got married. She couldn't immigrate to the United States right away because there was a hold on her because she owed some debt. [This is] how most of the camptowns work: they would try to force women to go into prostitution to pay off their debts. So it could've been that she was tricked into that and then she was on the run from that debt and then finally, when she got married to my dad, she wanted to leave the country, but then the debt got reported and she couldn't leave. So maybe that's what happened? I have no idea because she doesn't talk about it. [My dad] thinks that when he met her, she was on the run from a camptown that was trying to pressure her into—like a bar or wherever she worked—that was trying to pressure her into prostitution.

Jae's parents eventually married, and the family moved to Maine for a military assignment. However, Jae's mother experienced difficulties adjusting to life in the United States and expressed "a lot of culture shock," which was not unlike the experiences of many of the Korean military brides who migrated before her.[59] Subsequently, Jae's father asked to be restationed in South Korea, and the family moved back. It was there that their marriage fell apart and led to an international custody battle. This resulted in Jae and his older brother being brought back to the United States by his father to live with his paternal grandmother in Ohio. Jae's mother fought for custody and eventually moved to Ohio to be with her sons.

The family of Abby, a twenty-two-year-old participant who identifies herself as "half-Korean" and "Hapa,"[60] had a similar military-related immigration history. Abby was born into a military family: her White American father was in the U.S. Marines and stationed at the U.S. embassy in South Korea when he met her mother, a South Korean national. While Abby is unclear about the details of how they met, she does know that her parents moved around for some time because of her father's military assignments. Abby was born in Italy because her dad was stationed there. The family eventually chose to settle in Ohio because "they just liked it here in this area." Similar to the experience of Jae's mother, Abby recalls her Korean mother's struggle in adjusting to life in the United States:

> Yeah, actually it was very hard for her. I remember she was very lonely because she was following my father, you know, for his job. She went to Ohio, and I remember she would cry when I was little because she was so alone. She also told me [that] right when I was born, my father's mom, my grandma—right when [my grandma] saw me, she was a little disappointed. My mom could tell how disappointed [my grandma] was when she saw I had black hair and looked more Asian than White. Which, you know, that must be a struggle for my mom. I feel for her.

In Abby's account, her mother's adjustment struggles were partially driven by racist interactions with her in-laws. Unfortunately, loneliness, homesickness for South Korea, discrimination, and racism played a prominent role in the lives of many post-1950s Korean brides residing in the United States.[61]

Finally, the migration history of Anna, who was mentioned in the introduction, is different from those of the rest of this study's participants. However, her story represents one of the dominant historical narratives about how many Asian Americans ended up settling in the Midwest. Anna was part of a large group of Korean adoptees who were adopted by families (typically White) in the United States, beginning around the end of the Korean War in 1953. Since that period in the 1950s to the present, over 100,000 children from South Korea have been adopted by U.S. families.[62] The Korean adoptee movement began with child causalities of the Korean War. These children included mixed-race children (children of U.S. servicemen and Korean women), children left homeless by the war, and children left in the care of orphanages either permanently or temporarily.[63] They were adopted predominantly by White families moved to action by anticommunist sentiments, Cold War humanitarian efforts, and/or religious callings.[64] Many families in Minnesota responded to these influences, and Minnesota became home to the largest Korean adoptee population in the United States.[65] Growing up in this contextual space in the 1980s, Anna recalls knowing only Koreans who were also adoptees until she was seventeen years old. She describes Minnesota and this cultural dissonance: "In Minnesota our state's slogan is 'the land of 10,000 lakes.' It's also informally known as 'the land of 10,000 Korean adoptees' because there are so many of us. I didn't meet anyone who was Korean who wasn't adopted until I was seventeen, and they were all adopted by White families."

Despite growing up in this environment, Anna's interactions with other Korean adoptees were "all coincidental" and not planned, either by her or her family. She elaborates: "My experience had been—being taken into a White family, they made decisions about my connectedness with what I was at the time calling my biological culture. They chose not to send me to culture camps, not to connect me with other Korean adoptees or Korean Americans. I didn't have Korean food until I was seventeen years old. And so that—absolutely, I was assimilated as a result of my adoption." Growing up in this racialized Midwestern space heavily influenced Anna's experiences as a transracial Korean adoptee and an Asian American growing up in the United States. This influence is discussed in more detail in subsequent chapters.

The histories discussed in this chapter offer a glimpse of the diversity of Midwestern Asian American backgrounds and experiences. The family histories are tales of migration driven by politics, school, work, and family. They are the stories told by people who live in, belong to, and represent both Asian America and America's so-called heartland.

2

"I Only Knew It in
Relation to Its Absence"

Isolated and Everyday Ethnics
on Spatial Contexts,
Community, and Identity

Jill, a thirty-one-year-old who self-identifies as "Hapa; half-White and half-Filipina," grew up in a small town in southern Illinois with minimal exposure to her Filipinx community. Her mother's side of the family "came over ages ago," and she describes her mother as "White as White bread." In contrast, Jill's father left the Philippines in 1966 to attend medical school in St. Louis, Missouri. Jill describes her identity this way:

> I totally knew I was different. But it wasn't necessarily in a way that was problematic other than sort of the vague feeling of loneliness. . . . Growing up, Asians and Asian America . . . it was just an enigma. It was a mystery. It wasn't home. I only knew it in relation to its absence. Whereas my impression of California—I just imagine it has to be very different. I went on a recent trip there [and] went to Angel Island and I-Hotel. There is no counterpart to that where I'm from. Also, there were Asians everywhere! . . . [Growing up,] there weren't enclaves of Asians around. That wasn't an option. That was the way it was; there was only absence.

Jill's experience in the Midwest is an example of the theme of isolation (along with loneliness and absence) and the lack of an Asian community. Similar to Chung's narrative (discussed in the introduction), Jill's experience outside of the Midwest's physical spatial context was transformative in influencing how she made sense of her racial identity. Jill also notes about her visit to California:

> I was in a room full of Hapas: it was an experience. I mean your default mode is not fitting in, half Asian in the Midwest. That is the default. That is the baseline of your life. That's not a choice for you. There aren't enclaves—at least for me, there aren't enclaves of Asians around. It wasn't an option; it wasn't a choice. That was the way it was, there's only absence. That's why I think it was hilarious when I read—I like *Hyphen* [magazine] a lot, but their "About Us" page . . . is kind of hilarious to me in that regard because they're like, "No Asian American 101 here. We discovered our roots a long time ago, thank you." I think Asians in the Midwest, just even roots, that idea—that is not just casual, that's not personal, that is everything. That is political. That's your place in the world. So yeah, it's a different experience.

Jill acknowledges how physical geographic space can affect a person's access to panethnic community, racial history, and formation of racial identity. Jill's comment about the magazine *Hyphen*, a West Coast publication on Asian American culture and identity, emphasizes her perception of the unevenness of where Asian American communities are positioned throughout the United States. It explicitly highlights the critical role of space in regional racialized experiences—and, I argue, the need to examine differential racialization in different spaces. While the members of some Asian American communities feel as if they have moved past the need to educate other Asian Americans on basic group history, others (e.g., Jill) are searching for the history of their Asian American roots. Today, Jill proudly asserts an "achieved ethnic identity"[1] as "hapa."

Jill's story indicates the focus of this chapter, which empirically examines how Asian Americans experience a racialized co-ethnic community and culture and a panethnic identity while growing up in the Midwestern spatial context. Drawing on my in-depth interviews, this chapter is organized around the central question: What is the role of physical spatial context in how Asian Americans perceive and experience co-ethnic community and culture as well as panethnic identity as they come of age in the Midwest?

In addition to the importance of spatial context, previous scholars have highlighted the critical role of various other contexts in human development and identity formation.[2] In the 1970s, Urie Bronfenbrenner introduced an ecological model that noted how different contexts (e.g., the family) could have multidirectional influences on one another in human developmental processes.

Several decades later, Cynthia Garcia Coll and colleagues expanded on Bron-fenbrenner's model to include social, racial, environmental, and cultural factors in the development of racial-minority children.[3] More recently, Lisa Kiang and Andrew Supple built on these ideas to propose a conceptual model relevant to the heterogeneous experiences of new-destination Asian Americans. Their model consists of four broad factors of influence: social position and individual characteristics, community factors, cultural and family resources, and developmental outcomes. Within the category of community factors, Kiang and Supple point to the importance of "social reception" (or racism and discrimination), "segregation" (or ethnic isolation), and "infrastructure" (the lack of ethnic community support, which can lead to "further feelings of isolation").[4]

Other scholars similarly have argued that ethnic identity formation is a multistage process influenced by context, at both the group and individual levels. According to Jean Phinney and colleagues, group-level contexts influence our sense of "ethnic affirmation and belonging," while individual-level contexts either encourage or restrict "ethnic identity exploration."[5] Ethnic affirmation and belonging is based on Henri Taifel and John Turner's social identity theory, according to which an individual's sense of belonging and worth is tied to their ethnic group membership.[6] The concept of ethnic identity exploration is derived from Erik Erikson's theory of ego identity formation, which involves four stages ranging from a "diffuse identity" (no commitment to an unexplored identity) to an "achieved identity" (commitment to an explored identity).[7] This theory was later reformulated by Phinney to better account for identity formation among racial minorities. Phinney's three stages of ethnic identity formation are an "unexamined" or unexplored ethnic identity;[8] an "ethnic identity search (moratorium)", in which the individual becomes immersed in ethnic-related activities and cultural events; and an "achieved ethnic identity." In the final stage, participation in ethnic-related activities leads the individual to possess a "deeper understanding and appreciation of their ethnicity."

Migration studies and acculturation literature also have stressed the importance of ethnic identity formation in understanding the children of those who experience immigrant adaptation. While classic assimilation theory seeks to describe the adaptation process of the offspring of mainly European immigrants since the beginning of the twentieth century,[9] scholars of post-1960s immigration contest the applicability of such thinking to the post-1965 immigration wave's second generation. This group of scholars has proposed a more nuanced, segmented version of assimilation.[10] According to Min Zhou, "The effect of ethnicity depends on the microsocial structures on which ethnicity is based, as well as on the macrosocial structures of the larger society."[11] That is, adaptation is influenced by both structural (e.g., the quality of schools) and cultural (e.g., family and ethnicity) factors. Offering an alternative theory for how ethnic identity is negotiated, Pawan Dhingra's study of second-generation Korean and Indian American professionals in the understudied U.S. South finds that in addition to constantly navigating multiple spheres with different identities, they are engaging in "lived hybridity" and thus exist at the "margins in the mainstream."[12] Dhingra argues that members of the second generation are able to incorporate their multiple selves simultaneously into the U.S. mainstream via lived hybridity, rather than simply enacting one identity (ethnic, racial, or national) at a time while traversing different social spaces.

Finally, previous studies of ethnic communities and children of immigrants also have found that the salience of identity varies by neighborhood context.[13] For example, Nazli Kibria's study of second-generation Chinese and Korean Americans in the Los Angeles and Boston areas found that the existence of the ethnic community served to strengthen "ethnic consciousness and pride" because it reaffirmed what parents were teaching their children.[14] And in a study of third or later generation Asian Americans in Northern and Southern California, Mia Tuan found that Asian Americans who grew up in White-majority neighborhoods had a more salient racial identity, whereas those who grew up in an Asian-majority neighborhood experienced more flexibility in their racial and ethnic identities.[15] The role of a nearby ethnic community appears to help increase socioeconomic mobility, strengthen ethnic identity, and allow for flexibility.[16] In sum, the process of ethnic identity formation is highly complex, and physical spatial context matters in understanding people's racialized narratives.

"There's Not the Same Community": Racialized Visibility and Identity

My participants' comments show that Midwestern Asian American experiences are informed by racialized visibility and perceived differences between the Midwest and other spaces. Ashwin, who grew up in Ohio, provides a clear example of experiencing racialized visibility in his response to whether he has experienced racism: "Yes, definitely. Just because, I think—because of regions of America." I asked, "What regions?" He said: "I think just like more conservative areas. It's just like that . . . when you're in the middle of America, when you're in Indiana—most of Indiana, because I just hate Indiana in general—but in Indiana, like in smaller-town Indiana, you'll see it. When you're in small-town Ohio, you'll see it. Even when I was at Athens [Ohio], which is actually not as conservative as some areas. It's a small town, and you have people who've lived in Athens their entire life. They're still the same. . . . You'll just hear little remarks on it [your race]." I asked, "What remarks did you hear?" He said, "Just little racial slurs."

Additionally, the participants perceive their experiences as distinctly different—whether the difference is real or imagined—from those of others living outside their spatial region. This ultimately impacted their identity formation. For example, Molly, a twenty-four-year-old second-generation "Taiwanese American" who was born and raised in Michigan, describes such differences in recounting her experiences. Her family's history in the United States began when both of her parents migrated from Taiwan in the 1970s as graduate students. They were living in Detroit in 1982, when Vincent Chin was murdered there.[17] This murder galvanized the Asian American movement in the 1980s. Molly recalls that her parents, despite being relatively new immigrants at that time, joined "Justice for Vincent Chin" marches because they felt a connection to Chin and the plight of Asian Americans. Her family's journey led Molly to believe that Midwestern Asian American encounters with "everyday racism" differ from the encounters of Asian Americans who grew up outside the Midwest:

> I've always thought—and no disrespect—that Asian Americans that grew up in the Midwest, they definitely came out with the most radical sense of identities. Just because they did have to undergo such, you know, everyday racism that people in pockets of Asian American communities don't have to on the West Coast or on the East Coast. And like in my life, I've encountered a lot of, especially, . . . West Coast Asian Americans, who are like, "You know, racism is like dead. It's over. Stop fishing about it—God." And who are sort of really, really callous to the lived experiences of other Asian Americans. And I think that growing up Midwestern Asian American has really, really influenced the way I see the world. . . . I think me [sic] growing up Asian in the Midwest has had everything to do with where I am right now.

Molly's response clearly signifies the impact of racialized visibility on Asian Americans in the Midwest. In her view, the inescapable racialized experiences (including being marked as racially hypervisible) within Midwestern spaces frames identity making. As she explains, growing up in the Midwest "really, really influenced" how she views the world and her career choices. At the time of the interview, she was attending law school and applying for jobs in the public-interest field. She said that she pointed out in her job applications that "I want to do this work because of race, and because I think that it's really important to have more people of color in public defender offices."

John, a twenty-three-year-old who self-identifies as "Taiwanese American" and grew up in a predominantly White space in the Chicago suburbs, also believed that Midwestern Asian Americans' experiences were inherently distinct:

I think that there's a lot of Asian Americans in the Midwest who grow up without other Asian Americans around them, besides maybe their family. So there's not the same community. Whereas some friends that I've met from the West Coast or East Coast, they grew up with a lot more Asian Americans around them. And then so I feel like the passion for Asian American issues tends to be not as—not quite as much for a lot of them. Of course, there's always a few that do find a lot of passion in that stuff, which is—that's really great. But in either coast, Asian American issues don't seem to be quite as important to them. . . . I think I find that by comparing campuses. Like U of I [the University of Illinois] has a lot of Asian American activism going on and stuff like that. I don't know. I guess I always hear about activism going on in the West Coast as well, but in terms of . . . things that happen that are racist, like—I feel like it happens a lot more in the Midwest.

Like Molly, John believes that Midwestern Asian Americans have a greater exposure to racism and racialized issues compared to Asian Americans on "either coast." As a result, both participants believe that Midwestern Asian Americans are more "radical" and possess "a lot of passion" about issues pertaining to Asian America. As John explicitly states, "there's not the same community."

These sentiments are echoed by Ava, a thirty-eight-year-old who identifies as "Asian American" and was born and raised in northern Ohio. Her parents initially came to the United States in the 1960s for their medical residencies, and eventually they resettled in the United States. In response to whether she felt accepted as an "American," Ava replies, "Not always. Mostly because of race." Her quick reference to race highlights its influence on her identity growing up in the Midwest:

When I took my first Asian American studies class in college, it resonated with me because I always felt like I was foreign. [Others were] surprised that I spoke English, surprised that I was from Cleveland and not from Korea, [and would ask,] "When are you going to go back?" and all that stuff. So all that stuff to me is part of my experience. And I think growing up in the Midwest—[I was] very aware of race, always. I remember being in kindergarten and being aware of race and being different. And growing up in a very White community, like the very, very few African American kids that were in my whole high school or Latin[x] students . . . feeling drawn [to these students], almost like, I have something in common with that person because we're not White.

Ava's comments reveal, again, the role of racialized visibility and the salient role of race. Her admission that "I always felt like I was foreign" is evidence that she was unable to escape being marked and treated as racially different growing up. Also, being spatially isolated from co-ethnics, Ava felt a sense of kinship and an almost gravitational pull toward other students of color. After college, she spent nine months in California and describes that period as "a difficult experience, very painful":

> I was going to go to California, which was this mecca of Asian Americans, Korean America. I went there, and I thought, "this is not for me" or "I do not belong here" because people keep telling me that I was from Cleveland, that I didn't speak Korean, that I was engaged to someone who wasn't Korean, [and] I wasn't going to a Korean church. On top of that I was young, I was twenty-two, I was a woman and an outsider. And I have all these intentions and I get placed at this agency, and it's like no one will listen to you. The aunties would kind of be like, "This country girl coming from nowhere, can't even speak Korean, this is ridiculous."

The ostracism that Ava encountered in California led her to the realization of "okay, I'm not Korean in this way." The spatial marker of regional difference—as the "country girl"—is evident in Ava's retelling of intra-ethnic contact in California. She eventually returned to the Midwest because "the Midwest is harder, but I know how to do it. I know the language, and I've done it. And it's harder, but I like being able to connect to lots of different people because we have empathy for each other." Ava's experiences in California reveal that for her, there are clearly marked differences in being Midwestern Korean American in California versus in the Midwest.

Amar, a twenty-eight-year-old second-generation who self-identifies as "Indian," was born and raised in a "99 percent White" neighborhood in Minnesota. Living in this primarily White space meant that he was subject to racialized visibility and was made aware of his racial differences early on: "I mean, no one could pronounce my name in school—teachers, everything. I definitely knew that I wasn't the same as these other kids." I asked him, "Did you ever grow up embarrassed of being Indian or wanting not to be Indian?" He said, "Oh yeah, a lot of times. There was always like some embarrassing moment that happened as a child, and I wished I was just one of the White kids." When people ask him, "Where are you from?," Amar replies, "India." However, he was born and raised in Minnesota. He explains his answer this way: "I'm assuming they just want to know my ancestry and they're just wording it, 'Where are you from?' because if I answer Minneapolis, they'll usually answer, 'Where are you from, from?' As if repeating 'from' will make me change my answer." I said, "So just for convenience's sake you'll say that you're from India?" "Yeah," he said, laughing. "I'll just skip to that and just say India. And if it's people that I'll be talking to for a longer time, then I'll say I was born in Minneapolis or something of that nature. . . . If I say I'm from Minneapolis, the people will roll their eyes, like, 'Obviously, that's not what I'm asking.'"

Amar's response indicates that he engages in this strategy for convenience and to prevent uncomfortable situations (e.g., having people roll their eyes at him). He currently lives in Northern California, and he mentioned the surprise he felt when he saw Asian Americans represented in all labor sectors and socioeconomic statuses. He poignantly noted: "You also see Asian homeless people. I never thought I'd see that in America, where old Asian ladies [are] digging through the trash."

Isolated Ethnics: "And on Sunday We Would Become Korean"

In an examination of how co-ethnic community and culture are experienced, two broad patterns emerge: people are either isolated ethnics or everyday ethnics. The isolated ethnics—those who experience spatially defined isolation, live at a distance from Asian co-ethnics (at least outside their families), and experience ethnic community and culture only on weekends or occasionally throughout the year—made up the largest group of the study participants: forty-three out of fifty-two. The remaining nine participants were everyday ethnics—those who had consistent daily exposure to co-ethnics. For isolated ethnics, experiences with a larger ethnic community are not seamlessly integrated into their everyday lives. Rather, these experiences take place in specific social or spatial contexts and/or at specific times.

Given the relatively small Asian American population in the Midwest as a whole, it is not surprising that the majority of participants reported zero to minimal daily exposure to an ethnic community. However, there were several recurring points of access to social spaces in which participants experienced a sense of a larger co-ethnic community. Specifically, many participants made weekly or biweekly visits to one or more of the following social spaces: an ethnic enclave, a relative's home, ethnic language classes, and a place of worship. The potential for social spaces to serve as dynamic spaces full of history and meaning in ways influential to identity formation was especially noted by participants in this category.[18] At times, religious activities overlapped with language classes, as both were held at religious sites. Other occasional activities included ethnic events and festivals, visits to ancestral homelands, and summer camps. The category of isolated ethnics includes all people who had weekly, biweekly, or yearly exposure to, or engagement with, a co-ethnic community.[19] For the sake of brevity, and because most participants in this category predominantly engaged in ethnic activities on weekends, I use the term "isolated ethnics" to include all people who engaged in weekend and occasional ethnic activities.

The theme of isolation was consistent among participants in this category. This is the case for Adam, for example, who grew up in Wisconsin. However, unlike Jill, he experienced occasional (biweekly to monthly) visits to an ethnic enclave growing up. He shared his views on the influence of spatial context, growing up in the Midwest, and isolation:

> Geography is tied to how we socialize and connect with one another. And I think that's something that is unique to California—that you have such a large community of Asians, Southeast Asians, East Asians, and the ability to share and connect and talk about resources, problems, and be able to communicate. I feel like that opportunity doesn't really exist for Asian Americans in the Midwest. I feel like it varies, but it's much less successful. And so being in the Midwest, and Vietnamese American, you can expect to feel isolated; you can expect at times to feel alone and need that extra effort, and that extra connection.

Jill's and Adam's connections between the lack of ethnic community presence in the Midwest and their expectations of "feel[ing] isolated" reflect Kiang's and Supple's conclusion that "community factors" are a critical determinant of feelings of belonging.[20] Adam was exposed to the Vietnamese community only when his family drove two hours to another state (i.e., a different social space) for groceries and to visit relatives. Furthermore, Adam said that he felt ashamed of his Vietnamese identity in his everyday neighborhood context, where most people were either White or Black. He noted that visits to Chicago provided him with a sense of ethnic self-validation: "I think, when we went to Chicago, it kind of solidified what my mother did. In those opportunities, even though they were limited, I was able to see other people practice the same kind of things.... Definitely coming to Chicago, I did feel good.... It was where I smelled food that was being cooked that was the same food that my mother made, you know? So, in a sense, I didn't feel alone when I had that connection to Chicago." Adam's statement points to the importance of ethnic enclaves for identity maintenance and daily life not only for the individuals in those enclaves,[21] but also for those who live in regions where opportunities to interact with co-ethnics outside of the family are rare.[22] Adam's experience illustrates how space impacts identity formation and that Midwest spaces are not all identical.

Other participants were exposed to a co-ethnic community via a different type of social space: weekend language schools. This was the case for Andy, a thirty-nine-year-old who identifies himself as "Chinese American." Andy's family came to the Midwest because of educational opportunities. In the 1970s, his parents emigrated from Taiwan to the United States so his father could pursue his second medical degree at Indiana University. Back in Taiwan, Andy's father had been a doctor and his mother a nurse. Andy was born in Indiana shortly after his family's arrival in the United States. When Andy was a toddler, the family relocated to a small, predominantly White town in northeastern Ohio. Consequently, Andy had very little exposure to other Chinese Americans or Asian Americans growing up. His only interactions with Chinese co-ethnics his own age occurred during Chinese language classes held on Saturdays at the nearby university. Andy stated: "We did get coerced, or forced, to go to Chinese school on Saturdays. But it was interesting because I didn't take it seriously because I knew I wasn't gonna get measured by it. It was kinda a place where I could socialize with other kids, essentially. On the weekends, we'd see each other, but on the weekdays, we'd be in our normal school . . . and mostly, it was predominantly Caucasian." In Andy's K–8 school, Andy, his sister, and two Vietnamese boys who had been adopted by a White family were joined by just one other Asian student.

Another recurring theme among the participants in this category was the role religious activities and social spaces played in facilitating their co-ethnic interactions. Specifically, the schedule of religious activities framed these experiences on weekends. Hana, a nineteen-year-old who identifies herself as "Korean American," illustrated this point in sharing her experience of growing up in Michigan. In 1990, Hana's parents left South Korea to pursue graduate degrees at the University of Michigan, bringing their infant daughter with them. Growing up, Hana attended a predominantly Korean church every weekend, and these interactions served as her primary exposure to other Korean Americans outside her family. Hana's reliance on the Korean church for a "Korean connection" is clearly illustrated in her explanation of the importance of these weekly visits: "I was thinking if I didn't go to a Korean church, I don't think I would have anyone. I would have no Korean connection besides my family members or my family friends. No—actually even then, I wouldn't have anyone to really talk to." As a result of the racial segregation inherent in the social spatial contexts in which she moved, Hana grew up with two sets of friends: her weekend Korean American friends from church, and her weekday White American friends from school.

This was also the case for Mina, a twenty-seven-year-old who grew up in Minnesota and identifies herself as "Asian American." She recalls there being only a handful of Koreans in the area where she grew up. Referring to the role of religious activities and social spaces in connecting her to her co-ethnic community, Mina stated: "There's one Korean Catholic church in Minnesota, so we went there for a while. . . . You know, after the initial kind of contact with the church, it was mainly like we wanted to go because it was a place where I could interact with other Korean kids. And eventually my parents stopped going to the church. I kept going. I would visit once in a while, even when I was in college. . . . Other than [at tae kwon do classes], everywhere else was

White, except for the church." I asked, "Now, in retrospect, how does—what was it like growing up in that predominantly White space?" She replied: "It was very isolating. I think it was very—it was a very safe isolated space where, you know, my parents had some control over like who I hung out with, physically where I could be, you know? . . . I think that from the perspective of my friends, I was always 'the Korean friend,' you know? Like, I don't think that I was invisible to them. I don't think even if they would ever admit it, that they would always associate me with food, or my appearance, or you know, things like that."

Mina touches on themes of isolation and racialization. Her statement that "I don't think that I was invisible to them" highlights the role of racialized visibility in her experiences within White social spaces. Specifically, she was constantly rendered racially visible and racialized ("they . . . associate me with food, or my appearance").

Ajay, a twenty-year-old who grew up in Dayton, Ohio, and who identifies himself as "Indian; Indian American," also experienced this connection between religion and ethnic community during the weekends. Ajay's aunt and uncles sponsored Ajay and his parents to the United States when he was nine years old. In the United States, his parents initially worked in a hotel owned by members of their extended family; later, they took up factory work. When I asked Ajay about how often he interacted with co-ethnics or members of the broader Indian community, he responded: "It used to be pretty often, like two, three times a month. So, on the weekends—because all families that we grew up with were pretty religious—we would have little gatherings on the weekends where they would do a little religious thing, and the kids would get together. So pretty much it was on a weekly basis: on the weekends we would see each other. And it was more so done to get the community together." I asked, "Did people drive from far away?" He said: "Not so far. Maybe thirty, forty minutes max."

Weekend visits to a religious social space (in this case, a temple) were also part of Priya's experience. A twenty-one-year-old who self-identifies as "Indian; Indian American," Priya was born and raised in southern Ohio. Her maternal grandfather had migrated to the United States for graduate school. Priya's mother was born in India but came to the United States at the age of two, while Priya's father migrated for postgraduate education. Priya's parents had an arranged marriage. Like other participants discussed above, Priya spoke about feeling isolated and having separate sets of friends: "When I was in high school I kind of felt like I didn't fit in because I didn't listen to the same music, I didn't watch the same movies [as other people]. . . . It made me feel isolated; everything kind of felt like I was isolated."

Priya interacted with her Indian friends through the temple, the Indian cultural center, and an Indian dance group, and she interacted with her

"American" (White) friends at her predominantly White school. She spoke about participating in a "cultural show" for her White friends:

> I would always dance because it is what I enjoy doing, and I always enjoy sharing. But it always kind of made me feel like I was an exhibit or something. Like my [White] friends would always come and all of a sudden, for a day, they would be really interested in India and want to know everything. And then I just felt like I was being asked to speak for an entire country. I know what I know, and what I grew up with, but I don't know enough. And I don't think under any context one person can represent an entire country because there are so many experiences, and so many differences. So that kind of also made me feel like I stood out. Like, all of a sudden, I was an exhibit.

Priya's experience of being made to "feel like I was an exhibit or something" by her friends exemplifies a hyperracialized visibility that marked her experience growing up in the predominantly White social spaces of southern Ohio. These were common experiences that constantly reminded Midwestern Asian American that they were the racialized other.

Ava, who grew up in a household where religion played a dominant role, had a similar experience. Her mother was one of the female elders in the family's Korean church. Ava described the ethnic community as "far away because the community was so dispersed, so we'd drive on the highway for like forty-five minutes to get there." Although these visits occurred only once a week, they lasted the entire day. The day would begin at 9:30 A.M., with "Korean class in the morning, service in the afternoon, and my parents would do church meetings after, so we'd get home like after 6:00 P.M." Outside of these Sundays, Ava commented that she was surrounded by "all White people." She explained how distinct these two social worlds were when she was growing up: "Aside from home, everything we lived and did was in English. Except for Sunday at the Korean church where we did have language class, where we learned basic grammar, but it wasn't very effective. Monday through Saturday we were around all White people—television, everything was a certain way, and on Sunday we would become Korean. . . . I want to joke that I was like Ivory soap—I was 99.44 percent American. . . . I was the Twinkie. I was very, very, very Americanized, and I would joke about it."

Experiencing religious social spaces as an access point to a larger co-ethnic community was common among isolated ethnics. Their everyday lives and structured interactions with their ethnic community on weekends played a crucial role in their identity formation. Ava's view of herself as "Ivory soap" or "99.44 percent American" during the week and "Korean" on the weekend exemplifies a hyperawareness of her social spatial surroundings and their impact on her ethnic identity and sense of nationality. These experiences led her to internalize her racial differences and equate whiteness with Americanness. Today, she remains firmly rooted in the panethnic Asian American identity: "I identify most strongly as 'Asian American' versus 'Korean American.' I have a very complicated relationship with my ethnic community and ethnic background. But the reason why I identify as Asian American is a lot about racial politics, and looking beyond to see how I did in fact have a lot in common with other Asian Americans of my generation, regardless of ethnicity."

Ava's explanation touches on the allure of panethnicity not only an identity grounded in a "common" experience of political struggle in the United States but also as an identity that supersedes ethnic and regional differences.[23] Furthermore, her rationale for her panethnic identification reflects Phinney's concept of an "achieved ethnic identity," in which an individual arrives at an informed ethnic identity.[24] Finally, Ava's narrative of whiteness as "Ivory soap" is also not uncommon: many other isolated ethnic participants had similar narratives. This identity negotiation highlights the influential role of social spatial context.

As indicated above by the responses of many isolated ethnics, self-perceptions among the members of this group are largely influenced by mere existence in White social spaces. This was the case for Andrea, a twenty-six-year-old fourth-generation Japanese American and second-generation Chinese American who identifies herself as "Asian American" and who grew up in a small, predominantly White town in Ohio. She said: "I just thought I was just one of the kids. I thought I was a Caucasian kid with black hair. I just had darker skin sometimes." Despite being tormented by other kids for being racially different, Andrea still saw herself as "White" until middle school. Only then, prompted by a school assignment, did Andrea begin looking into and unpacking her family's multiethnic history.

Alice, a twenty-eight-year-old who identifies herself as "Vietnamese" and grew up in Kansas and Nebraska, told a strikingly similar story about living in a White social spatial setting and its influence on her identity formation: "For the longest time, growing up in Kansas, I thought I was White because by the time I was in elementary school, there weren't very many Vietnamese people left. They all went their ways to California, Texas . . . to more populated areas of Vietnamese people. And so I thought I was White for the longest time. . . . Like in Kansas, they were all White. The only Vietnamese people were my aunts or uncles that my parents sponsored from Vietnam to the United States."

According to Kiang and Supple, "segregation in new immigrant destinations can take the form of residential, social, economic, or ethnic isolation," and residing in mostly White spaces provides access only to "limited social, institutional, and community resources."[25] This results in limited access to the kind of social capital that can be beneficial in adaptation.[26] Alice's life, like that of many others, reflects this reality. Alice saw herself as "White." For isolated ethnics, the notion of cultural whiteness refers to American cultural identity (specifically, to dominant American cultural practices) rather than to the physical characteristics of whiteness.[27] Alice explained: "I did all the things they [White Americans] did, pretty much. Playing sports, being involved with activities if I could. But at home, I was not the White version really. Okay, I guess I was two layers—I don't know. But outside I was White. But when I went home, we still spoke English, but with our parents we still ate Vietnamese food and stuff like that. . . . I didn't see a difference between my [White American] friends . . . and me. In that sense, that's why I thought I was White for the longest time."

While Alice believed that engaging in the same cultural activities as her White American friends made her similar to them, her statement about possessing "two layers" of identity highlights her keen awareness of her difference. It is important to note that in these instances, participants relegated their ethnic culture to a personal family affair that was distinct and differed from the outside world or social space.

Additionally, isolated ethnic participants compared the Midwest to elsewhere in the United States to highlight the distinctions they perceived between the two spatial contexts, as well as how these differences subsequently impacted their identity formation. Ava said:

> I think growing up in the Midwest, I was very aware of race, always. I remember being in kindergarten and being aware of race and being different. . . . I had just come from [visiting] California, and I really felt a regional difference. And maybe it's not even region, but where you grew up. You're around a lot of other Asian Americans, it was easier . . . you could be different, and there are a lot more models and avenues to express your identity. And it was more okay. . . . But I think for me, there's one way to be Korean, and I'm not that.

For isolated ethnics, the weekend encounters and occasional trips with co-ethnics were undertaken purposefully and with the explicit goal of maintaining, if not reinforcing, ethnic identity. So while the time spent traveling may be similar across geographic community contexts, distance—both the physical distance and the symbolic distance from everyday life in predominantly White social spaces—plays a crucial role in perceptions of identity and belonging within specific racialized spaces.

Everyday Ethnics: "I Feel Strongly Rooted in My Ethnic Identity"

As noted above, a smaller portion of participants fall into the category I term "everyday ethnics." These participants lived in proximity and thus had access to an Asian co-ethnic community at the time of their interviews and/or previously in their lives. Also as noted above, Minnesota's Twin Cities are home to the largest Hmong concentration in the United States, and Illinois (specifically, the Chicago metropolitan area) is home to one of the largest Asian populations in the Midwest (see Table 1.3 for more details). The nine everyday ethnics who participated in this study grew up in one of these two spatial communities. Seven of them were Southeast Asians from St. Paul, Minnesota, and the other two were from the Chicago area.

The everyday ethnics offer a different perspective on the Midwestern Asian American experience. Their narratives convey a stronger connection than that of isolated ethnics to their ethnic communities. For example, for Mai, a twenty-two-year-old who self-identifies as "Hmong American," her closeness to her Hmong co-ethnic community defined her youth in Minnesota. Mai's family fled Laos after the Vietnam War. After living in Thailand for six years, the family were admitted to the United States as refugees. They settled in Wisconsin, where Mai was born. Shortly after her birth, the family moved to St. Paul, Minnesota, to be closer to the larger Hmong community already living there. When asked whether there was a strong ethnic community around her while she was growing up, Mai said that there was: "I think for the most part I would say so, because during the time growing up in Minnesota there were a lot of Hmong organizations that were established. So right away my parents put me into some Hmong program. I did a lot of traditional dancing, so I definitely felt like there was a lot of support in the Hmong community and the Hmong organizations."

Growing up in this space also provided her with a strong sense of ethnic identity:

> In middle school people would ask, "Oh, what's your ethnicity?" "Oh, I'm
> Hmong." But then through high school, when people asked [I said], "Oh,
> I'm Hmong American." Because I think during that time, learning more about
> my history and understanding it better, and then learning about the American
> history too and understanding that, I came to understand better about how
> I want to identify myself. I just personally felt like, I know by saying "I'm
> Hmong" I'm still valuing my tradition as a Hmong person and understanding
> my language and how everything works. As an American, I'm also a person
> who lives in the U.S. and a person who has the right to vote and a person who is
> able to have freedom of speech and just integrate that all together.

Mai's access to and involvement in her co-ethnic community provided her with an experience that differed from that of the isolated ethnics. Her identity was centrally focused on the salience of her Hmong ethnic identity and her sense of national American identity.

Kanya, a twenty-six-year-old who self-identifies as "Asian American; Cambodian-Chinese," also grew up surrounded by a co-ethnic community. In the late 1970s, her family fled Cambodia to escape the Khmer Rouge's genocidal regime. After temporarily finding shelter in Thailand, the family was eventually sponsored as refugees to the United States by a Catholic charity in Indiana. A short time later, the family resettled in Uptown Chicago, where Kanya was born in the mid-1980s. Kanya painted the picture of a tight-knit co-ethnic community:

> I grew up in Uptown Chicago. When I was growing up, there was a big Cambodian community, because that's where a lot of us just kind of settled around. A lot of us just grew up within a one- or two-block radius from each other, and the association wasn't too far from us either. So there was just like, you know, a community sense there. . . . We're deeply rooted in our Cambodian-Chinese identities for sure. We always celebrate both new years, and then we also have all the American counterparts like New Year's, Christmas, and Thanksgiving, and that's pretty much it. But I know that our identity, as who we are—that's very important, and that's something that I strongly remember. . . . I feel strongly rooted in my ethnic identity. I truly believe that I have a dual identity and not just one.

Dara, a twenty-three-year-old who self-identifies as "Khmer American" and also grew up in Uptown Chicago, had an experience similar to Kanya's growing up. Dara's family also fled Cambodia during the late 1970s to escape the Khmer Rouge and entered the United States as refugees. Dara recalls being surrounded by her co-ethnic community as well as diverse racial groups in her spatial context: "I grew up in Uptown Chicago. It's pretty diverse because there's a lot of Asians. The majority are Cambodian, Laotian, Vietnamese, Chinese, [and] Asian Indian. There's a mix of Hispanic, there's a good mix of African American, and there's also a good mix of White. So it's pretty diverse. But yet each community is like so segregated in their own communities." I asked, "Can you give me a better sense of how large the Khmer community is where you grew up?" She said: "So the majority of Khmer, at the time I grew up, lived in Uptown Chicago. There's a Cambodian Association of Illinois, and two Khmer temples—Muslim Khmer and Christian Khmer—so that also kind of breaks us into smaller subgroups." I then asked, "And you always had that network, that support, and that community growing up?" She answered, "Yes."

Furthermore, when I asked whether she had ever felt the desire to identify as White, Dara's response was concise: "Being White? No. I was always proud of being Asian, and I was definitely proud of being Khmer." Dara's response represents the sentiments of most everyday ethnics about the strength of and pride in their ethnic identity, which is clearly impacted by their spatial context and access to a co-ethnic community. These views present a stark contrast from the way isolated ethnics viewed their ethnic identity growing up.

Conclusion

This chapter has explored the variances in spatially dependent Midwestern Asian American experiences based on spatial context and access to a co-ethnic community. Many of the narratives discussed provide strong evidence that participants perceived differential racialization and/or racialized challenges (e.g., isolation, invisibility, and racialized visibility) while growing up in the Midwest. Midwestern Asian American experiences are explicitly informed by racialized visibility and the perception that their experiences were different from those of non-Midwesterners. It does not matter whether or not these perceptions were based on fact: in either case, they were ultimately influential on identity formation and notions of belonging.

Participants experienced their ethnic community and culture based on two distinct patterns of exposure within their social and spatial community contexts. In the first distinct pattern, the experiences of isolated ethnics reflect pervasive feelings of loneliness and isolation. They lacked an ethnic community and support (or infrastructure such as an extensive subway system), which led to feelings of isolation.[28] This finding is in keeping with Kim Park Nelson's research on Korean adoptees: she found that those who grow up in Minnesota tended to experience racial isolation. She argues that this is a form of "broad, socially rendered racism."[29] This implicit form of racism is consequential in that it prevented Korean adoptees from having any exposure to cultural experiences or any connections with (or, for that matter, from even seeing themselves as a part of) an ethnic or racial community. In this study, the isolated ethnics' narratives highlight the importance of access points to social spaces in minimizing this socially rendered form of racism among Midwestern Asian Americans. Their weekly, biweekly, or monthly engagements with a co-ethnic community were facilitated via specific access points to social spaces (e.g., ethnic enclaves or religious activities). This points to the social and material value of particular social spaces as influential both for the identity maintenance of those who live in close proximity to them and of those who live in locations where opportunities to interact with nonfamilial co-ethnics are rare.[30]

The outcomes when religious social spaces are used as facilitating access points are similar. They were particularly formational for participants like Ava, who said that "on Sunday we would become Korean." In contrast, the everyday ethnic participants had more (almost unlimited) access points to social spaces. This was so much the case that experiences in those spaces were not meaningfully distinguished from other elements of everyday life. In their narratives, members of this group expressed a more vocal sense of ethnic pride and support from their co-ethnic community. Within their communities, there were established ethnic organizations and/or social spaces (e.g., temples and ethnic associations).

Many narratives are defined by spatially driven exclusion, isolation from any co-ethnic community, the inability to be seen or heard at regional and national levels, and a hypervisibility as racialized others in their everyday lives. Their claim on spaces in America's heartland are often met with resistance. Race plays a crucial role in their lives inside and outside of the Midwest. Consequently, these experiences inform their self-perceived identities as Midwestern Asian Americans within racialized spatial contexts. The experiences also highlight the importance of examining social spatial contexts in understanding how racial groups are subjected to differential racialization.

3

"Why Couldn't
I Be White?"

On the Legacy of Colonialism,
Racism, and Internalized
Racism in the Midwest

> Growing up as a minority, I found
> independence in these mottled, urgent
> ways. At a water park, at age eleven,
> being called a [racial slur] was just another
> new occasion for me to disassemble and
> learn the English language. To claim it in
> all its pricking points of ugliness. To be
> bullied and loved, relentlessly, by the
> alphabet.... Banana. Twinkie. F.O.B....
> As a Chinese-American, I feel frequently
> caught in liminal space, floating in-between
> myth and a self-inflicted series of rules.
> —Carlina Duan, "Michigan in Color"

There is a town called Pekin in central Illinois, approximately 170 miles southwest of Chicago. The origin of the town's name can be traced back to one of its original settler colonialists, who believed that the town's location was on the exact opposite side of the globe from Peking, China.[1] Pekin's history of race relations is highly problematic at best. It is known historically as a sundown town,[2] and it served as the headquarters for the Ku Klux Klan's Illinois chapter in the early twentieth century.[3] From 1923 to 1925, the Klan owned and controlled the local newspaper, the *Pekin Daily Times*, which prominently published Klan propaganda.[4]

In 1984, the *Journal of the Illinois State Historical Society*, a publication of the University of Illinois Press, published an article by Carl Hallberg titled "'For God, Country, and Home': The Ku Klux Klan in Pekin, 1923–1925." This article provides a noncritical history of the Klan in Pekin. Hallberg describes the Klan's mission and purpose this way: "In Pekin the Klan did not view itself as possessing the power to enact change. Rather it portrayed itself as a social order whose guiding principles embodied Christian and patriotic virtues essential to community improvement."[5] Toward the end of the article, the author clearly empathizes with the Klan by noting the hate group's "sincerity": "the Klan thrived on a variety of fears and issues, while public appearances contributed to its credibility and sincerity."[6] Incidentally, Hallberg's biography notes that he is "a native of Pekin."[7] What does it mean when this pro-Klan work is considered academic scholarship? It means that this version of history is legitimized and taught. There is still Klan activity in the area as of the early twenty-first century.[8]

Contributing to Pekin's problematic racial legacy is its history of blatant anti-Asian racism. In 1964, the Pekin Community High School's (PCHS) basketball team won the state championship. As a result, the high school received attention in the statewide and national press. This attention exposed the school's team names—Ch-nks and Ch-nklettes—as racist slurs.[9] Local and national Asian American communities protested in response. In the 1970s, activists from the New Youth Center, an Asian American youth activist group from Chicago's Chinatown area, traveled to Pekin and held a teach-in to try to convince the school to change their team names. They were unsuccessful. However, some people argued that the teach-in was the first step in bringing the issue of "new social sensitivity" to light among the students.[10] The protest did appear to have impacted the PCHS student body. The February 1970 issue of the Pekinois, the school's monthly student newspaper, published a letter that the newspaper staff had received. Titled "Oriental Discrimination," the letter read:

> To the editor of the student body newspaper. The FIRST TUESDAY of the month, a program presentation of NBC, was viewed by our family here in Los Angeles.

The segment with regard to the basketball activities, in which your high school was identified as the Pekin "CH-NKS," surely must have been made in error.

If not, please cancel our subscription to the future generation.

Yours truly,
Robert Mochinaga
The Tokyo "J-p"[11]

A Japanese American who lived in Los Angeles, California, had written the letter, revealing how far the news had traveled nationally. Below the letter, the newspaper staff asked for student feedback on the issue: "Mr. Mochinaga obviously feels that each time a PCHS student refers to the 'Ch-nks,' he is being critical of people of Oriental descent. . . . What should be done about this? Change the long-traditional name of Pekin High's team members and students? Ignore people (after all, they are a minority) who are insulted by the name?" [12] The staff members made their position on the issue known with their flippant and dismissive suggestion that the protesters be ignored because "after all, they are a minority."

It was not until 1981 that the school changed its team name to the Dragons. This change was not without community protests and resistance, which apparently persists today. According to the *Chinese American Museum of Chicago*,[13] a letter to the editor was published on "a liberal website" in 2005 that expressed racist sentiments towards the mascot change. It was written by "1960 Ch-nk Bob Brown," a former PCHS student.[14] In the letter, Brown wrote that he had served with "great honor" as the school mascot during his tenure at the school, and that he was "still upset today that the school buckled under and changed the name to Dragons in 1981." He believed that the decision was the result of "pointy headed pablum sucking liberals who run the polictical [sic] correctness gestopo [sic] in this country." Brown noted that he would attend his forty-fifth high-school reunion that weekend in 2005 and "will proudly wear my PEKIN CH-NKS shirt. Liberal [sic] and their pathetic ilk can go to Hell!!"

Additionally, in April 2019, a White male social studies teacher at PCHS resigned after being accused of making numerous racist, anti-Semitic, and xenophobic comments in a private, White-nationalist online community.[15]

I have recounted this racist history to illustrate that stories of anti-Asian racism and discrimination are pervasive and institutionalized. They exist everywhere and, in some instances, are fervently defended as part of Midwestern history and culture. It is important to emphasize that the themes of isolation and being very aware of race that were expressed by participants in previous chapters are concrete reactions to tangible experiences of racism and discrimination. The racist encounters recounted by my participants all involved some form of othering, in some cases with the intent of marking individuals as foreign or outsiders who do not belong in the Midwest (or even in the United States). For example, Jack, a thirty-six-year-old who self-identifies as "Vietnamese American," said about growing up in southern Indiana: "All the racial slurs, name calling, being picked on by other kids. Just feeling the sort of feeling of knowing you were different when you walked into a room—whether it be a store or a restaurant or whatever—and feeling like eyes are on you. So yeah, those sorts of things all happened throughout my childhood in Indiana."

Vivian, a twenty-two-year-old who self-identifies as "biracial, Asian" and who like Jack was born and raised in Indiana, recounts similar racist interactions. Vivian's father was sponsored as a young teenager to northern Indiana by his aunt, a Korean military bride who was married to a U.S. serviceman. Vivian's mother is fourth- or fifth-generation German American. Growing up, Vivian and her brother were the only two Asians in their small town in south central Indiana. Their White peers subjected them to such racist acts as calling them "ch-nk" and asking whether they knew martial arts.

Bing, a twenty-one-year-old who self-identifies as "Chinese, Chinese American" and who was born and raised in northern Ohio, experienced similar acts of racism. She recalls a White classmate insisting that Bing was born in China, and Bing was told to "go back to where you came from" while working in her family's Chinese take-out restaurant. People constantly questioned her: "Where are you from?" "Where are you really from, from?"

These sorts of racialized interactions have a profound effect on how Midwestern Asian Americans view themselves, as well as their place in the Midwest and the nation at large. This chapter examines the consequences of racialized visibility and racism, and their impact on ethnic and panethnic identity making. The chapter began with a quote from Carlina Duan, a University of Michigan student who grew up in Michigan. Her words describe how racialized encounters comprehensively impacted her self-identity, specifically highlighting numerous instances of racialized visibility. Moreover, in a reference to the concept of Asian Americans as racial interstitial subjects, Duan expresses feeling "frequently caught in liminal space, floating in-between myth and a self-inflicted series of rules." Duan's brief statement makes clear that there are links among the spatial (both physical and symbolic), racism, racialization, and internalized racism. The aim of this chapter is to further unpack these connections to explore the United States and the Midwest as racialized spaces that perpetuate Asian American experiences of racism and discrimination—and to show how these experiences manifest internalized racism. The next section of the chapter draws on historical, psychological, sociological, and cultural studies to interrogate the vestiges of colonialism, racism, racialization, and internalized racism in the lives of Asian Americans. Following this I analyze the role of internalized racism in the lives of specific Midwestern Asian Americans.

The final section of the chapter is guided by the following broad question: What is the Midwestern Asian American experience with internalized racism?

Colonialism and Internalized Racism

In the mid-twentieth century, several anticolonial scholars wrote about the detrimental psychological effects of colonial oppression.[16] These writings centered on the colonized mentality of identity confusion, self-denigration, and perceived inferiority, along with the resulting desire to mirror the oppressor.[17] More recent scholarship has extended this line of inquiry by historically linking Asian or Asian American communities with European and U.S. colonialism and imperialism. For example, Kevin Nadal's work maps the history and psychological impact of colonization throughout Asia.[18] Specifically, Nadal chronicles the extensive history of European colonization throughout Asia, including the colonization of Malacca (now Malaysia) by Portugal and Great Britain, beginning in 1511; the Philippines by Spain for over three centuries, beginning in 1565; Indonesia by the Netherlands in 1605–1799 and 1825–1949; the Indian subcontinent (1633–1947) and Singapore (1824–1957) by Great Britain; and Vietnam and Indochina (1859–1954) by France.[19] A nonexhaustive list of the parts of Asia and the Pacific Islands colonized by the United States includes Hawai'i (1897–present), the Philippines (1898–1945), and Guam (1898–present).[20] These colonizing presences resulted in the infusion of ideas of European and White superiority over indigenous peoples throughout Asia and the Pacific Islands.[21] For example, in his research on the mental health of Filipinx Americans, E.J.R. David explores the significant impact of colonial mentality in the form of "the self-inferiorizing attitudes, beliefs, and behaviors developed by Filipinos during colonial times and passed on to later generations."[22] In the Philippines, there is an almost automatic preference for anything related to the United States. This sentiment is negatively correlated with personal and collective self-esteem and positively correlated with depression symptoms among Filipinx Americans. Thus, acknowledging the impact of oppressive colonial history is critical to understanding the mentality and behaviors of the oppressed.[23]

The idea of internalized racial oppression has been explained in scholarship that examines oppressive colonial relationships historically.[24] This body of literature explains that colonized oppressed subjects react to their social and political conditions by questioning their identity, often believing that they are inferior and experiencing self-doubt and self-hatred because they are the objects of denigrating acts and stigmatizing labeling.[25] Consequently, those who are subjugated and consistently made to feel inferior will eventually view their own history, culture, and phenotype as worthless. This reflexive process is captured in W.E.B. Du Bois's concept of "double consciousness," or the "sense of always looking at one's self through the eyes of others, of measuring one's soul by the tape of a world that looks on in amused contempt and pity."[26]

To understand internalized racism, we must start with systems of oppression, which can be found whenever one group has power and privilege over another, and proceeds to use its dominance to maintain its control.[27] Scholars who have examined large systems of oppression have argued that internalized oppression is an "inevitable" condition of oppressive structures.[28] Accordingly, oppression can unfold at multiple levels of interaction (e.g., institutional and individual), is expressed in both explicit and implicit ways, and takes aim at markers of difference (e.g., race, gender, and sexuality).[29] Previous studies have explored internalized racism in various permutations, ranging from colorism (the privileging of lighter skin tones) and its association with social, racial, and symbolic capital[30] to educational impacts.[31] For example, in addressing colorism, Evelyn Nakano Glenn's work points to the economics of skin bleaching as perpetuating a "legacy of colonialism, a manifestation of 'false consciousness,' and the internalization of 'white is right' values by people of color, especially women."[32] This also clearly marks the ideology of White supremacy as transnational: it can and does travel with migrants and transcends national borders.[33] In her transnational study of South Koreans and Korean Americans, Nadia Kim argues that Koreans are influenced by Western White-supremacist ideology—via mass media and popular culture, the U.S. military occupation of South Korea, and religious influences—before migrating to the United States.[34]

Internalized racial oppression, then, is a concept that refers to a process in which racially oppressed groups come to accept, believe, and internalize the negative views and demeaning images and behaviors produced by the dominant group.[35] What emerges from these oppressive relationships is the practice of internalized racism, which includes not only accepting, believing, and internalizing negative views but also projecting them through actions that shame oneself and the group to which one belongs. According to Andrew Choi, Tania Israel, and Hotaka Maeda, internalized racism can result from experience with "discrimination, negative stereotypes, racist doctrine, self-hatred, and White supremacy."[36] Over time, racialization and the indoctrination of White supremacy become institutionalized, which results in detrimental and lasting legacies. Hence, internalized racism is one of the consequences and impacts of colonialism.

The Racialization of Asian Americans and Internalized Racism

The broad history of racializing Asian Americans as forever foreigners and the model minority has been well documented.[37] The framing of racial discourses on Asian Americans has led to various social and institutional forms of anti-Asian racism, including the exclusionary acts and other legal barriers to Asian Americans' land ownership, their limited access to and mobility in the labor market, their limited access to resources in education, and the denigrating portrayals of them in the media.[38] For example, another of John Mellencamp's songs provides a glimpse into the history of Asian American racialization by the dominant White culture in the United States, and by White Midwesterners in particular. In the 1979 song "Welcome to Chinatown," Mellencamp sings about encountering "a slit-eyed" woman in Chinatown whom he associated with a "rickshaw ride."[39] This explicitly racist description refers to an Asian woman who is also a sex worker. The stereotypical rendering of Asian women as sex workers reflects one of the oldest racial projects in the literal and symbolic regulation of Asian bodies in the United States.[40] It has manifested itself through multiple forms throughout U.S. history. Examples include the 1875 Page Act, which characterized most women from "China, Japan, or any Oriental country" as prostitutes in an effort to bar their entry into the United States; the 1922 Cable Act, which revoked the U.S. citizenship of any Asian women who married "an alien ineligible for citizenship" (read: Asian male);[41] the subjugation of Asian female bodies during times of war all over Asia via military prostitution and its aftermath;[42] and racist mass-media depictions of Asians as threats to the nation, nerds, or hypersexualized.[43] These practices have culminated in the racialized trope of "Lotus Blossom, Geisha Girl, China Doll"—all images of the hypersexualized and subservient Asian women that are pervasive in popular culture (such as *The World of Suzie Wong*, *Full Metal Jacket*, and *Miss Saigon*).[44]

These racialized portrayals fall in line with what Patricia Hill Collins, in her work on the positionality of Black women, identifies as "controlling images," or images used by the dominant group to "dehumanize" and "control" the "other."[45] Other controlling images of Asian Americans include the trope of Asian American women as the sinister and untrustworthy "dragon lady" (e.g., Anna May Wong in 1931's *Daughter of the Dragon*), as well as the trope of Asian American men as both the asexual model minority (e.g., Charlie Chan) or the sexually threatening "yellow peril" villain who seeks world domination (e.g., Dr. Fu Manchu).[46] Yen Le Espiritu contends that "fighting the exoticization of Asian Americans has been central in the ongoing work of cultural resistance."[47] Pun Bandhu, a Thai American actor, sums up the history of Asian portrayals in Hollywood succinctly: "We're the information givers. We're the geeks. We're the prostitutes. We're so sick and tired of seeing ourselves in those roles."[48]

When internalized, racialization impacts intragroup relationships. Consequently, Asian Americans come to view themselves and other Asians through the racialized gaze of White dominance, as inferior subjects.[49] The legacy of racialization influences the framing of racial discourses and how racial minorities view themselves and each other. In 1969, the "Yellow Power movement" activist and poet Amy Uyematsu captured the process of internalized racism in her critique of Asian Americans who have assumed a "mistaken identity" and have "fully committed to a system that subordinates them on the basis of non-whiteness" by becoming "white in every respect but color."[50] Uyematsu writes: "In the process of Americanization, Asians have tried to transform themselves into white men—both mentally and physically. Mentally, they have adjusted to the white man's culture by giving up their own languages, customs, histories, and cultural values. They have adopted the 'American way of life' only to discover that this is not enough. Next, they have rejected their physical heritage, resulting in extreme self-hatred."

The political rhetoric of S. I. Hayakawa, a Japanese Canadian American who served as the president of San Francisco State University from 1968 to 1973, provides an apt example to illustrate the consequences of racialization on intragroup relationships. Hayakawa, a conservative who was supported by Ronald Reagan (then the governor of California), played a key role in opposing the establishment of ethnic studies. Ethnic studies stemmed from two strikes by the Third World Liberation Front: in 1968 at San Francisco State University[51] and in 1969 at the University of California (UC), Berkeley.[52] Capturing the political urgency of these strikes, Karen Umemoto writes:

> Batons were swung and blood was shed in the heat of the conflict. But this violence was only symptomatic of the challenge made by activists to fundamental tenets of dominant culture as manifested in the University. African American, Asian American, Chicano, Latino, and Native American students called for ethnic studies and open admissions under the slogan of self-determination. They fought for the right to determine their own futures. They believed that they could shape the course of history and define a "new consciousness." For Asian American students in particular, this also marked a "shedding of silence" and an affirmation of identity.[53]

Lasting several arduous months and ending in March 1969, the strikes eventually achieved success through the establishment of the School of Ethnic Studies at San Francisco State and the Ethnic Studies Department at UC Berkeley.[54] Asian American studies, along with other ethnic studies disciplines nationwide, grew out of these important movements that were fought for by students, faculty members, and community activists.[55]

In April 1969, a month after the strikes ended, Hayakawa gave a speech to an audience of six hundred members of the Japanese American Citizens League at the Disneyland Hotel in Anaheim, California. During the speech, he labeled the San Francisco State protesters as "dissident students" and "neo-Nazis."[56] In his speech, Hayakawa also advanced the ideas of Issei and Nisei exceptionalism and the model-minority myth by stating that the Japanese Americans exhibited "good behavior" during their incarceration and had since achieved economic success. He argued that the formerly imprisoned Japanese Americans are "one of the greatest stories in the history of immigration." He then engaged in anti-Blackness by accusing the sansei of "imitating" Blacks and discouraging them from continuing to do so: "The Sansei should not be imitating the Negro. He should be urging the Negro to imitate the Nisei."[57]

Interestingly, Hayakawa also related his own difficulties as a Japanese academic in the Midwest. He had migrated from Canada to the Midwest in the late 1920s to attend graduate school at the University of Wisconsin-Madison. After he earned a PhD in English, Hayakawa taught at various Midwestern colleges in Wisconsin and Illinois for over twenty years before moving to the West Coast. In the Disneyland Hotel speech, according to *Gidra*, Hayakawa "told of the difficulties he encountered when looking for a job, saying that it was 'a silly damn thing' to have a Japanese teaching English in a midwestern college."[58] He also said that he and his family had avoided being interned during World War II because they were in Chicago at the time. Despite Hayakawa's own experience with institutional racism, he denied its existence by arguing that "racism and institutionalized racism" are "absurd abstractions to which dogmatic and absurd young people are reacting to as if [they] were words with references."

While Hayakawa was giving his speech inside the hotel, Asian American students and community members were fervently protesting outside. They were holding signs that read: "Hayakawa is a banana—yellow skin, white inside," "Hayakawa is not our spokesman," "Hayakawa is NOT our leader," and "Down with Hayakawa."[59] The reality is that both Hayakawa and the protesters were engaging in internalized racism—Hayakawa in his White assimilationist stance, and the protesters in their labeling of him as a "banana."

In general, the scholarship that has examined internalized racism and Asians or Asian Americans can be divided into two categories. The first category includes mainly education and psychology research. It identifies and provides the structural explanation (e.g., colonial mentality and racialization) for individuals' engaging in internalized racism.[60] The second category consists mostly of research from psychology (psychometric studies) and the literature on the sociology of immigration. Numerous psychometric studies on Asian Americans have emerged to identify and measure internalized racism and its impact on psychological well-being.[61] For example, Frances Shen, Yu-Wei Wang, and Jane Swanson found evidence suggesting that stereotype internalization (defined as "the identification with characteristics of a stereotype") exists among Asian Americans and is associated with low self-esteem and relatively poor quality of life along psychological measurements.[62] Andrew Young Choi, Tania Israel, and Hotaka Maeda applied the Internalized Racism in Asian Americans Scale to measure the consequences of exposure to internalized racism. According to the authors, internalized racism consists of three parts: having self-negativity, using the weakness stereotype (the belief that Asian Americans are inherently weak and inferior), and using appearance bias (the desire to conform to European beauty standards).[63] The authors concluded that Asian Americans "may adopt the racist messages and negative experiences" when exposed to internalized racism and that internalized oppression is "a phenomenon with clear negative mental health consequences."[64] The literature on immigration identifies internalized racism, views it through the lens of agency, and defines it as an adaptive strategy.[65] For example, Karen Pyke and Tran Dang argue that the use of labels such as "FOB" ("fresh off the boat") and "whitewashed" serves as an adaptive strategy that Asian Americans use to cope with their own racialization.[66] However, the authors also acknowledge that these terms are problematic: "although these identities are constructed as a means of resisting a racially stigmatized status, they also reproduce the derogatory racial stereotypes."[67] In the following section of this chapter, I turn to my study participants to examine the legacy of racialization, the role of differential racialization, and the participants' experiences with internalized racism.

"Why Couldn't I Be White?": Internalized Racism in America's Heartland

Growing up in Cleveland, Ohio, in the 1980s, Ava keenly recalls being one of only a handful of students of color at school. Her self-perception was greatly influenced by how she compared to her White peers: "I was always self-conscious about how I looked. I always hated my eyes—they were too small; [I] wanted blonde hair; I was always too short; [I] always wanted to look different; and [I was] not popular. I had a small group of friends, mostly White friends, but never really had boyfriends, and I attribute that to being Korean." Moreover, in explaining what it was like growing up in her spatial context, Ava states:

> I always knew that I was different, but I was never really able to talk to my parents about that feeling because they didn't know what it was like, really, as a child growing up in that environment. They knew it as an adult, but I would sometimes say, "Oh, someone made fun of me," and they would be like, "Oh, just ignore them. Just work hard and ignore them." But it was never like a soothing or a safe place I could come [to], and they would hug me. It was just like, "Oh, you know, just prove them wrong. Be smart and succeed. That's all that matters." Even as I got older and went through the teen years [with] body image, dating, and all the insecurities about how I looked. And self-consciousness and confidence, and all that stuff—*all that was in isolation*. I really felt like I struggled with that by myself and would just write in my diary.

Ava's response clearly highlights the influential role of racism and spatial isolation (and the lack of social support) while she was coming of age in the Midwest. In the previous chapter, Ava was quoted as describing herself as "Ivory soap," "99.44 percent American," and "Twinkie." These powerful self-descriptions illustrate how she saw her own social positioning during that period of her life: she was someone who felt yellow on the outside and White on the inside. She saw herself as "very Americanized," an identity that Ava associated exclusively with whiteness. Moreover, she carried these sentiments into college: "The first year [in college], I remember meeting some Koreans through intervarsity [activities] and feeling really uncomfortable and saying, 'I'm not really Korean.' My experiences with Korean Americans have been really negative. I don't feel like I belong."

While Ava attributes her shortcomings to her Korean ethnicity, her use of the ascribed racial term "yellow" highlights the influence and inescapable nature of racial identity and racialization for Asian Americans. Ava explains the integral role of "racial discrimination" in her definition of what it means to be "Asian American":

> To me, being Asian American is a political identification more than just [a] description. When I claim that, I believe it's an acknowledgment and a commitment to being aware of otherness and difference, and working to change that or to support others. It's this category that's about race, but it's also about racial discrimination. It's not just this synthesis category or racial category, but it's about an experience that's been about discrimination; it's been about immigration restrictions; it's been about stereotypes and oppression and unfairness. Because historically, I've learned that—but I've also personally experienced it here. And it's this larger term which lots of people can sit under. And it's an affinity to other communities of color or other marginalized communities. So for me, it's about social justice. Because to me, being Asian American is very much about this history and current status of discrimination.

Ava is an example of an individual who has grappled with racial and ethnic self-doubt and harbored a sense of shame and inferiority. Her thoughts reflect how racial subordinates have internalized their own racial oppression.[68] However, as Ava explains, these are reactions to experiences with racism and discrimination while growing up in the Midwest.

Ava is one of many examples of Midwestern Asian Americans who experienced internalized racism. Although I did not ask directly about internalized racism, nearly all participants shared stories of facing and reproducing negative stereotypical perceptions when they were growing up Asian American in the Midwest. One example was Mike, a twenty-two-year-old who self-identifies as "American Vietnamese" and who was born in Oklahoma. When Mike was in middle school, his family moved to Cincinnati, Ohio, because of his father's job as an engineer. In Ohio, Mike was enrolled in a private and predominantly White Catholic school. He recalls being the "only minority out of 500 kids" and says that "everyone was very wealthy, except our family." He explains that growing up in the Midwest, he primarily sought to be perceived as "more than . . . just" Asian American. His desire to "fit in," in his words, also led him to ignore the racial "jabs" directed at him (e.g., being told his eyes were small):

> I make it a point to fit in but still be myself. . . . So even in high school—that's why I think I didn't let the [racial] jabs affect me because I was just like, it's not worth it. Because if I do that, I'm just gonna let them win. So I think people saw that I was more than that. I was not just an Asian American. I was also an Asian American who was interested in tennis, who was interested in singing, who was interested in community service. I guess I thought of myself as more multifaceted, so that way even if one person picked on one part, I still was like, well, I'm more than just that.

Within his isolated spatial context, Mike was subjected to racialized visibility. In other words, he was perceived as different based on his race, which led him to want to be "more than just" Asian. Due to his spatial isolation, he did not have other co-ethnics to turn to for support. At the start of his college career, Mike had no intention of participating in what he called the "Asian scene," because he did not want to be pegged as the "Asian who hangs out with all the other Asians, and not having White friends." At that point in his life, he admits that he "had a misconception that the Asian American associations were very 'Asian power'—like, we don't want to be friends with White people." However, by the end of his second year, Mike ended up joining the Vietnamese Student Association when he realized that "they were just like me." Mike felt that his co-ethnics shared his values, cultural background, and experiences of growing up in the Midwest within predominantly White spaces. In his fourth year in college, Mike became the association's president.

At the same time, Mike also actively disassociates himself from Asian international students. While he finds acceptance and camaraderie among other Vietnamese Americans, Mike is often called "whitewashed" by his friends. However, this does not offend him. He attributes this label to his "preppy style" and being from the Midwest. In drawing on common racialized tropes, Mike clearly distinguishes between being Asian American and being "fobby." He defines a "fobby" as a person who has recently come to the United States from Asia and speaks in "broken English, and [is] very anime-esque: huge glasses, and bracelets up the arm, and tacky accessories, like Hello Kitty everything."

Mike's portrait of the "fobby," when juxtaposed against his "preppy style," reveals his reactionary disassociation with Asians as forever foreign and his preference for what he perceives as normative whiteness.

Internalized racism as a reactionary by-product of dealing with experiences of racialization and discrimination was a prevalent theme among participants, as I noted above in this chapter. This also was made evident by Andrea, a twenty-six-year-old from Ohio who self-identifies as "Asian American" and who is of Chinese and Japanese ancestry. Andrea's father had migrated from Hong Kong to the United States in his early teens, and her mother is third-generation Japanese American: her grandparents migrated from Japan to Hawai'i. During World War II, Andrea's maternal grandfather and his family were incarcerated by the U.S. government at Tule Lake, California. Andrea's grandfather has never spoken to her about his experience there. Her family settled in the Midwest because her maternal grandmother had migrated from Hawai'i to St. Louis and then to northern Ohio to pursue a nursing career. Andrea's maternal grandfather's family was a part of the large wave of Japanese Americans who moved to the Midwest during and after their incarceration in World War II.[69] Her maternal grandparents met in northern Ohio and eventually married. Andrea discusses how growing up in a predominantly White area of northern Ohio, in a multiethnic (Chinese and Japanese) household with language barriers between generations, factored into her self-identification:

> You know, when I was growing up, in elementary school I would pretty much say, yeah, I thought I was White because I really didn't know much difference and all my friends were Caucasian. At that point I really didn't know too much about the Asian side. I didn't want to study Chinese because my grandmother, who only speaks Chinese—whenever she talks (she speaks Cantonese) it sounds like she's yelling, like, constantly. I think that dissuaded me from ever wanting to learn it, because why would I ever want to learn the language that this lady is yelling at me?

Like Mike, Andrea was unable to turn to co-ethnics for support due to spatial isolation. In addition to chronicling how growing up in this predominantly White space has influenced her self-identity, Andrea recalls how experiencing racism influenced it, too: "When I was growing up, I did experience racism. I experienced it as early as kindergarten. And so I think up until high school, I really didn't want to associate myself too much with my Asian side because I knew that being Asian, I was probably going to face racism, therefore it was bad."

Nineteen-year-old Gina, a second-generation Asian American who self-identifies as "Korean American" and was born and raised in Illinois, had a similar experience. The maternal side of Gina's family migrated from Korea to the United States for political reasons when her mother was fourteen. Gina's parents met in South Korea when her mother went back for a visit in her twenties. Both of Gina's parents went to college (her father attended a university in South Korea, and her mother went to the Art Institute of Chicago), and they currently own a small business. Gina was raised in a predominantly White, upper-middle-class neighborhood where her peers were "all White, blond hair, blue eyes, brunette, you name it." In looking back at her childhood, Gina recalls how she began questioning, and was ashamed of, her own identity because she was socially ostracized and bullied during that period: "At one point, I asked my mom, 'Why couldn't I be White?' You know? I have small eyes—when I was little, I got beat up because I had small eyes. I wrote a paper about how I got picked on a lot because I was the only Asian in the class. . . . Every day, they dragged me to the back of the bus. Ugh, it was terrible. So . . . because of that, I was a stronger person. But as I grew up, I realized I hated being Korean. I despised it. I didn't speak Korean. I hated Korean food."

Elsewhere in her interview, Gina describes the difficulty of being Asian, thus highlighting the role of racialized visibility in her experience: "when you go to different places, you just feel so outcasted [sic] that sometimes, being Asian is so . . . hard. . . . So at times I wish I was White." Moreover, her White peers marked her as "foreign" but also as "honorary White."[70] She explains: "They say I'm basically a Twinkie. They tell me, 'You're Asian. You're yellow on the outside, but you are so White on the inside that I wouldn't even consider you Asian sometimes.' . . . When I get to school, they all say to me, 'Oh, you have such an Asian accent. It's so cute.' I'm like, 'Uh, I was raised in America. I do not have an Asian accent.'"

The racialized visibility via the racialized assumption of foreignness (possessing an accent) because Gina is of Asian ancestry is prominent in this statement. These interactions suggest her peers' disregard for the fact that she was born and raised in the United States. Through her negative descriptions of racialized treatment, Gina indicates that she internalized not only her sense of shame at being Korean and Asian but also the racialized labeling her White peers used for her. Both were reasons for her being bullied and othered.

In contrast to many other participants, Mai, a twenty-two-year-old who self-identifies as "Hmong American," did not grow up in spatial isolation from her co-ethnic community. She grew up in an area that was "mainly populated by African Americans and Hmong." Even so, her comments convey the recurring themes of discrimination and the powerful influence of racialization, whiteness, and White supremacy: "I think growing up, having to go through the prejudice and discrimination, there was a point when I was a little child where I was just like, 'I just want to be an American. I just want to have blond hair, blue eyes so that nobody would judge me or that nobody would discriminate against me.'"

This was also the case for Abby, a twenty-two-year-old who self-identifies as "half-Korean, half-Asian" and who grew up in Ohio. Abby's experience with racism led her to want to be White, as she explains: "In junior high, I wanted to be White. I just wanted to not be Asian because I wanted them [her White classmates] to stop saying mean things to me, racial slurs."

The role of spatial racialized visibility is evident in the above responses. Participants said that they had consistently been subjected to racism and discrimination based on their physical appearance. Thus, the negative association between their phenotype and their racial and ethnic identity reflects an individual-level reactive adaptation. Consistent with previous literature,[71] participants engaged in internalized racism (e.g., defensive othering, disidentification, and disassociation) as a reactionary response to their experiences of discrimination for being Asian. Furthermore, for many participants, experiencing racism was accompanied by the desire for whiteness. The majority grew up within predominantly White spatial contexts in the Midwest and were socialized by the pervasive White racial frame.[72] For example, their desire for blond hair and blue eyes and their failure to view terms like "whitewashed" as problematic reflect their socialization that led them to view Whites as normative and representing default Americanness. In their eyes, to be White was to be a normal American.

"I Took a Class!": Critical Exposures to Ethnic History and Organizations and to Co-Ethnics

Jack had experienced racist bullying and racialized feelings of otherness in small-town Indiana, and he describes how it "felt great" to attend college in California. He acknowledges that he sought out a "heavily Asian American environment" because, in his words, "growing up in such a White environment I craved that sort of thing. . . . And it was also the time when I was first exploring Vietnamese American history, Vietnamese American identity—that sort of stuff was in college. Of course, I think—being reflective and looking back, I didn't always consciously [ask questions] . . . but those kinds of questions were always there: 'Who am I?,' that sort of thing."

Jack is an example of how some of the study participants responded to change in their lives. Some of the major life changes participants experienced had to do with self-identity, spatial contexts, and access to racial and/or ethnic resources and communities. Consequently, beyond providing strong evidence of engaging in practices that reproduce internalized racism, some participants also exhibited changes in behaviors that shift away from reproducing inequality. This section of the chapter focuses on identifying factors that reduce the perpetuation of internalized racism. The findings show that the factors leading to shifts in perceptions and behaviors are framed by critical exposures to three central themes. The three central themes that recur throughout most of the participants' narratives are: critical exposures to ethnic and racial history, ethnic organizations, and co-ethnic social ties.[73]

For Ted, a twenty-six-year-old who self-identifies as second-generation "Vietnamese-American" and who grew up in Minnesota, critical exposure to all three themes played a major role in his self-perception and racial identity. According to Ted, his family relocated from California to Minnesota when he was young because his parents felt that moving the family to a predominantly White environment was the best adaptive strategy for their children: "I think [my parents] wanted me to improve my English, because the whole point of my pop's moving me out of the hood was for me to interact with White people, and compete with White people, and do better than White people." Ted "experienced a lot of racism" growing up, which adversely influenced his self-perception. He recalls asking his father in middle school whether he could change his Vietnamese last name to a more Anglo-sounding last name because "the kids thought [his last name] was funny and stuff" and were making fun of him. At that moment, his Vietnamese name was a source of shame for him. In retrospect, Ted views this incident as something "that's really sad now," because he is no longer ashamed of his ethnic identity. Ted describes going through a transformation:

> I guess I just always felt really different growing up. I think it's not only about learning—it was about finding who I was. I think part of that was trying to figure out where I came from, why my skin is this color, what does it mean to be Vietnamese, and what is Vietnamese? Like on a deeper level. I think taking classes and connecting that with what I was doing in the community was really empowering. It kind of made everything understandable. I don't know how to explain it . . . interacting with other Vietnamese Americans, and they would invite me to stuff. . . . [And] I took a class! I think that's what inspired me. It was 'Introduction to Asian American Studies.' . . . [The professor] talked about Chinese American history, Asian American immigration to the U.S., and later [about] refugees. . . . This really made me think about stuff. I mean, they have questions that I never really had to answer before, so it challenged my views. So it was good, really good. Once I did that, it really started getting the ball rolling in terms of working with multicultural organizations.

Ted credits his sense of empowerment and shift in self-identity to these various critical exposures through ethnic studies courses and participation in ethnic organizations.

John, who grew up in a predominantly White suburb in the Chicago area, is another participant whose feelings of shame gradually shifted. John's father was sponsored from Taiwan to the United States in the early 1970s by an aunt.

In Taiwan few years later, his father was introduced by a friend to John's mother, and eventually he brought her to the United States. Both parents sought higher education: John's father obtained an associate's degree, and his mother obtained a master's degree in engineering. In elementary school, John was already aware that he was different from his predominantly White classmates. He recalls an incident in which a White child taunted John's cousin by pulling his own eyes back and saying, "Your eyes look like this." John recalls laughing at his cousin. John explained that he laughed because "I didn't wanna feel left out or something." In retrospect, John acknowledged how this "little thing" still impacts him today: "[I] always kinda wished I was the type of person that stood up for my cousin."

In response to a question regarding his past perceptions of other first-generation Asians growing up, John evinces not just internalized racism but preconceptions about generational distinctions among Asians and Asian Americans and about what constitutes normative behavior (i.e., cultural markers provided via language and popular culture references) in the United States: "I think when I was younger, it was always a running joke about "fobs," you know?" I asked, "F.O.B.s?" He said, "Yeah, "fresh off the boat." . . . I don't know; I mean part of it is because it's like, as Asian Americans and being with Asian American friends, you identify with having parents that speak English in funny ways, you know? I always felt a disconnect with first-generation Asian Americans. . . . In general, yeah, I never found a lot of community with them. . . . The only way I ever really connect with them [was] usually [through] what I know about Asian pop music and stuff like that."

John also discusses his exposure to other co-ethnics through a summer camp organized by the Taiwanese American Foundation (TAF). One of the camp's goals was to teach children about Taiwanese cultural identity. According to John, "The community of TAF was really, really important for me in finding identity, and being okay with myself as a Taiwanese American." At the camp he met others who had experiences similar to his. John spoke extensively about the seminal role that TAF played in his life as a buffer from the isolation, discrimination, and bullying he endured in school:

I think part of it was because growing up, in school, and stuff, I always felt very isolated, and I think that finding the community and friends from TAF, I guess, made me feel a lot better about my situation. Yeah, especially when people would be mean or pick on me, and stuff like that. . . . Yeah, I think especially in seventh grade, I used to get bullied by these two guys every day in my English class. They would just ask me a lot of questions that made me feel very isolated and different. It was like to make sure that I felt different from them, you know? Like: "What kinda music do you listen to? What religion are you?" and things like that, even though they were trying to expect a certain kind of music or religion, and stuff like that. I would just answer their questions, but I guess they were really curious. But at the same time, they would say things in ways that tried to make fun of me, and they would spit [pencil] erasers at me, and stuff like that. I remember one day, one guy just straight up punched me in the arm as hard as he could. It hurt so bad that I cried. It was, like, silent tears, and I never told on them for that stuff because I didn't wanna be a narc and be even more uncool, you know?

Isolation was a central theme that reverberated throughout John's life. During his senior year in high school, he decided to join the U.S. military. His explanation for enlisting reflects the void he felt in terms of both community and citizenship, as well as the gendered racialization of Asian America: "Even when I was eighteen and nineteen, I still felt isolated. I still felt like people saw me as being Asian first and not American. . . . If I'm really honest with myself, I feel like part of why I joined the military also was claims to citizenship and patriotism and stuff like that . . . but maybe even being an Asian American male, more so, made me feel like I was really searching for ways to claim masculinity because of all of the ways that people tend to emasculate Asian American males."

John's response shows the complicated relationship that Asian Americans have had with the U.S. military. Historically, Asian Americans have enlisted as a way to demonstrate their patriotism. Such was the case with the 442nd Infantry Regiment, the nearly all Japanese American unit in World War II.[74]

In college, John decided to major in Asian American studies, a choice that he credits with providing him with the tools to critically access his identity. This education, along with learning more about his parents' immigration history, served as a humbling "eye-opener" for him:

I think the day that I was learning about the history of U.S. immigration laws and stuff like that and the 1965 [Immigration] Act—I felt like that was like a really eye-opener day for me, in that I think after that day, the next time I saw my parents, I asked them about their immigration. You know, they talked about all the same things that I had learned about. How they had these preferences for engineers and stuff like that. And it made my book come to life, you know? But then knowing that my parents actually experienced that stuff and then asking them about what it was like to come over, whether they were scared or if anything was hard. They told me all about how the language was really hard, and a long time ago people were really racist. They always made [my parents] feel like they didn't belong. I think for my parents—for me growing up, when I was little, I always searched for ways to claim "Americanness," and I think I didn't realize that my parents had been doing that for many more years than me, you know?

John's statement establishes that his learning about U.S. history was a bridge both to his parents' past and to the realization that they had also endured racism and have been searching for a sense of national belonging in America's heartland. Today, John continues this intellectual work by creating films that address Asian American identity. In making the connection between racialization and his own racial identity, John notes: "I feel like there's a space that the rest of America has sort of carved out for people who look like me. They're always going to see me as being Asian American first, or they'll see me as being Asian first—before anything else, you know? The only thing left for me to do is to claim that identity and to celebrate it, you know? I think that's the only way people will start to see other Asian Americans as individuals and complex."

For Anna, who self-identifies as "Asian American" and a "transracial Korean adoptee," the journey toward dismantling her internalized racism was couched in a narrative that differed from those of participants discussed above. However, the results were similar. Anna's mother raised her in a color-blind household where she was taught, "You're just like everyone else. Everyone's purple; race doesn't matter." Anna recalls identifying herself as "White" growing up and checking the "White" race box on school forms. Unlike the majority of my study participants, Anna was able to identify her own racial bias against "Asian-Asians" as "internalized racism":

> I have a lot of work to do, because I am fully aware that I have my own biases. I think I've been socialized and culturalized partially by living in the Midwest, partially by having a White family, to have somewhat negative perceptions of immigrants.... And I needed people to know that I was an Asian American, and that that was somehow distinctly different, and—if I'm being completely honest—somehow valued in my mind as distinctly better than an Asian-Asian. And so I have a lot of unpacking to do around my own internalized racism, because clearly there's something there. I definitely struggled with it.... In the area that I grew up [in]—there was a large Hmong immigrant community in the Twin Cities, and I did my best to disassociate with [sic] them. I think that it wasn't so much about my negative feelings towards them as immigrants or as other Asians or Asian Americans, it was more [that] I didn't feel Asian enough.... I felt like I would be judged for being too White because I had a White family, and I didn't know another Asian language and all of that.

In response to questions about what factors prompted changes in her life and whether she views herself as White, Anna said:

> Graduate school. When I started grad school, I did a counseling and personal services master's program, studying college student development. And seeing

language around identity development, studying Asian identity development, and being like, "Whoa, that's not relevant because this is talking about culture that's supposed to influence you, and family, and household. And that's not me." So mostly identifying with bi- and multiracial identity development, in terms of straddling two different communities. But then, also, learning about the construct of whiteness, and about privilege, and it really doesn't matter if I identify with certain tradition or community. The reality is, I don't have the same privilege as a White person because I don't show up in a room as White. So unpacking all of that. . . . I don't [view myself as White] anymore, but I did. I actually wrote [an essay in] my . . . application to get into graduate school entitled "I'm a Twinkie." The thesis of it was, "don't be mistaken, I might look Asian but I really am White." Grad school was really transformative for me. I have now come to understand that even though I was raised in a White family and in a predominantly White community, that my experience is still Asian, and that it's just a different experience—that it's more complex.

Anna's response highlights the impact that other Asian ethnic interactions in the Midwestern spatial context (specifically, the Twin Cities) had on her identity formation and internalized racism.

It is also interesting to highlight that while the narratives of Ted, John, and Anna referred to the influences of ethnic studies courses, not all participants acquired their education through formal channels. Some conducted their own research and/or reached out to their social networks because formal courses were not available. For example, Jill, a self-identified "Hapa; half White and half-Filipina," engaged in self-education through what she describes as "public study." In college, Jill never took any race-specific courses or joined any ethnic organizations. However, she was an active participant in antiwar movements in her college community. During her independent research on political movements, she stumbled across the 1960s Asian American "Yellow Power" movement and the brutal killing of Vincent Chin (discussed in detail in chapter 4):

Just reading how the idea that Asian American identity and Yellow Power, it's not about "I'm really proud of Japanese aesthetics" or "I love Chinese food." It was about people trying to forge something new, not on the basis of genetics but on a shared American experience. And that Yellow Power was about a counternarrative to White supremacy at the time. That Yellow Power was inherently about solidarity because they were trying to form a pan-Asian movement before it existed. And they operated in solidarity with the Chicanos, organizing school walkouts. They organized in solidarity with the Native American students occupying Alcatraz. . . . They organized in solidarity with the Black Power movement. Of course, as Asian Americans, they spoke out against Vietnam. And so, once I read all of that stuff, I felt like, there's a legacy here that I'm already a part of. . . . I think that all those really vague feelings that Asian Americans feel as a result of not being a part of the conversation about race in America, for the most part, [are] based on assumptions about being a model minority. All of these sort of vague feelings I think a lot of people feel, like not really fitting in, or just the kind of alienation you feel from your own story never being told, it's always there on some level or another—whether it's immediately on the surface for you or buried below. But I feel like understanding Asian American history, and not even the most radical part in the sixties, but all the experiences before that—that are so much about being immigrants chasing the American dream, faced with racism. The idea that Asian Americans too—that our bodies have been moored on [sic] and legislated against, and that people have organized, and that change has happened. I feel like I definitely understand the legacy. These people might not be my ancestors in DNA but they're my ancestors in spirit, and I will say that that's felt very genuine and it's meant everything.

For participants like Jill, learning about the history of Asian Americans' contributions to the counternarrative against White supremacy provided them with an understanding of their larger legacy and a place to belong in Asian American history.

Andy, a thirty-nine-year-old who self-identifies as "Chinese American" and who was born in Indiana and grew up in northeast Ohio, began his self-education at college. Andy's parents had come to the United States as part of the "brain drain in the seventies." Back in Taiwan, his father had been a physician and his mother a nurse. They migrated "probably on a student visa" so that his father could attend medical school at Indiana University. Andy had this to share about growing up in a predominantly White space: "Through high school, I did have [a] stereotypical perception of Asian Americans, Chinese Americans. Because we were all kinda a little bit dorky, a little nerdy, at least the ones that I knew, and that would include myself. So you tried to distance yourself from it."

Andy's statement signals his spatial isolation from other co-ethnics. His sentiments began to shift in the summer before college, when his mother forced him to attend a summer Taiwanese cultural immersion program, popularly known in his community as "the Love Boat."[75] During this trip, Andy met other co-ethnics who shattered his stereotypical images: "One of the reasons I was trying to disassociate myself with [sic] some of the Asians in high school was sort of this perceived 'geekiness and nerdiness, not very fun kinda crowd,' and these guys were almost the opposite of that. I would be the conservative one. They're crazy, partying people. I mean they pretty much blew away any potential stereotype you might have had of that group, which was a really good thing."

After this critical exposure to other co-ethnics, Andy went to the University of Pennsylvania and was exposed to a larger group of Asian Americans from across the United States: "I would say soon after that, when I got to Penn . . . I actually read up on a lot of Asian American stuff. There was a section in the library that was very small that had Ronald Takaki's *Strangers from a Different Shore.* . . . In college . . . I had started meeting more Asian Americans, and I started perceiving them more like people, like individuals, rather than ethnic groups."

Consequently, Andy became involved in a "bit more social justice, Asian American issues." He currently serves on the board member of Asian American organizations and fights to bring Asian American studies to his campus. The exposure he had to other co-ethnics via the Love Boat, the education he acquired on his own through the college library, and his interactions with ethnic organizations and co-ethnic friends all played a large role in altering his previous perceptions of Asian Americans and his self-identity.

Adam, a "Vietnamese American" who grew up in Wisconsin, similarly said that it was "definitely college" when he was exposed to Asian American history and began identifying as Asian American. He was introduced to relevant readings by an Asian American organization that he belonged to. To Adam, identifying as Asian American

> means significance; it also means [being] a part of the base group. It means that even though my family's only been here for thirty or so years, we've made a contribution to America. And other Asian groups have made a contribution to this country. I feel like a bunch of my experiences, discrimination experiences—a bunch of them have insinuated this foreign or separate "I don't belong to it" mentality. And I think that that term ["Asian American"] for me [means], "No, I do belong. It's you that, maybe, should think about if you need to evaluate where you belong." I mean, everything from what I've learned—Chinese immigrants that were brought over, how they suffered in [working on] the railroads, the detention of Japanese Americans—that history of oppression runs just as deeply in the Asian American community. So it makes me feel like I'm a part of the United States. I'm a part of America.

Regardless of how participants obtained their education (inside or outside the academy), it is important to highlight the critical role that educational materials played in their knowledge acquisition. Educational materials written largely by and about members of oppressed racialized minority groups were transformative. This was precisely the intentions of those who fought for including ethnic studies in the academy in the first place. In 1969, the editorial team of *Gidra* wrote:

Ethnic studies is the study of the culture and history of <u>this</u> country, our country—America—and of the contributions we have made to its growth and development. Asians have been in America for over a century. . . . We helped to build this country, but you would never know this from reading the history books used in most of our high schools and colleges. Ethnic studies will tell everyone about the contributions of the heretofore ignored people of color. It will dispel the all too common notion that white men alone built this country and that peoples of color are his guest to be told, "Go back to wherever you came from if you don't like it here." But the knowledge that builds respect and understanding to bring people together also reveals the uniqueness of each ethnic minority. We want to explore and come to understand our unique situation for it is only through such understanding that we can deal with the many problems—both individual and community—that confront us. This is why we need ethnic studies.[76]

It is precisely this exposure to ethnic history and community that helped another participant grapple with the evolution of her identity. Kia, a nineteen-year-old who self-identifies as "Hmong American" and who grew up in the Twin Cities, shares her experience of navigating internalized racism and her influential exposure to a co-ethnic community. While Kia acknowledges that there is a supportive ethnic community in the vicinity, she reveals that she never really had a Hmong American mentor growing up. Thus, while Kia did not experience immediate spatial isolation growing up because she was surrounded by the Hmong community, her response still reflects the impact of racialization and a disconnect from the Hmong and Asian American community. When I asked whether she ever felt ashamed of being Hmong growing up, Kia said:

Yes. I'm not afraid to admit that because I have learned why that is, and why I shouldn't be ashamed of it. I think I was ashamed of it because I've always felt like [sigh]—I don't know, it's hard to say. I just know that growing up, I've always wanted to be White, like a White girl. I wanted to have blond hair, blue eyes. . . . I remember as a child, whenever I went to the mall with my mom, I didn't want to be with her because she didn't know how to speak English, you know? It's like, "You should know how to speak English," that kind of mentality. So I think I was ashamed of those things and not really understanding why she couldn't speak English.

I asked, "At what point did that change for you?" She said: "I think because I went to this weekend conference where the Hmong author, Kao Kalia Yang . . . I think she really inspired me to really appreciate who I am. It's okay to speak Hmong; it's okay to be bilingual; it's okay to be different. . . . I think that was the turning point for me in knowing that I shouldn't be ashamed of my skin color, my hair color, you know." Kia credits the beginning of her shift away from shame to an encounter with a fellow Hmong American who served as her inspiration.

Conclusion

The Midwest is the source of nuanced Asian American narratives that go beyond the "vast banana wasteland."[77] However, this does not mean that Midwestern Asian Americans are not racialized to view themselves as "banana" within the Midwestern spatial context. The narratives of racism and discrimination documented in this study highlight the impacts of differential racialization (via spatial isolation, invisibility, and racialized visibility at both the local and national levels) and experiences with racism, both of which are clearly central to growing up Asian American in the Midwest. Specifically, the study highlights how existing in spatially defined isolation away from co-ethnics and encountering racialized visibility and invisibility impacts Midwestern Asian Americans' navigation of identity and belonging in different social spaces. These experiences are both distinct from and similar to those of Asian Americans who grew up in other regions of the United States.

Furthermore, this chapter has gone beyond merely identifying the existence of internalized racism and resulting behavior among children of immigrants: it has also empirically examined the fluidity of (or potential for shifts in) individuals' perceptions and the behaviors that perpetuate internalized racism. The study reveals three types of specific critical exposures, which have the potential to shift participants away from perceptions and behaviors that reproduce internalized racial oppression in their everyday lives: ethnic and racial history, ethnic organizations, and co-ethnic social ties. In the end, these critical exposures ultimately lead to what Paulo Freire calls a sense of critical consciousness (*conscientização*), which is necessary to divert Asian Americans away from behaviors that perpetuate internalized racism.[78] This study confirms Freire's findings, as my participants were able to recognize their oppression and intervene in their lived experience through concrete actions. Furthermore, the findings show how critical exposures and the emergence of a critical consciousness can lead individuals to resist the notion of whiteness as normative and to embrace a more positive self-image as Asian Americans.[79]

To return briefly to Ava: like other participants, she experienced a shift in perspective during her later years in college, when she became more interested in her pan-ethnic Asian American identity and sought to learn more about it. Ava describes the period in which she shed her internalized oppression this way: "I was taking the classes and understanding the structural aspects of racism and the history of it—that really was so empowering to me. I became very aware of being Asian American and wanting to do something about it and be with other people who felt that way."

For Ava, now a thirty-eight-year-old "Asian American," this was her period of "healing": "I kind of felt like all the stuff—the healing I did after that—happened when I went to college." Ava's journey captures the fluidity of racialized self-perceptions and how practices of internalized racism can persist but can also be mitigated or diminish over time. In other words, at the individual level, change (or "healing") is possible when racial subordinates are critically exposed to their own racialized and oppressed positions within various spatial contexts.

4

Crafting "Sharp Weapons" in the Heartland

The Making of Cultural Productions as Racialized Subjects

As a second-generation [Asian American], because I came over [to the United States] at an early age, I think I got a taste of, perhaps, maybe the sense of isolation? Uh, that I think people that immigrate here are kinda trapped within. But further, I think, I felt attracted to just kinda this . . . liminal, third space that I think these people occupy—and that we occupy. That oftentimes gets caught in the conversation as being caught between two worlds. Which I think is somewhat accurate, but as, you know, as we kind of get further in generation, especially our generation, it feels more and more like it's its own thing.
—Steven Yeun

In the quotation above, the Korean American actor Steven Yeun, best known for his roles in *The Walking Dead* and *Minari*, describes what it is like to grow up as an immigrant in the United States—specifically, in the Midwestern state of Michigan. In his comment, Yeun cites themes that are nearly identical to those mentioned by my study participants: living in perceived isolation, feelings of liminality, the role of agency, and the possibility of change. The "own thing" to which Yeun refers is Asian American identity and culture. With this identity comes the creation of new Asian American cultural productions.[1] In his case, the creation was helping make the award-winning film *Minari*.

Cultural forms and productions are central components of sustaining group memory and identity. In writing about Asian American culture as historical preservation, Amy Ling contends that documenting Asian American culture is about more than chronicling the reaction of how Asian Americans are treated by the dominant society: rather, it is "about recapturing various histories differentiated by the specificities of each group, histories of survival and endurance, stories of love and heroism, which would otherwise be lost."[2] While telling stories of "love and heroism" is a powerful and necessary act of preserving group identity, Lisa Lowe notes that [Asian American] culture also serves as "a mediation of history, the site through which the past returns and is remembered, however fragmented, imperfect, or disavowed. Through that remembering, that re-composition, new forms of subjectivity and community are thought and signified."[3]

Lowe explains that "the making of Asian American culture includes practices that are partly inherited, partly modified, as well as partly invented; Asian American culture also includes the practices that emerge in relation to the dominant representations that deny or subordinate Asian and Asian American cultures as 'other.'"[4] In her work on Latinx migrant imaginaries, Alicia Schmidt Camacho further develops this idea when she writes that "cultural forms are not a reflection of the social, or merely a detached 'set of ideas,' but rather the means by which subjects work through their connections to a larger totality and communicate a sense of relatedness to a particular time, place, and condition."[5] Thus, it is through culture that groups and individuals are able to mediate their (imperfect and fragmented) pasts and simultaneously construct new cultural forms to define their futures within specific spatial and temporal contexts. Culture must be understood as a relational concept to dominant racial representations, or racialization.

For John, one of my study participants, creating films is an outlet for expressing his differentially racialized experiences (such as isolation and racialized visibility, as noted in previous chapters). John intentionally creates films to contribute to Asian American cultural production: "I think I'm a legacy kind of person, and that's probably why I'm getting into film. Because I feel like a lot of people fall into two categories. One is like they want to enjoy life as much as they can, and other people want to do something significant with their life. . . . More of my goal is to leave having done something that has made the world a little bit better."

Both Steven Yeun and John seek to play a part in mediating Asian American history through visual storytelling. But how do other Midwestern Asian Americans respond artistically to their experiences with differential racialization? This chapter aims to contribute to the larger project of mediated historical preservation by examining Midwestern Asian American cultural productions and exploring how Asian American culture serves as "a mediation of history" to impact Asian American cultural production within the Midwestern spatial context.[6] Two questions frame this chapter: What are the roles of space, race, and art in Midwestern Asian American identity making? And what stories are being conveyed through Midwestern Asian Americans' cultural productions? The data used for this chapter draw on the in-depth interviews discussed in previous chapters and cultural materials produced by Midwestern Asian American artists (specifically, filmmakers, musicians, and poets).

I seek to analyze the connections between space (physical and symbolic) and racialization by interrogating the role of cultural productions in the spatial positioning of Midwestern Asian Americans as a "racially interstitial" population, or as those occupying a liminal, intervening space.[7] As Yeun's statement indicates, this is a conceptual lens that Asian Americans also apply to themselves. Using this perspective allows us to see the importance of agency, which creates possibilities for intervention and the emergence of cultural hybridity[8] and reveals the influence of structural forces (i.e., differential racialization) that regulate and oppress.[9] As Camacho argues, examining cultural productions can reveal different "forms of political subjectivity" that "resist subordination to the nation-state."[10] In particular, it can reveal resistance to the nation-state's racialized framing of Asian American identity.

Asian American Cultural Productions

The history of Asian American cultural productions can be traced to the mid-nineteenth century.[11] While the West Coast is credited as being where Asian American art emerged and flourished,[12] several influential artists of Asian descent were influenced by other regions of the United States. Isamu Noguchi, arguably one of the most successful Asian American modernists, was one such individual.[13] Noguchi was a sculptor, who was born in the United States to a Japanese father and White American mother. He was taken to Japan at the age of two and spent much of his youth there. In 1918, at the age of fourteen, Noguchi was sent back to the United States and enrolled in school in La Porte, Indiana. Going by the name Sam Gilmour, Noguchi lived in the

Midwest until he was eighteen, graduating from LaPorte High School.[14] His time in the Midwest would eventually influence his art production. According to Elaine Kim, Noguchi's work was partially impacted by "his studies of abstract painting and sculpture in California and the Midwest."[15] In particular, Noguchi's landscape design piece, *Monument to Plough*, "refers to the vast open spaces of the Midwest and to the American pioneer spirit"[16] while also representing his "wish to belong to America, to its vast horizons of the earth."[17]

Another early example is George Masa, a Japanese American mountaineer and photographer who lived and worked in North Carolina and is known as the "Ansel Adams of the Southern Appalachians."[18] Born in Japan as Masaharu Iizuka, Masa migrated to the United States in his early twenties to attend school in Colorado. He eventually made his way to Asheville, North Carolina, where he became a photographer with his own studio. Masa's mountaineering and photography played a seminal role in the mapping of the Appalachian Trail and the designation of Great Smoky Mountains as a national park in 1934.[19] Masa's photos were heavily used in promotional materials to advertise this region of the South.

Not surprisingly, neither Noguchi nor Masa escaped being racialized under the Orientalist gaze—that is, by virtue of the widely held practice of "setting [European culture] against the Orient as a sort of surrogate," a surrogate that is perpetually exoticized and consumed.[20] In 1935, the New York art critic Henry McBride "predicted" that Noguchi "would not amount to much in the public's eye": McBride derogatorily dismissed Noguchi with the attitude of "once an Oriental[,] always an Oriental."[21] Similarly, in *The Mystery of George Masa*, a 2002 documentary on Masa's life, he is described by the narrator within the first three minutes of the film as a "mysterious" person who "worked very hard," was a "wonderful little bundle," and was "kind of an Eastern mystic more than a Western photographer."[22] The persistent racialization of the Asian other, even in laudatory works, reflects the manner in which Asian Americans are subjected to stereotypes about their cultural productions and them as cultural producers.[23] In addressing Asian American "cultural artistic representation," Lowe argues that the Asian American movement "has struggled for access to means of representation in order to create alternatives to the stereotypical or fetishistic images of Asians as barbaric, sexualized, or unassimilable foreigners."[24]

In the 1960s and 1970s, Asian American culture reflected the temporal context of a movement and people with a political objective.[25] According to the historian William Wei, the Asian American movement's activist approach was heavily influenced by a 1942 speech by Mao Tse-tung later published as "Talks at the Yen'an Forum on Literature and Art."[26] Mao argued that art should serve a political purpose before an aesthetic one. According to this view, Asian American artists should see themselves as "cultural ambassadors" who had a "moral responsibility to the community": their cultural production should serve a "social purpose."[27]

A number of Asian American activists answered this call, including a particularly notable trio: Chris Iijima, Nobuko Miyamoto, and Charlie Chin. In 1973 they recorded the first Asian American folk album, titled *A Grain of Sand*. According to Daryl Maeda, the group's pioneering music addressed issues of panethnic unity, cross-racial coalitions, and anti-imperialism.[28] The album expressed its themes of anti-imperialism and antiracism through songs such as "Imperialism Is Another Word for Hunger" and "We Are the Children." The latter song contains references to being a part of the global Third World peoples' movement.[29] Years later, when reflecting on the group's formation, Iijima explained that the band had come together and toured in the 1970s as a "way to try to further organize and connect the localized APA [Asian Pacific American] activities happening around the country."[30] The group's intent was to instill a "consciousness about how racism affected us and others; how many poor communities, communities of color and of Asians, needed to be given greater voice; and the ways in which we could respond, as Asian Americans and as concerned beings."

By the mid-1970s, however, the Asian American artistic community began to fracture. Public criticism appeared against Asian American cultural productions that embodied a primarily aesthetic approach that was more concerned with achieving "artistic vision and standards" than with political activism—which many people viewed as "consciously individualistic" and apolitical.[31] For example, in 1975, the anti-imperialist organization Wei Min She (Organization for the People) published an open critique of Asian American writers for being overly "hungup [sic] on identity" without a "political focus."[32] In the organization's view, it was insufficient to focus strictly on pride and identity at the expense of political objectives. As a radical organization, Wei Min She was "dedicated to the ideal of culture as a political tool" and argued for "'reevaluating our cultural work' in order to 'make our culture a sharp weapon in the hands of the people.'"[33] From its standpoint, Asian American cultural productions needed to have political utility so they could be used as a "weapon" against social injustice. Recent scholarship, such as that of Oliver Wang, is skeptical of this binary contrast between "aesthetics" and "political" art.[34] Wang argues that this viewpoint is reductive, given that artists can operate in both realms—whether consciously or unconsciously. Furthermore, this artificial divide does not address the impact of art on consumers, irrespective of artists' original intentions.

The existence of this debate points to the importance of understanding Asian American cultural production. In *Asian American Art: A History, 1850–1970*, Gordon Chang poses the question: "Why have historians dedicated to studying the Asian American past themselves neglected to appreciate the importance of art in Asian American lives?"[35] He argues that almost all historical works produced before 1990 were characterized by this neglect. According to Chang, there are two plausible explanations. The first is related to the social consciousness of the 1960s Asian American movement, which was dedicated to recounting history from the people's perspective, or "from the bottom up."[36] In other words, the movement centered on history and resistance among the working-class community. The movement was interested in staking a claim to an American identity, which resulted in a shift away from distinctions among ethnic groups and toward a more politically driven, panethnic collective identity.[37] Consequently, transnational connections to the Asian diaspora were downplayed. Chang's second explanation for why pre-1990 scholarship largely failed to examine Asian American art has to do with the complexity of the topic. For Chang, the topic includes such questions as: What is Asian American art? What does it entail (e.g., in terms of style and form)? Who produces it? What is the "relevance" of examining Asian American art for "understanding Asian American lives in the past?"[38]

Contemporary Asian American studies scholarship has expanded its definition of the scope of Asian American experiences by incorporating transnational narratives. The transnational lens examines Asian or Asian American experiences in the context of the global economy, decentering the nation-state and its boundaries.[39] Asian Americanists thus have taken up the challenge of examining the role of art and artists in Asian American history in a multitude of ways. In assessing the contemporary moment, Yen Le Espiritu argues that the current generation is engaging in "corrective resistance," specifically in writing its own history, and she note that "given the historical distortions and misrepresentations of Asian Americans in mainstream media, most cultural projects produced by Asian American[s] . . . perform the important tasks of correcting a politics of resistance, and opening spaces for the forcibly excluded."[40]

Fighting Invisibility and Isolation and Defining Space

Two common themes emerge from my interviewees' responses in regard to Midwestern Asian American cultural productions: such productions fight invisibility and isolation, and they define space with political intent. In facing isolation, invisibility, and racialized visibility in the Midwest, Midwestern Asian American cultural producers engage with the politics of resistance by claiming and defining both physical and symbolic space.

Documentation of the long history of Midwestern Asian Americans' feeling isolated and invisible can be traced back to the beginning of the formation of an Asian American panethnic identity. In *My America: Honk If You Love Buddha*, a documentary film about locating Asian America, Renee

Tajima-Peña, the film's Japanese American director and producer, shares what it was like to grow up as Asian in the Midwest in the 1960s:

> Whenever I've gotten the same crap my grandfather got ("Go back from where you came from!") I think to myself, what do you mean? Chicago? I was born about two blocks from Wrigley Field. Mom and Dad were the Japanese version of Ozzy and Harriet. Every summer we would pile into the Ford Fairlane and took [sic] off for the open road. But I noticed something odd. We'd drive clear across five states and never catch a glimpse of an Asian face. [A picture of the young Tajima-Peña in front of Mount Rushmore appears on the screen.] . . . I think back to growing up here during the 1960s: talk about being invisible. If one Asian showed up for ten seconds on TV, the whole family would come running to see it. Dad would race in from the yard. Grandma would grab her walker. And then you could never be sure it was a real Asian [Images of White actors in yellowface appear on the screen].[41]

Tajima-Peña's narration makes evident the themes of isolation, invisibility, and racialized visibility. These themes repeatedly appear in cultural works produced by Midwestern Asian Americans.

For example, the Rice Paper Collective (the progressive Asian American student organization at the University of Wisconsin–Madison mentioned in the introduction), began publishing a zine called Rice Paper in the summer of 1974. The zine included essays, artwork, poems, and other forms of expression.[42] It described the Midwest as a "vast banana wasteland."[43] In this way, the collective drew attention to the way non-Midwestern Asian Americans perceived its members—namely, as culturally assimilated, racially hypervisible, and living in isolation. Reacting to their experienced racialization and perceived racial positioning, the members resisted what they saw as the national erasure of Asian Americans. In the zine's second issue, published in 1975, the collective boldly focused on institutional racism and White oppression: "Who built the railroads, did heavy mining, reclaimed wastelands, among other grueling tasks? We did! But these are facts that white writers censor. Our history and the history of other third world peoples has [sic] not been written for and by ourselves, but to perpetuate the myth of the American Dream. In our eyes, the media and educational institutions are the worst offenders [sic] of this crime. . . . We ask white Americans to recognize that these problems are not unique to Asian Americans, nor people of color; but are a product of white America's problems."[44]

In addition to calling for political action, the zine included statements by student organizations at various Midwestern universities that described their purpose and concerns. For example, in the same 1975 issue, the Asian student organization at the University of Michigan noted: "We should extend our base and appeal to AA [Asian Americans] throughout the Midwest, most of whom are middle-class and come from areas isolated from other Asians."[45] Such statements further substantiate the feeling of isolation in the narratives of Midwestern Asian Americans.

These themes continue to frame the narrative of growing up Asian American in the Midwest. I argue that Midwestern Asian Americans negotiate their racial identities by claiming spaces, which they do by creating a sense of place and identity for themselves within these physical spaces. The cultural productions that Midwestern Asian Americans create are informed by the history and experiences that emerge from the Midwestern space. In other words, in their art Asian Americans link their personal history to the larger Midwestern history. What are the pivotal moments in Midwestern Asian American history? According to the interview responses, one of the most mentioned historical incidents is the brutal murder of Vincent Chin in 1982 in Detroit, Michigan.

This murder and its aftermath constitute one of the most defining moments in Asian American protest history. Vincent Chin, a Chinese American, was murdered by two White men, Ronald Ebens and Michael Nitz, who were both affiliated with Detroit's auto industry. In the 1980s, Japan's auto industry became the scapegoat for the struggles of the U.S. auto industry and corresponding economic recession. Detroit unions were sponsoring events in which participants could take a sledgehammer to a Japanese car for a dollar, and the chairman of Chrysler Corporation joked about dropping nuclear bombs on Japan.[46] Ebens and Nitz racialized Chin as the Japanese "enemy" and unleashed their xenophobic anger on him during a bar fight.[47] It was precisely Chin's racialized visibility—his being marked as the Asian other (the "Japanese enemy")—that made him a target in this particular spatial context in Detroit. Witnesses reported hearing Ebens call Chin racist slurs and saying, "It's because of motherf-ckers like you that we're out of work!"[48] The two White men ended up chasing Chin out of the bar and bludgeoning him with a baseball bat. Chin died from his injuries four days later in the hospital, at the age of twenty-seven. Ebens and Nitz never served a day in prison for their crime. In a ruling that outraged the Asian American and other activist communities, Charles Kaufman, a Wayne County circuit judge, stated, "These aren't the kind of men you send to jail. . . . You fit the punishment to the criminal, not the crime."[49]

The killing of Chin holds great significance for all Asian Americans, but especially for the Midwestern Asian American who are aware of this history. This was the case for the Midwestern Asian American activist Soh Suzuki, who cofounded the Detroit Asian Youth Project with other activists (Scott Kurashige, Emily Lawsin, and Michelle Lin) in 2004.[50] The project is a social justice–oriented, leadership-focused organization for Asian American youth centered on multiracial coalition building in the Detroit area. Since its inception, the project has contributed to important work such as revitalizing Detroit's Chinatown, creating a mural of Asian American activists and activism there, and archiving Asian American oral histories.[51] Suzuki credits his learning about Chin and Grace Lee Boggs during his time at Michigan State University as his motivation for becoming an activist and community organizer.[52] According to Suzuki, the organization began "in response to questions being raised at the 20-year anniversary of the Vincent Chin incident. . . . Where has the Asian American community in Detroit gone? What does it mean to organize Asian Americans in Detroit today? What does it mean to be Asian American in Detroit today?"[53]

Suzuki's story about the influence of Chin is not uncommon: strikingly similar narratives were shared by study participants. Those who knew Chin's history had learned it from college courses or relatives. In chapter 2, I referred to Molly, who grew up influenced by her parents' participation in the "Justice for Vincent Chin" marches in Michigan. This history is a source of pride for her. It has also fueled her ambition to become a lawyer fighting for criminal justice reform. The case impacted others as well. For example, Kanya, who grew up in Minnesota, recalls feeling as if Midwestern Asian Americans "had no voice" until she learned about Chin: "The whole Vincent Chin thing was also a turning point in my life because it was in Michigan. It's like, oh, it's not in California, not in the East Coast, but in Michigan. It was kind of close to home, and that's where I kind of felt like our voice in the Midwest, it's really important."

Chin's murder allowed Kanya to locate the significance of Midwestern Asian American voices within the national history of Asian America—essentially, to stake a claim based on spatial affiliations. Kanya's statement also highlights the important connection between seeing oneself in spatial (geographic) history and feeling a sense of belonging within both Asian American history and U.S. history. In short, the history of Asian Americans in the Midwest plays a critical role in Midwestern Asian Americans' identity formation.

Chin's murder was the first incident that Jill (who grew up in Illinois) mentioned when she explained how she began to explore Asian American political consciousness: "I read a lot of politics, and I came across a mention of Vincent Chin. I mean, you know that story, it's just—once you read it, it just blows you away." Jill elaborates on the case's significance for contemporary race relations: "And just knowing about Vincent Chin in 1982, I think knowing about that means that you know that no one gets to say our era of being scapegoated is over, you know what I mean?" Similarly, Donna, a twenty-one-year-old who self-identifies as "Vietnamese American" and grew up in central Ohio, foregrounds Vincent Chin in describing her recently acquired knowledge of historical injustices toward Asian Americans: "I think growing up, Asian [American] history definitely wasn't emphasized in my schools, definitely wasn't incorporated into the curriculum at all. Yeah, I've been able to learn a lot more about discrimination cases against Asians or Asian Americans like Vincent Chin. Growing up I never knew who he was and what happened to him. I've just been able to learn a lot more about the injustices that Asians, Asian Americans have endured over the past few years."

Learning about this landmark hate crime in the Midwest has provided a way for participants to stake a claim to, and project a voice and visibility in, Asian America. They do this to counter their differential racialization in the Midwest. Chin's critical role in Midwestern Asian American history is clearly reflected by Gina, who bluntly states, "I always try to tell my friends about Vincent Chin."

"I'd Fight Back": Resistance from Midwestern Asian American Cultural Producers

It is in the context of defining self within space that forms of resistance emerge. In viewing Midwestern Asian Americans as racial interstitial subjects and examining their cultural productions, more light is shed on these processes. As mentioned above, art has long played a role in resistance and change. For example, in her examination of the Kanaka Maoli's (Native Hawaiians') resistance to U.S. colonialism, Noenoe Silva documents the important role of art (e.g., *mele* and hula).[54] Beyond my study participants, Chin has proved a popular subject more broadly in Midwestern Asian American cultural productions. His murder and the protest movement that followed were chronicled in the 1987 documentary *Who Killed Vincent Chin?*,[55] directed and produced by the filmmakers Christine Choy and Renee Tajima-Peña. By making the documentary, Choy and Tajima-Peña provided seminal cultural material for creating and sustaining Asian American historical memory. The film also serves as what James Scott defines as resistance in "public transcripts" that function as "works of negation," or forms of resistance that exist among subordinate people in response to their domination.[56]

As mentioned above, Tajima-Peña, a Japanese American, spent part of her youth in the Midwest. During World War II, her Japanese American father served in the U.S. Army while her mother's family was incarcerated behind barbed wire by the U.S. government. In *My America: Honk If You Love Buddha*, Tajima-Peña comments that she was raised to "just blend in" because "Mom believed that being too Japanese got her sent to the camps."[57] In other words, to counter the effects of being a hypervisible racialized subject, Tajima-Peña's mother taught her to "just blend in." Tajima-Peña learned about the Japanese internment camps only when she interviewed her grandparents for a family history project. When she presented this material to her class, her teacher accused her grandparents of lying and said that something like that could never happen in the United States. It was then that Tajima-Peña knew she could no longer stay silent. This experience of suppression and erasure served as the origin of her resistance. She says in the documentary: "And in that moment, I knew that it was racism that defined my life. And that I would never turn the cheek as my parent had. I'd fight back. I joined up with other young people who were just as angry as I was. That was the end of being an outsider. And I decided to become a filmmaker to show the world."

Years later, Tajima-Peña reflected on the role of the past on her cultural productions:

> Ever since the beginnings of the Asian American movement, we've strained under the burden of aesthetics, following the politico-cultural footprints of third world nationalist movement, within and without America. . . . Although I began filming with the question "Who are we as Asian Americans?" by the time I'd finished, I realized the real question is "What are we here to do?" . . . It's not enough to come here [to the U.S.] in search of the "Gold Mountain"— to make money and raise our families. There is a social contract involved in living in a democracy. People in [*My America: Honk If You Love Buddha*] such as Bill and Yuri Kochiyama and Alyssa Kang really resonated for me. They translated their personal experiences of struggle and racism into a moral obligation to fight injustice wherever they see it—and not only for Asian Americans. They get involved—and that's what I think we're here to do.[58]

Tajima-Peña's body of work on documenting social injustices[59] reflects one political legacy of the Asian American movement: the creation of art with a sociopolitical purpose. Cultural productions, whether created expressly with political intent or solely with an aesthetic purpose, have served as "mediation[s] of history" and have influenced generations of Asian Americans who came of age in the years that followed their production.[60] Twenty years after the making of *Who Killed Vincent Chin?*, another documentary about Chin was released, titled *Vincent Who?*[61] Directed by Tony Lam and written and produced by Curtis Chin, this film addresses Vincent Chin's impact on subsequent generations. It serves as a call to arms for political action and resistance within Asian America. Like Tajima-Peña, Curtis Chin was born and raised in Michigan.

In other artistic media, references to Vincent Chin can be found in the works of I was Born with Two Tongues, a trailblazing Chicago-based Asian American collective that gave spoken-word performances. The collective was active from 1998 to 2003, and its members included Emily Chi-Hua Chang, Marlon Unas Esguerra, Anida Rouquiyah, Yoeu Esguerra, and Dennis Sangmin Kim.

In her analysis of the collective, Jane Hseu argues that its spatial focus was both national and local, in that it was "protesting the national image of Asian Americans" and providing "specific Chicago spatial references . . . [that] present spaces of racial alienation."[62] In this context, feelings of belonging were missing from both geographic and symbolic spaces. The group's 1999 piece "Excuse Me, AmeriKa" exemplifies this point of national and local spatial influences.[63] The piece simultaneously addresses the multiple forms of oppression (from hate speech to hate crimes) of Asian Americans in the United States, and specifically the Midwest. The line in the piece "Bashing the heads of all our Vincent Chins" evokes all the racialized violence—whether psychological or physical—against individuals of Asian ancestry who have lived in the United States. The direct references to the Ku Klux Klan explicitly refer to White-supremacist violence against Asians. At the end of the piece, this point is further emphasized by listing Asian Americans who were murdered in hate crimes in the United States. This powerful piece documents both the physical and the emotional trauma associated with Asian American racialized visibility in its deadliest form. The victims are named so their lives (and murders) can never be erased from U.S. historical memory. In such instances, music and other arts serve as powerful media that can preserve a legacy both of pain and of political power. As the ethnomusicologist Deborah Wong has argued, "music is performative and . . . it 'speaks' with considerable power and subtlety as a discourse of difference . . . and the Asian American musicians who make this noise have a lot to say about what they are doing."[64]

More than four decades after his death, the legacy of Vincent Chin continues to influence the lives of Midwestern Asian Americans. For Midwestern Asian American artists, Chin's murder has played an extremely influential role in cultural productions, panethnic identity making, and inspiring resistance. This is evident in the work of Bao Phi, an acclaimed Midwestern performance poet and writer who grew up in Minneapolis, Minnesota, as a Vietnamese refugee. Phi's poem "The Measure" is explicitly about Chin's murder.[65] The haunting poem serves to document Chin's murder and reflect the tenuous Asian American positionality in the United States. On the thirty-year anniversary of Chin's death, Phi commented:

30 years later, and we can't forget Vincent Chin. And we shouldn't.

There is no way for me to make sense of this case. I try to write intelligently about it, and all I have is unbridled, bottomless anger. I feel provoked, to my core. That one of my earliest memories is that kids were calling me ch-nk and I had to ask my dad what it meant. To have a lifetime of micro-aggressions and not-so-micro aggressions directed at you, stacked on top of people telling you your experience and insisting that racism doesn't exist towards your people, and to top it all off, that people can murder you in the street in front of McDonalds and get a slap on the wrist for it. And though Vincent Chin's tragic murder is relatively invisible, it's horrifying to think his case is actually one of the more visible, known cases of anti-Asian violence. I feel that there is no room for love, or reason, in a world like this. I feel tired, and defeated. Stupid and useless.

Of course, if there is any bright side at all to this, it is that the memory of Chin and the blatant injustice has galvanized many Asian Americans to activism.[66]

"Our Politics is in Our Writing": Resistance by Cultural Producers

The handful of artists who participated in my in-depth interviews spoke about isolation and invisibility, the desire to leave a legacy behind, and the wish to contribute to humanity in a meaningful way (e.g., by fighting racism and being politically active). Their cultural productions (films, poetry, and paintings) were inspired by and created within the context of navigating interstitial space and touch on the feelings the artists associate with identity, racism, loss, and belonging in the context of growing up in the Midwest.[67] They were also interested in creating art with a political purpose and engaging in "corrective resistance."[68]

For example, Dara, a twenty-three-year-old who self-identifies as "Khmer American" and who grew up in Illinois, began her journey into writing and poetry in high school while participating in an after-school program. The program's mentors exposed her to the larger Khmer and Asian Pacific American community, as well as to artist activists in the community and elsewhere. She learned about issues such as "Asian Pacific Islander American identity, stereotypes, and gender" and how to apply them in activism and writing: "[The] mentors, they were spoken-word artists and they pretty much taught how to express yourself—but with powerful voices and through writing, through improvising theaters, and through marching for . . . May 1 [International Worker's Day]. They taught us a lot of that."

Dara comments about writing and performing poetry: "I felt really powerful because I can voice myself. I can write it out and perform a piece in my way, myself." However, she acknowledges the relative lack of spatial visibility for Midwestern Asian American artists: "People just don't know that Asian Americans exist in the Midwest because compared to [artists in] California, [on the] East Coast—their works are known, their works are viewed worldwide." Interestingly, Dara says that two of her mentors were members of I Was Born with Two Tongues. This connection eventually led her to participate in the Asian Pacific Islander American Spoken Word and Poetry Summit. Dara is still engaged in activism work and constantly asks herself, "How can I still help, how can I still get engaged?"

Gurman, a second-generation "South Asian" who also grew up in Illinois, touches on the theme of spatial invisibility when he speaks about the need to contribute to the arts, because he only saw "people who didn't look like me or didn't share my experience" in the works he was studying at his small liberal-arts college in Missouri. He explains why he currently writes poetry and performs as a spoken-word artist:

> I studied theater in college, and I studied arts in high school a lot, as well. I think for me, it was in college and I was studying theater that I realized that a lot of what was written, or a lot of the work that we were studying in our drama courses were [sic] primarily written for people who didn't look like me or didn't share my experience, and I realized that if I wanted to express myself theatrically in that space, I would have to write my own thoughts, creative speaking my voice, because I didn't see it in what I was reading. I think that's why I started to write more. And then I connected with a friend, and the two of us started writing together and started sharing our own personal experiences, our own histories, our own memories of being, when we were young, and growing up. We started to funnel those into our work and started to really take ownership of those stories, in our own words.

Like other participants discussed above, Gurman is invested in giving voice to the invisible by telling his story. And like others, he is politically active: he petitions government officials, attends community events and rallies, and reads up on issues to advocate knowledgeably for his political positions. Gurman says that his work in performance poetry is decidedly political. He explains the objective of his poetry performance group: "Our politics is in our writing. It's less about passing certain legislation and more about broader political issues. And I think our political angle, our emphasis, is on addressing issues—I think cultural issues and issues of intolerance and open-mindedness—and bringing together folks that wouldn't necessarily see themselves as being together."

For Jack, a second-generation "Vietnamese American" who was born and raised in Indiana, his interest in filmmaking is based on a desire to leave something behind for the next generation: "I think partly my interest in filmmaking . . . I would be lying if I didn't say that my kids—I see them as one of my target audiences, especially for my current documentary project about [family]. . . . If anything, I want them to know about the war, about how racism affected people here, and other 'isms,' and that sort of thing." Today, Jack describes himself as "politically active" in his daily life: he has participated in community organizing, marching in protests, and walking in peace and anti-war demonstrations. He is also active in several artist collectives in his local community.

Conclusion

To find a place for oneself in this culture is a political act.

—May Sun[69]

"Asian American culture" thirty years ago was, in essence, the cumulative political and ideological acts of many different Asian Americans contesting subordination in many different ways. All that we did was sing about it.

—Chris Iijima[70]

In examining the role of space, race, and Asian American art, this chapter has revealed how Midwestern Asian American cultural productions are simultaneously a reflection of and forms of resistance against their producers' subordinate racialized subjectivity. The creation of cultural forms and productions is influenced by and serves as a form of identity making, fighting invisibility, resisting isolation and racialized visibility, defining space, and engaging in resistance. The producers fight against their invisibility not only by documenting it and the trauma of racialized visibility (e.g., in *My America* and *I Was Born with Two Tongues*) but also by leaving behind a legacy via cultural productions for future generations. Midwestern Asian Americans are engaging in historical preservation and, as Amy Ling has noted, fighting to preserve marginalized and invisible histories that "would otherwise be lost."[71] In doing so, I argue, these racial interstitial subjects are engaging in corrective resistance in the way they write their own history.[72]

This chapter has shown that Midwestern Asian Americans' cultural productions are influenced by Asian Americans' spatially influenced differential racialization. The relevance of cultural productions in Midwestern Asian American lives is starkly clear: the productions serve as a type of political action. The producers are continuing to answer Wei Min She's 1975 call to "make our culture a sharp weapon in the hands of the people" by creating Asian American narratives with political utility.[73] This is evident in examples such as Tajima-Peña's personal history of fighting back by becoming "a filmmaker to show the world"—thereby enacting the process that Lowe suggested would emerge from Asian American cultural productions and the mediation of history, in the form of "new forms of subjectivity and community."[74] These productions are also a reflection of interstitial subjects existing in liminal spaces or in the world of the beyond and creating new cultural forms and art.

Furthermore, the Midwestern Asian American cultural producers who participated in my in-depth interviews live and operate with a heightened sense of racialized challenges and purpose. This is reflected in how they live their lives (being politically engaged) and their cultural productions (e.g., poetry and documentary films). This chapter has focused particularly on how Midwestern Asian Americans have drawn on Chin's tragic murder to mediate reflections of their (imperfect and fragmented) pasts, while simultaneously constructing new cultural productions—via the claiming of "all our Vincent Chins" that are relayed through films, poetry, and music—to define themselves and their futures within a specific spatial and temporal context.[75] Through their work, we can see that human agency is thriving and that change is possible.[76]

Using racial interstitiality as a conceptual lens to understand Midwestern Asian Americans has revealed how White supremacy is upheld, negotiated, and contested in the lives of Asian Americans. It also has allowed us to move beyond the metaphor of the Asian American as being wedged in the middle of a Black-White binary. Instead, emerging from Midwestern Asian Americans' spatial context are cultural productions with themes of resistance and collective memory making.

In *The Walking Dead*, Steven Yeun's character, Glenn Rhee, is killed in a manner eerily similar to Chin's death: he is bludgeoned to death by a baseball bat.[77] The fictional Korean American Rhee and the real Chinese American Chin both grew up in Michigan. Whether the nature of Glenn's death was consciously intended to resemble Chin's or whether the similarity is a mere coincidence is irrelevant. While the violence was jarring to watch, the gruesome scene was especially difficult for me to see because of its heavy social and historical significance for Asian Americans. In short, I saw Asian America embodied in Glenn. Interestingly, aside from one published piece, the utter lack of social commentary connecting Chin to this scene speaks volumes about the invisibility of (Midwestern) Asian American history in the U.S. educational system.[78] I would characterize this scene and Yeun's work in the film as an important part of Midwestern Asian American cultural production. As Asian America grows, it is important to continue to ask: What will the future of Asian American art be, as more Asian Americans become cultural producers?

Conclusion

We are a landscape of all we have seen.
—Isamu Noguchi, "Isamu Noguchi's
'Lunar Landscape' (1943–44)"

[Asian Americans] in the Midwest may
have a different experience than an AA
[Asian American] from the East or West
coast or Hawaii, but our common bond
is what our role in the future will be.
—Bill Wu, "University of Michigan-
Ann Arbor, MI. East Wind Position
Paper"

The origins of this book can be traced to more than a decade ago. It began with my journey to the Midwest to take up an academic position. To tell the truth, moving to Columbus, Ohio, was a challenge for me, a nearly lifelong Californian. I recall constantly longing for the familiar sounds, smells, tastes, and warmth of my California-centric Asian America. I had a difficult time adapting to the expansive, flat land and the bitterly cold and snowy winters. Most of all, I missed the diversity in the faces and places that I had taken for granted in Northern California. However, in the midst of this experience, change was happening. By living outside of my comfort zone, I was forced to think about and experience Asian America in new and more nuanced ways. In crossing paths with Midwestern Asian Americans, I found myself constantly wondering about their stories. How did their families end up in the Midwest? What is it like to grow up Asian American in the spatial context of the Midwest?

I have now lived in the Midwest for over a decade. Several years after arriving in Ohio, I moved to central Indiana and took a new faculty position. What is the Midwest to me now? The winters are still bitterly cold, and I still greatly miss California, but this vast stretch of America's so-called heartland feels different now. The cold may be bitter, but it also provides comfort. The Indiana skies are brilliantly clear, with minimal pollution. At dusk, the sky has the most beautiful orange, red, and purple glow. Sometimes there are pockets of peace within long stretches of land and silence. Most important, I have had the privilege of interacting with many remarkable Midwestern Asian Americans along the way. They invited me into their personal journeys and shared with me intimate details about their family histories, intergenerational dynamics, struggles with identity, friendship networks, hopes and dreams, and overall experiences of growing up Asian American in the Midwest. Their rich oral histories serve as a testament to the fact that Asian America is so much more than the little that has been documented in history books.

In the process of writing this book on Midwestern Asian Americans, I too have become a part of Midwestern Asian America. This space and its people have taught me so much. My experiences as an Asian American woman of color navigating a predominantly White institution within a predominantly White and conservative state in the Midwest has been challenging and transformative. I have experienced numerous racialized incidents in both individual and institutional settings. Existing within the Midwest has provided me with my own experiences of contested belonging and differential racialization—of existing in isolation and invisibility, but still being subjected to hyperracialized visibility. Over the years, I have experienced a range of emotions due to these racialized encounters. Cathy Park Hong has identified these emotions as "minor feelings," or "the racialized range of emotions that are negative, dysphoric, and therefore untelegenic, built from the sediments of everyday racial experience and the irritant of having one's perception of reality constantly questioned or dismissed."[1] Hong explains that minor feelings can be triggered by being told that it is perhaps all in your head after telling someone about your encounter with racism. The accumulation of these interactions—being consumed by minor feelings—can lead to feelings of "paranoia, shame, irritation, and melancholy." I know that these emotions are not unique to Asian Americans living in the Midwest. However, Asian Americans who grow up in the Midwest generally occupy liminal spaces and different spatial contexts. Whether accurate or not, their views on their experiences of racialization and limited access to resources are real to them. Additionally, their narratives and cultural contributions have been largely missing from the national discourse on Asian American history. As a result, Midwestern Asian Americans have focused on the handful of historical narratives they can access (e.g., the murder of Vincent

Chin). As I attempt to convey in this book, their stories are filled with "minor feelings" that tend to be dismissed by U.S. culture at large. These Asian Americans need to be seen and heard.

Midwestern Asian Americans represent Asian America. The oral histories of the Midwestern Asian Americans presented in this book reflect the multiplicity of experiences that are a part of, and embody, Asian America. The varied experiences of these lives cannot simply be reduced to the stereotypical racial binary of model minorities and perpetual foreigners who exist in a "vast banana wasteland."[2] While Midwestern Asian Americans are heavily influenced by these racializing processes, they are also distinct individuals. Their stories encompass loneliness, pain, and suffering but also love, joy, triumph, and resistance. They come from diverse backgrounds, as discussed in chapter 1. They are children of successful and highly educated immigrants, refugees fleeing from war-torn countries, and military brides or children adopted transnationally. They tell stories of negotiating identity, belonging, racism, educational settings, and access to resources within larger co-ethnic communities to create a pan-ethnic cultural community. And they are grappling with all of this within a racialized spatial context. These racialized bodies exist in racialized Midwestern spaces that are impacted by differential racialization reflecting themes of isolation, invisibility, and racialized visibility. Their identities and sense of belonging within both the United States and Asian American history are influenced by these lived experiences. Their varied lives show that there is no single way of existing as an Asian American, even within a particular space. Using a spatial lens reveals a more nuanced portrait of Asian America by showing how Midwestern Asian Americans are differentially racialized, and how this process has individual and societal consequences.

While some readers will dismiss the previous paragraph as expressing nothing more than common sense, I hope that I have shown in this book that nothing should be taken for granted in the Midwest. As Jill, one of my participants, noted, what some may consider "Asian American 101" can serve as a necessary beginning or even a lifeline for others. Chapter 2 presented evidence that while many Midwestern Asian Americans live in predominantly White spaces as isolated ethnics, there are also everyday ethnic experiences. While less common, the latter experiences show that not all of my participants exist within a Black-White binary. That is, there are pockets of relatively large Asian ethnic communities in the Midwest (e.g., the Hmong community in Minnesota). Therefore, spatial context strongly influences access points to ethnic communities and, thus, to ethnic and racial identity formation. Chapter 3 explored the consequences of Midwestern Asian Americans' experiences with racialized visibility and racism and the impact of those experiences on their identity. The chapter also reviewed the colonial roots of internalized racism within Asian

America, and I argued that critical exposures to ethnic and racial history, ethnic organizations, and co-ethnic social ties ultimately can lead to the emergence of an empowering critical consciousness. Such a consciousness is necessary for diverting Asian Americans from behaviors that perpetuate internalized racism. Chapter 4 explored how Midwestern Asian Americans artistically respond not only to their racialized experiences but also to their symbolic spatial context of in-betweenness as racial interstitial subjects. In this chapter, I chronicled the role of art in Midwestern Asian America's resistance movements. For many Asian Americans in the Midwest, their sense of belonging and positionality within Asian American history is rooted in events specific to the geographic Midwestern space. Along those lines, references to themes of isolation, invisibility, and the murder of Vincent Chin are found throughout their cultural productions. The art they have produced reflects an engagement with corrective resistance in their writing of their own history.[3] Midwestern Asian Americans are producing resistance culture while existing in interstitial spaces, or "the beyond."[4]

Finally, while I have attempted to cover numerous topics related to Midwestern Asian America, many questions remain to examine. Some questions for future research include: How do the experiences of Midwestern and coastal Asian Americans differ? What are the experiences of Asian Americans from rural regions or so-called new destinations (or, new locations with growing immigrant populations) who move to larger metropolitan cities later in life? Does their self-perception change in a new spatial context? How do social activism and community organizing differ among Asians and Asian Americans across various spatial regions of the United States and transnationally? What is the role of technology in disseminating information between different regional communities across the United States and around the globe? What does community mean in the new digital and transnational context? These are all pertinent questions for future researchers to address in efforts to further our understanding of the roles of space and race, especially in rural and new destinations, for children of Asian immigrants and refugees.

Epilogue

A Final Note on Moving Forward for Asian America

> Asian Americans can no longer afford to watch the black-and-white racial struggle from the sidelines. They have their own cause to fight since they are also victims—with less visible scars—of the white institutionalized racism. A yellow movement has been set into motion by the black power movement. Addressing itself to the unique problems of Asian Americans, this "yellow power" movement is relevant to the black power movement in that both are part of the Third World struggle to liberate all colored people.
> —Amy Uyematsu, "The Emergence of Yellow Power in America"

There have been vast changes in the sociopolitical landscape of the United States since I conducted my first interview for this book. The early 2010s was an era characterized by the term "postracial America," or the idea that the United States had moved past its race-related problems with the election of the nation's first Black president, Barack Obama. Back then, more than half of my study participants expressed optimism—or at least, in some cases, cautious optimism—about the future of race in the United States. While sharing their pain and struggles with racism, they still expressed hope about future race relations. Their responses contained multiple references to a mixed-race future and the blurring of color lines. Following are some of the study participants' thoughts, along with their racial self-identifications and places of birth and/or residence.

> Chung, "Taiwanese American; Asian American," from Illinois: "Our census will probably show [that] we become very multicultural. As there are more interracial marriages, . . . even in the small towns of America, at least just in this country, people [will] start to see more diversity. We will see it on TV. And as we become more global in nature, people cannot afford to be racist. I think it is just going to have to change. It will change faster and faster as time goes on."

> Eric, "Asian American; Indian American," from Ohio: "I remember I saw a *Time* magazine article. I think [its title] was like, "The Face of the New America," and it was a picture of somebody . . . they had combined pictures of people who were all different races. If that's what the new America is like, it's kind of hard to be racist if everybody . . . —actually, I remember the Indian comedian, Russell Peters, he had this one act where he was saying that everybody in the world is mixing, we're all going to become like one shade of beige, and that's kind of true."

> Ashwin, "South Asian American," from Ohio: "I think it's definitely getting better. I don't see why it would get worse. I think with more influential people of minority status—like they're getting more in the political eye. Or the public eye, you know? They are breaking down standards, I would say."

> Kia, "Hmong American," from Minnesota: "I think it'll improve, but I personally believe it's a gradual process. . . . People think that we're past racism, but in terms of Asian Americans, we still have a long way to go in terms of not being discriminated against; not having jokes be said about us and it being funny. So I think it'll improve, but it's going to be a really long process."

At the other end of the spectrum, a handful of participants were skeptical about the future of race relations. Their statements reflect reactive responses to the postracial rhetoric of that period. For these individuals, ignoring the problems of race does not make the problems go away. Their statements foreshadow the racist attitudes that have since come to dominate the racial politics of the 2020s. Below are some of their statements on the future of race:

> Ava, "Asian American," from Ohio: "I don't know, it's kind of like I feel a little bit frustrated. Like when Obama was elected, it was a huge thing. But then I felt like a lot of people were saying, 'Race is over. We're postracial America. We did it.' . . . It's almost like we've got to a point now where if anyone mentions racism, people get really offended: 'I'm not a racist,' and blah, blah, blah. Because it's almost like it's harder to talk about it than in the fifties when everything was more blatant, and everything was more in your face. So I think that in a way means that yes, we've made progress. But it's harder in a way to talk about race these days because no one wants to talk about it. The post–affirmative action debates now—we can't talk about race at all, we shouldn't talk about it, we should not even use it. And I know it's a flawed category, there's all this stuff that's happening demographically with multiracial people, but we're losing a tool in our language to talk about some things that continue and structures that continue. So I don't know how I feel about that. . . . I'm kind of conflicted. I think we're moving towards an era where we're not talking about race relations because they're not as severe. But almost to a point where people are—it's not even something people want to talk about or can talk about anymore, and I don't think that's right."

> Ted, "Vietnamese American," from Minnesota: "I think one of the problems is that . . . a lot of White people feel uncomfortable talking about [diversity] because if you speak against diversity, you're labeled a racist. But I think the issue is that we've never really talked about why it is important to talk about diversity and how diversity benefits society. . . . You're not creating a demand for people to care. I think that's the biggest problem. Until that is fixed, I don't really see it getting better. I actually think it's probably getting worse. Statistics show that too."

> Anna, "Asian American; Korean adoptee," from Minnesota: "My mom always used to say things get a lot worse before they get better. . . . The rate at which people are open to having conversations, sharing experiences, moving beyond stereotypes—I don't know how fast that's gonna happen. My guess is there's gonna be some really messy places before we get to good places."

In retrospect, Anna's statement reads like a prediction of the years that followed. Her comment about "some really messy places" arguably describes the current state of race relations in the United States. The ephemeral postracial fog has dissipated for those who had believed in its existence, and racial discourse is now front and center. As I write this epilogue, we are in a highly politicized epoch in which Donald Trump's America, the Black Lives Matter protest movement, and the COVID-19 pandemic all coexist.

The pandemic altered the lives of all humans on Earth in 2020–2021. At the onset of the pandemic, Trump, who was then president, politicized COVID-19 by labeling the deadly virus the "invisible China virus" and "the kung flu" to signal its alleged origin in Wuhan, China, and to rouse his supporters. What enables the existence and continuation of anti-Asian racial projects? The long-standing racialization of Asian Americans as perpetual and expendable foreign pawns to be managed, regulated, and legally defined is continuously given the air to survive and expand.[1] Politicized xenophobic language like Trump's has dire consequences.[2] Between March 2020 and March 2021, more than 6,600 anti-Asian hate crimes have been documented.[3]

One of the more prominent contemporary acts of anti-Asian violence occurred approximately one year after the start of pandemic-related anti-Asian rhetoric. On March 16, 2021, eight people were murdered in a killing spree across three spa and massage parlors in Atlanta, Georgia. Six of the eight victims were women of Asian ancestry. Following this heinous crime Captain Jay Baker of the Cherokee County Sheriff's Office described the White male murder suspect, Robert Aaron Long, as having an "issue with porn" and said that Long's actions constituted "attempting to take out that temptation."[4] Baker stated that Long "had a bad day, and this is what he did." Officials noted that the suspect's actions did not appear to be racially motivated.[5] It was later reported that Baker had promoted an anti-Asian COVID-19 T-shirt on his personal social media account.[6]

In response to the tragedy, and in stark contrast to actions of the Trump administration, President Joe Biden's White House issued a statement on March 30, 2021, that identified and condemned anti-Asian violence. The statement read, "Across our nation, an outpouring of grief and outrage continues at the horrific violence and xenophobia perpetrated against Asian American communities, especially Asian American women and girls. As President Biden said during his first prime time address, anti-Asian violence and xenophobia is wrong, it's un-American, and it must stop."[7] Despite these statements, reports of anti-Asian violence have continued to rise since the Atlanta spa murders.[8]

At the same time, the murder of Vincent Chin continues to be relevant and galvanize Asian America. In the words of Viet Thanh Nguyen, the murder "remains a rallying cry."[9] The case has been widely cited in writings about Asian American responses to Black Lives Matter (and other antiracism movements) and anti-Asian racism during the COVID-19 pandemic.[10] The journalist Claire Wang directly linked Chin's murder with Trump's racist use of the term "Kung Flu": "This year, Chin's death has taken on renewed urgency as Asian American Pacific Islanders are again being scapegoated for an international crisis they have no control over: the coronavirus pandemic. Hate crimes have spiked while business at Asian restaurants has plummeted. And anti-Asian rhetoric has been endorsed at the highest level: At a Saturday [June 20, 2020] rally in Tulsa, Oklahoma, President Donald Trump referred to the coronavirus as the 'Kung Flu.'"[11] In another example, on May 21, 2021, Connecticut Attorney General William Tong created a short video for NowThis News to educate the public on the Chin case and its relevance to combating anti-Asian racism.[12] The case continues to serve as a critical teaching tool for educating people on Asian American history. This is one of the lasting legacies initiated by events and activism stemming from the Midwest.

The role of Asian American studies, and ethnic studies broadly, is at the center of antiracism work. The Midwestern Asian American experiences described in this book provide compelling evidence for the importance of knowing Asian American history to identity formation, forming a sense of belonging in local and national spatial settings, and combating racism (including internalized racism). It has been over fifty years since activists arduously fought for the creation of ethnic studies courses, yet much work remains. It has been over thirty years since Asian American studies programs were established at the University of Michigan in 1989 and the University of Wisconsin–Madison in 1991.[13] Today, with a few exceptions (e.g., the University of Illinois Urbana-Champaign is today a department), Asian American studies exists at most Midwestern universities merely as programs (if that) rather than departments, and positions in the field remain understaffed and underfunded. Universities must prioritize improving their institutional support of ethnic studies. The substantial increase in anti-Asian violence emerging in this political moment has shown us that knowledge of Asian American history—really, knowledge of the history of all marginalized communities—is critical for everyone.

In the Midwest, Asian Americans have organized politically to inform the public about this history via Illinois's Teaching Equitable Asian American Community History (TEAACH) Act, which sought to incorporate Asian American history into the curriculum of every K–12 public school in the state.[14] The act specifies as its goal the teaching of "Asian American history, including the history of Asian Americans in Illinois and the Midwest, as well as the contributions of Asian American towards advancing civil rights from the 19th century onward."[15] Asian Americans Advancing Justice in Chicago and local community stakeholders lobbied for passage of the act, which was cosponsored by Illinois Representative Jennifer Gong-Gershowitz, a third-generation Chinese American who is the second Asian American to be elected to the Illinois House of Representatives.[16]

Gong-Gershowitz explains the act's significance: "Asian Americans are a part of the American fabric but we are often invisible. Empathy comes from understanding. We cannot do better unless we know better."[17] On July 9, 2021, the bill was signed into law by Governor J. B. Pritzker, making Illinois the first state in the nation to mandate the inclusion of Asian American history in its public-school curriculum.[18] This is a monumental contribution to Midwestern Asian American, Asian American, and U.S. history. It should serve as a blunt reminder Asian American history *is* U.S. history.

As we think about the future of Asian American racial positionality, it is critical to shift away from focusing solely on individualized emotional and material losses within the Asian American community. Dorothy Fujita-Rony argues that we need to apply the lens of "militarized rupture" in examining Asian American transnational history and archives.[19] She argues that many scholars' fixation on "emotional loss" leads them to "individualize" history, which serves to "deemphasize" the role of structural and institutional forces (e.g., the U.S. empire and military) that have produced this loss.[20] Along these same lines, I have attempted to show in this book that to achieve a more equitable future we also must examine the structural forces that perpetuate inequality. Taking this more holistic approach allows us to identify the root causes of inequities and work toward solutions. As I explored in chapter 3, doing so will enable us to identify the structure of White supremacy and acknowledge Asian Americans' complicity in perpetuating this structure.[21] For example, the murder of George Floyd, a forty-six-year-old Black man, by police officers in Minnesota has made this complicity blatantly clear. One of the police officers was Tou Thao, a Hmong American and Midwestern Asian American. Thao stood guard while another police officer, Derek Chauvin, suffocated Floyd with his knee.

In response to this tragic murder, the Hmong American poet Mai Der Vang wrote a poem titled "In the Year of Permutations."[22] The poem sharply criticizes Asian Americans who attempt to mimic whiteness and perpetuate White supremacy: "To be complicit in adding to the / perpetration of power on a neck, / there and shamed, / court of ancestors to disgrace / you, seeing and to have done nothing. / Think you can be like them. / Work like them. / Talk like them. / Never truly to be accepted, / always a pawn."

Will the line "always a pawn" continue to haunt Asian America's future? The use of Asian Americans as pawns has been an issue of concern since the beginning of the Asian American movement in the 1960s.[23] In the 1980s, the legal scholar and critical race theorist Mari Matsuda explicitly addressed the topic in her speech "We Will Not Be Used: Are Asian Americans the Racial Bourgeoisie?" In the speech, Matsuda asks:

> If white, as it has been historically, is the top of the racial hierarchy in America, and black, historically, is the bottom, will yellow assume the place of the racial middle? The role of the racial middle is a critical one. It can reinforce white

supremacy if the middle deludes itself into thinking it can be just like white if it tries hard enough. Conversely, the middle can dismantle white supremacy if it refuses to be the middle, if it refuses to buy into racial hierarchy, and if it refuses to abandon communities of black and brown people, choosing instead to forge alliances with them.[24]

While Matsuda's speech operates strictly within the Black-White binary—thus reminding us of Richard Delgado's caution against falling into the "trap of exceptionalism"—the point remains salient.[25] What happens if all Asian Americans, as an interstitial collectivity, resist being used as pawns and fight against White supremacy—not just for themselves but on behalf of (and in concert with) all marginalized communities? Asian America has the ability to create social and cultural change if "it refuses to be the middle."

In closing, I ask Asian Americans: Where do we go from here as a nation? Will our lives cease to tragically echo those of the past? What legacy will we leave behind? We must continue to ask ourselves the question about social justice that Renee Tajima-Peña posed twenty years ago: "What are we here to do?"[26] My study participant Jill reminds us that in our reckoning with Asian American racial positioning, we should not forget our history of building movements:

I feel like an approach that Asian Americans can make as a contribution . . . is to sort of broaden an understanding of how racism plays out in our society. Not to say, "Well, but actually our people suffer worse in this regard," but to say, "there's a systemic problem, a systemic problem in all of our communities." We need to try to make it better. We need to try to change it. I think that these are facts. These are not nice, warm, fuzzy feelings. It's a fact that there's a problem with housing in America. It's a fact that there's a problem with employment. It's a fact that, in the richest country in the history of the world, . . . people are going hungry, across different types of communities. And that is something that people can potentially agree on. I'm very idealistic. I would say there's a ton of potential right now. But I also would say that knowing your history— reading books also says that we can build things. *We can build these movements. We can build solidarity.*

Let us never forget that Asian America and Asian American history have not yet arrived. They will forever be in the making. As Asian American activism— especially activism from America's heartland—has shown us time and again, there is still hope.

Appendix

Selected Characteristics
of Study Participants

Table A.1
Selected Characteristics of Study Participants

Pseudonym	Age	Gender	Ethnicity	Generation	State grown up in	Religion	Highest level of education	Class
Abby	22	Female	Multiracial	2	Ohio	Agnostic	Some college	Working
Adam	33	Male	Vietnamese	1.5	Wisconsin	Buddhist	Bachelor's degree	Working
Ajay	20	Male	Asian Indian	1.5	Ohio	Hindu	Some college	Working
Ajit	29	Male	Asian Indian	2	Ohio	Hindu	Professional degree	Upper middle+
Alice	28	Female	Vietnamese	2	Nebraska	Catholic	Bachelor's degree	Working
Amar	28	Male	Asian Indian	2	Minnesota	Hindu	Bachelor's degree	Middle
An	22	Female	Vietnamese	1.5	Wisconsin	Buddhist	Bachelor's degree	Working
Andrea	26	Female	Chinese Japanese	2	Ohio	None	Professional degree	Working
Andy	39	Male	Chinese	2	Ohio	Christian	Professional degree	Upper middle+
Anna	26	Female	Korean	1.5	Minnesota	Christian	Professional degree	Working class
Ashwin	20	Male	Asian Indian	2	Ohio	Agnostic	Some college	Upper middle+
Ava	38	Female	Korean	2	Ohio	None now	Professional degree	Upper middle+
Betty	34	Female	Chinese	2	Illinois	None	Professional degree	Upper middle+
Bing	21	Female	Chinese	2	Ohio	None	Some college	Working
Bob	23	Male	Chinese	2	Iowa	None	Professional degree	Upper middle+
Cassie	26	Female	Taiwanese	2	Wisconsin	None	Professional degree	Upper middle+
Chenda	30	Female	Cambodian	1.5	Minnesota	Buddhist	2-year technical college degree	Working
Chung	39	Male	Taiwanese	1.5	Illinois	None	Professional	Upper middle+
Corey	22	Male	Taiwanese	2	Illinois	Protestant	Bachelor's degree	Upper middle+
Dara	23	Female	Cambodian	2	Illinois	None	Bachelor's degree	Working
Donna	21	Female	Vietnamese	1.5	Ohio	Christian	Some college	Middle
Emily	19	Female	Vietnamese	2	Illinois	Buddhist	Some college	Working
Eric	19	Male	Asian Indian	2	Ohio	Christian	Some college	Upper middle+
Gina	19	Female	Korean	2	Illinois	Christian	Some college	Upper middle+

Name	Age	Gender	Ethnicity	Generation	State	Religion	Education	Class
Gurman	28	Male	Asian Indian	2	Illinois	None	Professional degree	Middle
Ha	22	Female	Chinese-Vietnamese	2	Illinois	Buddhist	Bachelor's degree	Working
Hana	19	Female	Korean	1.5	Michigan	Christian	Some college	Upper middle+
Jack	36	Male	Vietnamese	2	Indiana	None	Bachelor's degree	Working
Jae	22	Male	Multiracial	2	Ohio	None	Some college	Working
Jane	20	Female	Multiracial	2	Ohio	None	Some college	Middle
Janice	22	Female	Multiracial	2	Ohio	Buddhist	Some college	Working
Jill	31	Female	Multiracial	2	Illinois	None	Bachelor's degree	Working
John	23	Male	Taiwanese	2	Illinois	Christian	Bachelor's degree	Upper middle+
Kanya	26	Female	Cambodian-Chinese	2	Illinois	Agnostic	Professional degree	Working
Kia	19	Female	Hmong	2	Minnesota	Shamanist	Some college	Working
Leah	25	Female	Multiracial	2	Minnesota	Agnostic	Professional degree	Upper middle+
Lucy	19	Female	Korean	2	Illinois	None now	Some college	Upper middle+
Mai	22	Female	Hmong	2	Minnesota	None	Bachelor's degree	Working
Makiko	33	Female	Japanese	2	Ohio	None now	Professional degree	Working
Mike	22	Male	Vietnamese	2	Ohio	Catholic	Bachelor's degree	Upper middle+
Mina	27	Female	Korean	1.5	Minnesota	None	Professional degree	Upper middle+
Molly	24	Female	Taiwanese	2	Michigan	None	Bachelor's degree	Middle
Nina	24	Female	Taiwanese	2	Illinois	Agnostic	Professional degree	Upper middle+
Phong	22	Male	Chinese-Vietnamese	2	Iowa	Christian	Bachelor's degree	Middle
Preeti	18	Female	Asian Indian	2	Ohio	Jain	Some college	Middle
Priya	21	Female	Asian Indian	2	Ohio	Hindu	Bachelor's degree	Upper middle+
Sadie	24	Female	Filipino	2	Illinois	Catholic	Bachelor's degree	Upper middle+
Ted	26	Male	Vietnamese	2	Minnesota	None	Professional degree	Upper middle+
Todd	21	Male	Filipino	2	Illinois	Agnostic	Some college	Upper middle+
Vanly	24	Female	Laotian	2	Minnesota	Buddhist	Professional degree	Middle
Vinh	21	Male	Vietnamese	1.5	Ohio	Buddhist	Some college	Working
Vivian	22	Female	Multiracial	2	Indiana	Christian	Some college	Upper middle+

Acknowledgments

Writing this book has allowed me to contribute to Asian American historiography in ways that I could have never dreamed of growing up in the East Bay, California, as a 1.5-generation Asian American. As a child and young adult, I constantly grappled with questions embedded in issues of race, space, and identity. I navigated situations in which racism and whiteness were seen as normative, I questioned my placement and belonging in America, and I did not know about or understand the expanse of Asian American history and culture. I have written this book through the lens of Midwestern Asian America to address the ever-evolving social, cultural, and political history of Asian America. I hope that the book will serve as a resource for young Asian Americans grappling with the same questions I had growing up.

This book also is a reflection of the evolution of my scholarship. I have many people to thank who have helped me along my journey in crisscrossing multiple disciplines and writing this book. First and foremost, I want to thank the Midwestern Asian American participants in this study. This book would not have been possible without their generosity, support, and trust. Thank you for entrusting me, a complete stranger, with your personal histories and providing me with the privilege of telling your stories. I am deeply indebted to you.

I began my journey in the Midwest at The Ohio State University (OSU), where I was generously funded by the Social and Behavioral Sciences Diversity Postdoctoral Fellowship. The seed for this book was planted during my time there and thanks to the institutional support I received at OSU. I am extremely thankful for my supportive OSU friends and colleagues in the Sociology and Asian American Studies Program. I want to especially thank the following individuals: Tasleem Padamsee, Judy Wu, Zhenchao Qian, Joe Ponce, Yuri Doolan, Lynn Itagaki, Kimberly McKee, Juwon Lee, Christopher Brown, and Sachi Sekimoto.

When I first joined Purdue University's American Studies in the School of Interdisciplinary Studies in 2014, I could not have imagined all the ways in which my scholarship would grow within this academic unit. I could not ask for a more supportive environment and colleagues. Thanks go especially to Rayvon Fouché, Bill Mullen, Shannon McMullen, and Cheryl Cooky. Also, I thank Brandi Plantenga, Andrea Furrer, and Edie Moffitt for their invaluable administrative support. All of my past and present undergraduate and graduate students have played a very influential role in my academic growth. I credit their inquisitive questions for motivating me and pushing me past my own disciplinary-bounded comfort zones. I am very thankful for my American studies family.

My Asian American studies colleagues at Purdue have provided me with so much support over the years. These past and current colleagues include Beth (Bich Minh) Nguyen, Hana Lee-Moore, Pamela Sari, David Atkinson, Dada Dacot, Patsy Schweickart, Patricia Morita-Mullaney, Minjung Ryu, Aparajita Sagar, Jerilyn Tinio, Wayne Wright, Xiang Zhou, Kate Agathon, Annagul Yaryyeva, Michelle Lee, Yu Dou, Rachel Bonini, and Melvin Villaver. Thank you for all you have done to sustain Purdue's Asian American studies.

In addition I thank my friends and colleagues at Purdue and elsewhere for all the encouragement throughout the years: the late JoAnn Miller, Susan Curtis, Venetria Patton, Alfred Lopéz, Song No, and Rachel Einwohner. A very special thanks goes to Jean Beaman and Su'ad Abdul Khabeer, whose friendship sustains me in academia.

I am grateful to have received Purdue's College of Liberal Arts' Engage Award, which enabled me to workshop this book with a team of amazing Asian American studies scholars. Pawan Dhingra, Andrea Louie, and Chia Youyee Vang provided incredibly sage advice and constructive criticism that made this book exponentially better. Thank you all so much for your time, care, support, and belief in my work.

Many thanks go to those people who have directly contributed to the making of this book through helping me with recruiting participants and retrieving, coding, and transcribing data, as well as by reading and editing drafts. They include Hana Lee-Moore, Charlie V. Morgan, Michele Bendall, Marc Diefenderfer, Nicholas Vargas, Yuri Doolan, and Rachel Bonini.

I also thank Rutgers University Press for seeing the value in this book and my research. Thanks go especially to Huping Ling, the editor of the Asian American Studies Today series, for your belief in and support of my work. And thanks so much to the press's anonymous reviewers, editors, and editorial staff members (Jasper Chang, Kimberly Guinta, Laura Lassen, and Carah Naseem) for all of your assistance and advice in turning this book into a tangible reality.

I am also indebted to my two long-standing mentors, Linda Trinh Võ and Rubén G. Rumbaut, for their steadfast belief, encouragement, and unwavering support in my scholarship and career in academia. Thank you both for teaching me that all our personal biographies mattered in history—it is a lesson that I have never forgotten. I also wish to acknowledge and sincerely thank all the teachers who educated me along the way, from my first undergraduate Asian American studies course at the University of California (UC), Davis to my final graduate Asian American studies course at UC Irvine. You have all had a huge impact on my life and career, and I am forever grateful.

Also, I owe many thanks to Mai Der Vang for her generosity in allowing me to reproduce parts of her brilliant poem, "In the Year of Permutations" (Academy of American Poets, 2020), which was originally published through the Shelter in Poems initiative on poets.org (https://poets.org/poem/year-permutations). An earlier version of chapter 2 was published as "The 'Isolated Ethnics' and 'Everyday Ethnics': Region, Identity, and the Second-Generation Midwest Asian American Experience," in *National Identities* 20, no. 2 (2018): 175–195, and parts of chapter 3 previously appeared in "Asian Americans and Internalized Racial Oppression: Identified, Reproduced, and Dismantled" (coauthored with Hana C. Lee), in *Sociology of Race and Ethnicity* 4, no.1 (2018): 67–82, and in "Understanding the Use of 'Twinkie,' 'Banana,' and 'FOB': Identifying the Origin, Role, and Consequences of Internalized Racism within Asian America," *Sociology Compass* 13, no. 3 (2019): 1–12.

Finally, thank you to my mom, Penny, Jenny, and Demeter, and the Stainback family for all your unconditional love and support. I especially want to thank my older sister, Penny, who was the first person to expose me to Asian American history and activism outside of the classroom. Our early conversations about these subjects had a profound effect on me. Thanks for leading by example, sis. Last, but certainly not least, thanks to my husband and partner in life, Kevin M. Stainback. Not a day goes by that I am not filled with gratitude for our love and life together. Your love, laughter, patience, and support will always be my home.

Notes

Introduction

1 One of the fifty-two study participants. All fifty-two study participants are listed under pseudonym in the appendix. See *Appendix* for more details.

2 My use of the terms "Midwest" and "Midwestern" follows the U.S. Census Bureau's definition of the region to include twelve states: Illinois, Indiana, Iowa, Kansas, Michigan, Minnesota, Missouri, Nebraska, North Dakota, Ohio, South Dakota, and Wisconsin. See U.S. Census Bureau, "Census Regions and Divisions of the United States," https://www2.census.gov/geo/pdfs/maps-data/maps /reference/us_regdiv.pdf.

3 All cited interview sources draw from the fifty-two study participants, listed under pseudonym in the appendix. See *Appendix* for more details.

4 William Wei, *The Asian American Movement* (Philadelphia: Temple University Press, 1992), 29–30. Wei quoted from the Rice Paper Collective's publication, *Rice Paper*. Rice Paper Collective, Madison Asian Union, "Rice Paper," *Rice Paper* 1, no. 1 (Summer 1974): 3.

5 Chapter 3 provides a more in-depth discussion of the term "co-ethnic" and racialized ideology.

6 For example, Yen Le Espiritu, *Home Bound: Filipino American Lives across Cultures, Communities, and Countries* (Berkeley: University of California Press, 2003); Nazli Kibria, *Becoming Asian American: Second-Generation Chinese and Korean American Identities* (Baltimore, MD: John Hopkins University Press, 2002); Sunaina Marr Maira, *Desis in the House: Indian American Youth Culture in New York City* (Philadelphia: Temple University Press, 2002); Alejandro Portes and Rubén G. Rumbaut, *Legacies: The Story of the Immigrant Second Generation* (Berkeley: University of California Press, 2001); Mia Tuan, *Forever Foreigners or Honorary Whites? The Asian Ethnic Experience Today* (Piscataway, NJ: Rutgers University Press, 2001); Min Zhou and Carl L. Bankston III, *Growing Up American: How Vietnamese Children Adapt to Life in the United States* (New York: Russell Sage Foundation, 1998).

7 Pawan Dhingra, "Introduction to *Journal of Asian American Studies*, Special Issue on the Midwest," in "Special Issue on the Midwest," edited by Pawan Dhingra.

Special Issue, *Journal of Asian American Studies* 12, no. 3 (2009): 239–246; Erika Lee, "Asian American Studies in the Midwest," in "Special Issue on the Midwest," edited by Pawan Dhingra. Special Issue, *Journal of Asian American Studies* 12, no. 3 (2009): 253 and 256.

8 Dhingra, introduction, 322; E. Lee, "Asian American Studies in the Midwest," 265.

9 For example, Charlotte Brooks, "In the Twilight Zone between Black and White: Japanese American Resettlement and Community in Chicago, 1942–1945," *Journal of American History* 86, no. 4 (2000): 1655–1687; Huping Ling, *Chinese St. Louis: From Enclave to Cultural Community* (Philadelphia: Temple University Press, 2004), and "Reconceptualizing Chinese American Community in St. Louis: From Chinatown to Cultural Community," *Journal of American Ethnic History* 24, no. 2 (2005): 65–101; Barbara M. Posadas, "Teaching about Chicago's Filipino Americans," *Organization of American Historians Magazine of History* 10, no. 4 (1996): 38–45.

10 For example, Linda Furiya, *Bento Box in the Heartland: My Japanese Girlhood in Whitebread America* (Berkeley, CA: Seal Press, 2006); Bich Minh Nguyen, *Stealing Buddha's Dinner: A Memoir* (New York: Penguin, 2007); Ira Sukrungruang, *Talk Thai: The Adventures of Buddhist Boy* (Columbia: University of Missouri Press, 2010); Eleanor Wong Telemaque, *It's Crazy to Stay Chinese in Minnesota* (Bloomington, IN: Xlibris, 2000).

11 Helen B. Marrow, "Assimilation in New Destinations," *Daedalus* 142, no. 3 (2013), 107.

    For exceptions, see Noreen Naseem Rodríguez, "'This Is Why Nobody Knows Who You Are': (Counter)Stories of Southeast Asian Americans in the Midwest," *Review of Education, Pedagogy, and Cultural Studies* 42, no. 2 (2020): 157–174; Pao Lee Vue, *Assimilation and the Gendered Color Line: Hmong Case Studies of Hip-Hop and Import Racing* (El Paso, TX: LFB Scholarly Publishing, 2012); Sook Wilkinson and Victor Jew, eds., *Asian Americans in Michigan: Voices from the Midwest* (Detroit, MI: Wayne State University Press, 2015).

12 Stacey J. Lee, *Up against Whiteness: Race, School, and Immigrant Youth* (New York: Teachers College Press, 2005).

13 Nancy Abelmann, *The Intimate University: Korean American Students and the Problems of Segregation* (Durham, NC: Duke University Press, 2009).

14 Kim Park Nelson, *Invisible Asians: Korean American Adoptees, Asian American Experiences, and Racial Exceptionalism* (New Brunswick, NJ: Rutgers University Press, 2016), 104.

15 Nelson, *Invisible Asians*, 123–124.

16 For example, George Lipsitz, "The Racialization of Space and the Spatialization of Race: Theorizing the Hidden Architecture of Landscape," *Landscape Journal* 26, no. 1 (2007): 10–23; Brooke Neely and Michelle Samura, "Social Geographies of Race: Connecting Race and Space," *Ethnic and Racial Studies* 34, no. 11 (2011): 1933–1952; Laura Pulido, *Black, Brown, Yellow, and Left: Radical Activism in Los Angeles* (Berkeley: University of California Press, 2006); Homi K. Bhabha, *The Location of Culture* (London: Routledge, 1994); Leslie Bow, *Partly Colored: Asian Americans and Racial Anomaly in the Segregated South* (New York: New York University Press, 2010); Elaine Kim, "Interstitial Subjects: Asian American Visual Art as a Site for New Cultural Conversations," in *Fresh Talk/Daring Gazes: Conversations on Asian American Art*, ed. Elaine Kim, Margo Machida, and Sharon Mizota (Berkeley: University of California Press, 2003), 1–50.

17 For example, Richard Delgado, "Derrick Bell's Toolkit—Fit to Dismantle That Famous House?," *New York University Law Review* 75, no. 2 (2000): 283–307; Claire Jean Kim, "The Racial Triangulation of Asian Americans," *Politics & Society* 27, no. 1 (1999): 105–138; Pulido, *Black, Brown, Yellow, and Left.*

18 For example, Bow, *Partly Colored*; E. Kim, "Interstitial Subjects."

19 Pulido, *Black, Brown, Yellow, and Left*; Richard Delgado and Jean Stefancic, "Critical Race Theory and Criminal Justice," *Humanity & Society* 31 (2007): 133–145; Claire Jean Kim, "Unyielding Positions: A Critique of the 'Race' Debate," *Ethnicities* 4, no. 3 (2004): 337–355, and "The Racial Triangulation of Asian Americans."

20 For example, Erika Lee, *The Making of Asian America: A History* (New York: Simon and Shuster, 2015); Junaid Rana, *Terrifying Muslims: Race and Labor in the South Asian Diaspora* (Durham, NC: Duke University Press, 2011); Nancy Wang Yuen, *Reel Inequality: Hollywood Actors and Racism* (New Brunswick, NJ: Rutgers University Press, 2016).

21 John Mellencamp, "The Great Midwest," track 4 on *John Cougar* (UK: Riva, 1979), compact disc.

22 Kristin L. Hoganson, *The Heartland: An American History* (New York: Penguin, 2019), xiv.

23 Emily Badger and Kevin Quealy, "Where Is America's Heartland? Pick Your Map," *New York Times*, January 3, 2017, https://www.nytimes.com/interactive /2017/01/03/upshot/where-is-americas-heartland-pick-your-map.html.

24 "The French Lead the Way: c. 1500–1763," Library of Congress, accessed August 23, 2022, https://www.loc.gov/collections/pioneering-the-upper-midwest/articles-and -essays/history-of-the-upper-midwest-overview/french-lead-the-way/; R. David Edmunds, "Introduction: A People of Persistence," in *Enduring Nations: Native Americans in the Midwest*," ed. R. David Edmunds (Champaign: University of Illinois Press, 2008), 1–14.

25 Jack Blocker, *A Little More Freedom: African Americans Enter the Urban Midwest, 1860–1930* (Columbus: Ohio State University Press, 2009); Leslie Schwalm, *Emancipation's Diaspora: Race and Reconstruction in the Upper Midwest* (Chapel Hill: University of North Carolina Press, 2009).

26 Juan R. Garcia, introduction to *Mexicans in the Midwest*, ed. Juan R. Garcia, Ignacio M. Garcia, and Thomas Gelsinon (Tucson: University of Arizona Press, 1989), viii.

27 H. Ling, *Chinese St. Louis*, 25–54, and *Chinese Chicago: Race, Transnational Migration, and Community since 1870* (Stanford, CA: Stanford University Press, 2012), 29–57.

28 Posadas, "Teaching about Chicago's Filipino Americans," 38–39.

29 Brooks, "In the Twilight Zone between Black and White," 1657.

30 Nelson, *Invisible Asians*, 92–120.

31 David Urias and Carol Camp Yeakey, "Analysis of the U.S. Student Visa System: Misperceptions, Barriers, and Consequences," *Journal of Studies in International Students* 13, no. 1 (2009): 72–109.

32 Chia Youyee Vang, *Hmong America: Reconstructing Community in Diaspora* (Champaign: University of Illinois Press, 2010).

33 Wei, *The Asian American Movement*, 29–37.

34 Helen Zia, *Asian American Dreams: The Emergence of an American People* (New York: Farrar, Straus and Giroux, 2000), 55–81.

35 Robert D. McFadden, "Grace Lee Boggs, Human Rights Advocate for 7 Decades, Dies at 100," *New York Times*, October 5, 2015, https://www.nytimes.com/2015/10/06/us/grace-lee-boggs-detroit-activist-dies-at-100.html.

36 Cathy Park Hong, *Minor Feelings: An Asian American Reckoning* (New York: One World, 2020), 165.

37 Michelle Caswell, "Seeing Yourself in History: Community Archives and the Fight against Symbolic Annihilation," *Public Historian* 36, no. 4 (2014): 26–37.

38 For example, Tuan, *Forever Foreigners or Honorary Whites?*; Espiritu, *Home Bound*; C. Kim, "The Racial Triangulation of Asian Americans"; Keith Osajima, "Asian Americans as the Model Minority: An Analysis of the Popular Press Image in the 1960s and 1980s," in *Reflections on Shattered Windows*, ed. Gary Okihiro et al. (Pullman: Washington State University Press, 1988), 165–174; William Peterson, "Success Story of One Minority Group in the U.S.," *U.S. News and World Report*, December 26, 1966, 73–78; Luther Spoehr, "Sambo and the Heathen Chinee: Californians' Racial Stereotypes in the Late 1870s," *Pacific Historical Reviews* 43, no. 2 (1973): 185–204; Ellen D. Wu, *The Color of Success: Asian Americans and the Origins of the Model Minority* (Princeton, NJ: Princeton University Press, 2014).

39 For more information about the history of the racialization of Chinese in California, see Tomás Almaguer, *Racial Fault Lines: The Historical Origins of White Supremacy in California* (Berkeley: University of California Press, 1994); Sucheng Chan, *Asian Americans: An Interpretive History* (New York: Twayne, 1994); E. Lee, *The Making of Asian America*.

40 E. Lee, *The Making of Asian America*, 89–136.

41 C. Kim, "The Racial Triangulation of Asian Americans," 116 and 124; E. Lee, *The Making of Asian America*, 89–136.

42 C. Kim, "The Racial Triangulation of Asian Americans," 117.

43 E. Wu, *The Color of Success*; Madeline Y. Hsu, *The Good Immigrants: How the Yellow Peril Became the Model Minority* (Princeton, NJ: Princeton University Press, 2015); Robert G. Lee, *Orientals: Asian Americans in Popular Culture* (Philadelphia: Temple University Press, 1999).

44 E. Wu, *The Color of Success*; Rosalind S. Chou and Joe R. Feagin, *The Myth of the Model Minority: Asian Americans Facing Racism* (Boulder, CO: Paradigm, 2008); E. Lee, *The Making of Asian America*.

45 C. Kim, "The Racial Triangulation of Asian Americans," 118; E. Wu, *The Color of Success*, 242–258.

46 For example, Chou and Feagin, *The Myth of the Model Minority*; Espiritu, *Home Bound*; Grace Wang, *Soundtracks of Asian America: Navigating Race through Musical Performance* (Durham, NC: Duke University Press, 2015).

47 For example, see details of California Alien Land Law of 1913 & 1920 in Keith Aoki, "No Right to Own?: The Early Twentieth-Century 'Alien Land Laws' as a Prelude to Internment," *Boston College Third World Law Journal* 19, no.1 (1998): 37–72.

48 Yen Le Espiritu, *Asian American Women and Men: Labor, Laws, and Love* (Lanham, MD: Rowman and Littlefield, 2000), 86–107; E. Lee, *The Making of Asian America*; Lisa Lowe, *Immigrant Acts* (Durham, NC: Duke University Press, 1996); Mae M. Ngai, "The Architecture of Race in American Immigration Law: A Reexamination of the Immigrant Act of 1924," *Journal of American History* 86, no. 1 (1999): 67–92; Kent A. Ono and Vincent Pham, *Asian Americans and the Media* (Malden, MA: Polity Press, 2009); Yuen, *Reel Inequality*.

49 For example, Suyin Haynes, "As Coronavirus Spreads, So Does Xenophobia and Anti-Asian Racism," *Time*, March 6, 2020, https://time.com/5797836/coronavirus -racism-stereotypes-attacks/.

50 Nelson, *Invisible Asians*, 101–103.

51 For more information about the first documented settlement, see E. Lee, *The Making of Asian America*, 33, Renee Tajima-Peña, dir. and prod., *My America: Honk if You Love Buddha* (Public Broadcasting Service, 1997), DVD.

52 For example, Tuan, *Forever Foreigners or Honorary Whites?*; Jennifer Lee and Frank D. Bean, *The Diversity Paradox: Immigration and the Color Line in Twenty-First Century America* (New York: Russell Sage Foundation, 2010).

53 Delgado, "Derrick Bell's Toolkit," 283; see also 290–291.

54 Delgado, "Derrick Bell's Toolkit," 283.

55 C. Kim, "The Racial Triangulation of Asian Americans," 105.

56 C. Kim, "The Racial Triangulation of Asian Americans," 106.

57 C. Kim, "The Racial Triangulation of Asian Americans," 106. See also Almaguer, *Racial Fault Lines*; Delgado, "Derrick Bell's Toolkit"; Pulido, *Black, Brown, Yellow, and Left*; Delgado and Stefancic, "Critical Race Theory and Criminal Justice"; C. Kim, "Unyielding Positions"; Mari Matsuda, "We Will Not Be Used," *University of California Los Angeles Asian American Pacific Islands Law Journal* 1, no.1 (1993): 79–84.

58 C. Kim, "The Racial Triangulation of Asian Americans," 107.

59 Pulido, *Black, Brown, Yellow, and Left*, 4.

60 For more information about space, race, and unequal power relations, see Lipsitz, "The Racialization of Space and the Spatialization of Race"; Dorsey Massey, *Space, Place, and Gender* (Minneapolis: University of Minnesota Press, 1994); Neely and Samura, "Social Geographies of Race."

61 Massey, *Space, Place, and Gender*, 2.

62 Massey, *Space, Place, and Gender*, 2–3.

63 George Lipsitz, "Space," in *Keywords for American Cultural Studies*, 2nd ed., ed. Bruce Burgett and Glenn Hendler (New York: New York University Press, 2014), 227, 231.

64 Lipsitz, "The Racialization of Space and the Spatialization of Race," 12.

65 Lipsitz, "The Racialization of Space and the Spatialization of Race," 16–17.

66 Neely and Samura, "Social Geographies of Race," 1934.

67 Bhabha, *The Location of Culture*, 3; Also see E. Kim, "Interstitial Subjects"; Bow, *Partly Colored*; John Kuo Wei Tchen, "Believing Is Seeing: Transforming Orientalism and the Occidental Gaze," in *Asia/America: Identities in Con- temporary Asian American Art*, ed. Margo Machida, Vishakha N. Desai, and John Kuo Wei Tchen (New York: Asia Society Galleries, 1994): 13–25.

68 Bhabha, *The Location of Culture*, 1–2.

69 Bhabha, *The Location of Culture*, 4.

70 Bhabha, *The Location of Culture*, 1–2.

71 Bhabha, *The Location of Culture*, 4.

72 Elaine Kim, preface to *Charlie Chan Is Dead: An Anthology of Contemporary Asian American Fiction*, ed. Jessica Hagedorn (New York: Penguin Press, 1993), viii.

73 E. Kim, "Interstitial Subjects."

74 E. Kim, "Interstitial Subjects," 1.

75 Bow, *Partly Colored*, 5.

76 Bow, *Partly Colored*, 11.

77 Wen Liu, "Complicity and Resistance: Asian American Body Politics in Black Lives Matter," *Journal of Asian American Studies* 21, no. 3 (2018): 437.

78 For more information about this topic, see C. Kim, "The Racial Triangulation of Asian Americans" and "Are Asians the New Blacks? Affirmative Action, Anti-Blackness, and the 'Sociometry' of Race," *Du Bois Review* (2018): 1–28; Yoshiko Uchida, *Desert Exile: The Uprooting of a Japanese American Family* (Seattle: University of Washington Press, 1982).

79 Brooks, "In the Twilight Zone between Black and White," 1665. See also Eugene Shigemi Uyeki, "Process and Patterns of Nisei Adjustment to Chicago, 1953" (PhD diss., University of Chicago, 1953), 117 and 147.

80 Brooks, "In the Twilight Zone between Black and White," 1665.

81 Bow, *Partly Colored*, 11.

82 IPUMS-CPS, 2008–2018. University of Minnesota, www.ipums.org. The merged Integrated Public Use Microdata Sample and Current Population Survey (a joint effort of the Census Bureau and the Bureau of Labor Statistics) is a national survey that collects demographic data and is supplemented by labor statistics. I used this data set because it is the only large national data set that allows for a detailed generational breakdown (into first, 1.5, and second generations, for example) by racial and ethnic categories.

83 The American Community Survey consists of information from sixty samples of the U.S. population drawn from fifteen federal censuses.

84 See the appendix for more details on participants' characteristics.

85 Rubén G. Rumbaut, "Ages, Life Stages, and Generational Cohorts: Decomposing the Immigrant First and Second Generations in the United States," *International Migration Review* 38, no. 3 (2004): 1160–1205.

86 Elizabeth M. Hoeffel et al., "The Asian Population: 2010," United States Census Bureau, 2012, 2, https://www.census.gov/content/dam/Census/library /publications/2012/dec/c2010br-11.pdf.

87 Juliet Corbin and Anselm Strauss, *Basics of Qualitative Research: Techniques and Procedures for Developing Grounded Theory*, 3rd ed. (Thousand Oaks, CA: Sage Publications, 2007).

88 John Lofland, David Snow, Leon Anderson, and Lyn Lofland, *Analyzing Social Settings: A Guide to Qualitative Observation and Analysis* (Belmont, CA: Wadsworth Publishing, 2006).

89 For example, Peggy Levitt and Mary C. Waters, eds., *The Changing Face of Home: The Transnational Lives of the Second Generation* (New York: Russell Sage Foundation, 2002); Portes and Rumbaut, *Legacies*.

90 Urias and Yeakey, "Analysis of the U.S. Student Visa System."

91 Wei, *The Asian American Movement*, 29–30.

92 Bhabha, *The Location of Culture*, 4.

93 Bow, *Partly Colored*; Michael Omi and Howard Winant, *Racial Formation in the United States: From the 1960s to the 1990s*, 2nd ed. (New York, Routledge, 1994).

Chapter 1   Who Is Midwestern Asian America?

1 All participants' ethnic and/or racial identities are placed in quotes to emphasize that this is how they self-identify.

2 For more detailed examinations of the different Asian American ethnic groups and their members' reasons for migrating, see Catherine Ceniza Choy, *Empire of*

Care: Nursing and Migration in Filipino American History (Durham, NC: Duke University Press, 2003); Charles Hirschman, Philip Kasinitz, and Josh DeWind, eds., *The Handbook of International Migration: The American Experience* (New York: Russell Sage Foundation, 1999); Lisa Lowe, *Immigrant Acts* (Durham, NC: Duke University Press, 1996); James P. Lynch and Rita J. Simon, *Immigration the World Over: Statutes, Policies, and Practices* (Lanham, MD: Rowman and Littlefield, 2003); Ji-Yeoh Yuh, *Beyond the Shadow of Camptown: Korean Military Brides in America* (New York: New York University Press, 2004).

3 Yen Le Espiritu, "Asian American Panethnicity: Contemporary National and Transnational Possibilities," in *Not Just Black and White: Historical and Contemporary Perspectives on Immigration, Race, and Ethnicity in the United States*, ed. Nancy Foner and George M. Fredrickson (New York: Russell Sage Foundation, 2004), 224.

4 Espiritu, "Asian American Panethnicity"; Lowe, *Immigrant Acts*; Mae M. Ngai, "Transnationalism and the Transformation of the 'Other': Response to the Presidential Address," *American Quarterly* 57, no. 1 (2005): 59–65.

5 Leslie Bow, *Partly Colored: Asian Americans and Racial Anomaly in the Segregated South* (New York: New York University Press, 2010), 11.

6 Jigna Desai and Khyati Y. Joshi, "Introduction: Discrepancies in Dixie: Asian Americans and the South," in *Asian Americans in Dixie: Race and Migration in the South*, ed. Khyati Y. Joshi and Jigna Desai (Urbana: University of Illinois Press, 2013), 1–30.

7 Arthur Sakamoto, ChangHwan Kim, and Isao Takei, "Moving out of the Margins and into the Mainstream: The Demographics of Asian Americans in the New South," in *Asian Americans in Dixie*, 160–161.

8 Erika Lee, "Asian American Studies in the Midwest," in "Special Issue on the Midwest," edited by Pawan Dhingra. Special Issue, *Journal of Asian American Studies* 12, no. 3 (2009): 248–249.

9 Pew Research Center, "The Rise of Asian Americans," April 4, 2013, https://www .pewresearch.org/social-trends/2012/06/19/the-rise-of-asian-americans/.

10 Sucheng Chan, *The Vietnamese American 1.5 Generation: Stories of War, Revolution, Flight, and New Beginnings* (Philadelphia: Temple University Press, 2006), 67. For more information about the history of refugees of the Vietnam War, see Yen Le Espiritu, "Beyond the 'Boat People': Ethnicization of American Life," *Amerasia Journal* 15, no. 2 (1989): 49–67; Jeremy Hein, *From Vietnam, Laos, and Cambodia: A Refugee Experience in the United States* (New York: Twayne Publishers, 1995); Rubén G. Rumbaut, "A Legacy of War: Refugees from Vietnam, Laos, and Cambodia," in *Origins and Destinies: Immigration, Race, and Ethnicity in Contemporary America*, ed. Silvia Pedraza and Rubén G. Rumbaut (Belmont, CA: Wadsworth Publishing, 1996), 315–333; Chia Youyee Vang, *Hmong America: Reconstructing Community in Diaspora* (Champaign: University of Illinois Press, 2010).

11 The "New Economic Zones" were remote areas with uncultivated land and harsh living conditions. In the aftermath of the war, many Vietnamese and ethnic Chinese were forced to resettle in these areas. This was the Vietnamese communists' attempt to turn the bourgeois and petit bourgeois classes into "productive" citizens (Chan, *The Vietnamese American 1.5 Generation*, 67.

12 Chan, *The Vietnamese American 1.5 Generation*, 67, 172 and 218–222.

13 For more information about the ethnic Chinese from Vietnam, see Chan, *The Vietnamese American 1.5 Generation*; Steven J. Gold, *Refugee Communities:*

A Comparative Field Study (Newbury Park, CA: Sage Publications, 1992); Hein, *From Vietnam, Laos, and Cambodia*; Monica M. Trieu, *Identity Construction among Chinese-Vietnamese Americans: Being, Becoming, and Belonging* (El Paso, TX: LFB Scholarly Publishing, 2009).

14 Sihanouk was placed on the throne by France in 1940 and served as king from 1941 to 1955. Cambodia gained independence from France in 1954, and in 1955 Sihanouk abdicated the throne to become prime minister and later head of state (Sucheng Chan, "Cambodians in the United States: Refugees, Immigrants, American Ethnic Minority," *Oxford Research Encyclopedia of American History*, September 3, 2015, https://doi.org/10.1093/acrefore/9780199329175.013.317).

15 Chan, "Cambodians in the United States."

16 Mark Philip Bradley, *Vietnam at War* (New York: Oxford University Press, 2009); Judy Tzu-Chun Wu, *Radicals on the Road: Internationalism, Orientalism, and Feminism during the Vietnam Era* (Ithaca, NY: Cornell University Press, 2013), 252.

17 Chan, "Cambodians in the United States," 5 and 6–7.

18 Chan, "Cambodians in the United States," 7.

19 Chan, "Cambodians in the United States," 7.

20 Chan, "Cambodians in the United States," 11.

21 Erika Lee, *The Making of Asian America: A History* (New York: Simon and Shuster, 2015), 318; C. Vang, *Hmong America*.

22 Bradley, *Vietnam at War*, 2009, 158; J. Wu, *Radicals on the Road*, 252.

23 See E. Lee, *The Making of Asian America*, 319; C. Vang, *Hmong America*.

24 Irene Bloemraad, *Becoming a Citizen: Incorporating Immigrants and Refugees in the United States and Canada* (Berkeley: University of California Press, 2006), 128.

25 Sharon Park, "Indochinese Refugee Resettlement Office, 1975–1986," *MNOPE-DIA*, November 6, 2017, http://www.mnopedia.org/group/indochinese-refugee -resettlement-office-1975-1986.

26 U.S. Citizen and Immigration Services, "Legislation from 1981–1996," accessed August 25, 2022, https://ilw.com/resources/Immigration_Legal_History _Legislation_1981-1996.pdf.

27 Robert D. Ray et al., "Report of the Indochinese Refugee Panel" (Washington: Department of State, 1986).

28 Chan, *The Vietnamese American 1.5 Generation*, 83.

29 Chan, *The Vietnamese American 1.5 Generation*, 84. For more information, see Ray et al., "Report of the Indochinese Refugee Panel"; Edwin B. Silverman, "Indochina Legacy: The Refugee Act of 1980," *Publius* 10, no. 1 (1980): 27–41.

30 For more information about the Office of Resettlement and other impacts of The Refugee Act of 1980, see Silverman, "Indochina Legacy."

31 E. Lee, *The Making of Asian America*; Rubén G. Rumbaut, "Vietnamese, Laotian, and Cambodian Americans," in *Asian Americans: Contemporary Trends and Issues*, ed. Pyong Gap Min (Thousand Oaks, CA: Sage Publications, 2005), 262–289.

32 For more information about the history of student visas in the United States, see Chad C. Haddel, "Foreign Students in the United States: Policies and Legislation," (Washington: Domestic Social Policy Division, Congressional Research Service, 2008); Mary Helen Reeves, "A Descriptive Case Study of the Impact of 9/11 on International Student Visa Policy in the 20 Months Following the Attacks" (PhD diss., University of Oklahoma, 2005).

33 Chinese Exclusion Act of 1882. Pub. L. No. 47-126, 22 Stat. 58 (1882).

34 For more information about the origin of the model minority myth, see Madeline Y. Hsu, *The Good Immigrants: How the Yellow Peril Became the Model Minority* (Princeton, NJ: Princeton University Press, 2015).

35 E. Lee, *The Making of Asian America*, 176.

36 Barbara M. Posadas, "Teaching about Chicago's Filipino Americans," *Organization of American Historians Magazine of History* 10, no. 4 (1996): 39.

37 Yu-Wei Wu. "Transnational Teacher Mobility: Patterns, Qualities, Institutional Actors and Policy Implication." PhD diss., The Pennsylvania State University, 2012, 76.

38 Haddel, "Foreign Students in the United States"; Reeves, "A Descriptive Case Study."

39 David Urias and Carol Camp Yeakey, "Analysis of the U.S. Student Visa System: Misperceptions, Barriers, and Consequences," *Journal of Studies in International Students* 13, no. 1 (2009): 80. This act also provided a pathway for all Asians to become naturalized U.S. citizens.

40 E. Lee, *The Making of Asian America*, 270–271.

41 Janine Keil, "Voices of Hope, Voices of Frustration: Deciphering U.S. Admission and Visa Policies for International Students" (Washington: Institute for the Study of Diplomacy, Edmund A. Walsh School of Foreign Service, Georgetown University, 2006).

42 Haddel, "Foreign Students in the United States," 10.

43 This figure includes all F-1 visa students enrolled in associate, bachelor's, master's, or doctorate programs in the United States. See Neil G. Ruiz and Jynnah Radford, "New Foreign Student Enrollment at U.S. Colleges and Universities Doubled since Great Recession," Pew Research Center, November 20, 2017, http://pewrsr .ch/2hFbZCf.

44 Neil G. Ruiz, "Key Facts about the U.S. H-1B Visa Program." *Pew Research Center*, April 27, 2017. http://www.pewresearch.org/fact-tank/2017/04/27/key -facts-about-the-u-s-h-1b-visa-program/.

45 Ruiz and Radford, "New Foreign Student Enrollment." However, on July 6, 2020, the administration of President Donald Trump completely reversed long-standing U.S. immigration policies for international students. Under the guise of working in the national interest in response to the COVID-19 pandemic, the Department of Homeland Security issued a directive banning international students from entering or remaining in the United States if their full course load was strictly online, stating: "Nonimmigrant F-1 and M-1 students attending schools operating entirely online may *not* take a full online course load and remain in the United States" (U.S. Immigration and Customs Enforcement, "SVEP Modifies Temporary Exemptions for Nonimmigrant Students Taking Online Courses during Fall 2020 Semester," July 6, 2020, https://www.ice.gov/news/releases/sevp-modifies -temporary-exemptions-nonimmigrant-students-taking-online-courses-during). This change in policy was met with major backlash from over two hundred universities and colleges and resulted in at least eight lawsuits against the federal government from universities and states (Collin Binkley, "Trump Administration Rescinds Rule on Foreign Students," *AP News*, July 14, 2020, https://apnews.com /38b6562b7aaa73ea66fb72b06472e05d; Elizabeth Redden, "Government Rescinds International Student Policy," *Inside Higher Education*, July 15, 2020, https://www .insidehighered.com/news/2020/07/15/trump-administration-drops-directive

-international-students-and-online-courses). As a response to the backlash, the Trump administration rescinded the new directive on July 14, 2020. This was considered a major win for universities and colleges. On July 16, 2020, the State Department's Bureau of Consular Affairs quietly issued another directive that lifted the travel ban on students traveling to the United States from Europe. The July 16 directive states that "students traveling from the Schengen Area (which consists of 26 European countries), the UK, and Ireland with valid F-1 and M-1 visas, do not need to seek a national interest exception to travel" (University of Colorado Boulder. "National Interest Exceptions for Certain Travelers from the Schengen Area, United Kingdom, and Ireland," Accessed September 17, 2022, https://www.colorado.edu/isss/2020/07/20/national-interest-exceptions-certain-travelers-schengen-area-united-kingdom-and-ireland). According to that directive, the change in policy was motivated by economic reasons: "Granting national interest exceptions . . . will assist with the economic recovery from the COVID-19 pandemic and bolster key components of our transatlantic relationship." It is important to point out that the United Kingdom and Italy—both of which, at the time of the directive, ranked among the world's top fifteen countries in numbers of confirmed COVID-19 cases—were included. As of July 20, 2020, the United States was ranked number one in numbers of COVID-19 cases, the United Kingdom ninth, and Italy fourteenth. World Health Organization. "Coronavirus disease (COVID-19): Situation Report—193." Accessed September 17, 2022, https://www.who.int/docs/default-source/coronaviruse/situation-reports/20200731-covid-19-sitrep-193.pdf. The language here is clear: international students from European countries are to be welcomed into the United States during the pandemic. Everybody else is not.

46 Dudley L. Poston Jr. and Hua Luo, "Chinese Student and Labor Migration to the United States: Trends and Policies since the 1980s," *Asian and Pacific Migration Journal* 16, no. 3 (2007): 323–355.

47 E. Lee, *The Making of Asian America*, 284–300.

48 U.S. Citizenship and Immigration Services, "H-1B Specialty Occupation, DOD Cooperative Research and Development Project Workers, and Fashion Models," accessed May 1, 2020, https://www.uscis.gov/working-united-states/temporary-workers/h-1b-specialty-occupations-dod-cooperative-research-and-development-project-workers-and-fashion-models.

49 See Frank D. Bean and Gillian Stevens, *America's Newcomers and the Dynamics of Diversity* (New York: Russell Sage Foundation, 2003); James P. Smith and Barry Edmonston, eds., *The New Americans: Economic, Demographic, and Fiscal Effects of Immigration* (Washington:National Academy Press, 1997); U.S. Citizen and Immigration Services, "Legislation from 1981–1996."

50 E. Lee, *The Making of Asian America*, 286.

51 Neil G. Ruiz, "Key Facts about the U.S. H-1B Visa Program," Pew Research Center, April 27, 2017, http://www.pewresearch.org/fact-tank/2017/04/27/key-facts-about-the-u-s-h-1b-visa-program/.

52 Yen Le Espiritu, "Filipino Navy Stewards and Filipina Health Care Professionals: Immigration, Work and Family Relations," *Asian and Pacific Migration Journal* 11, no. 1 (2002): 48.

53 Espiritu, "Filipino Navy Stewards and Filipina Health Care Professionals"; E. Lee, *The Making of Asian America*; Choy, *Empire of Care*; Paul Ong and Tania Azores, "The Migration and Incorporation of Filipino Nurses," in *The New Asian*

Immigration in Los Angeles and Global Restructuring, ed. Paul Ong, Edna Bonacich, and Lucie Cheng (Philadelphia: Temple University Press, 1994), 164–195.

54 For example, Yuh, *Beyond the Shadow of Camptown*; Nadia Y. Kim, *Imperial Citizens: Koreans and Race from Seoul to LA* (Stanford, CA: Stanford University Press, 2008); Yaejoon Kwon, "Transcolonial Racial Formation: Constructing the 'Irish of the Orient' in U.S.-Occupied Korea," *Sociology of Race and Ethnicity* 3, no. 2 (2017): 268–281; Kimberly D. McKee, *Disrupting Kinship: Transnational Politics of Korean Adoption in the United States* (Urbana: University of Illinois Press, 2019).

55 E. Lee, *The Making of Asian America*, 267.

56 Ji-Yeoh Yuh, "Moved by War: Migration, Diaspora, and the Korean War," *Journal of Asian American Studies* 8, no. 3 (2005): 278.

57 E. Lee, *The Making of Asian America*, 267.

58 Yuh, "Moved by War," 278.

59 For a more in-depth examination of the lives of Korean military brides, see Yuh, *Beyond the Shadow of Camptown*.

60 This is her own term. However, I want to acknowledge the fact that some Indigenous activists consider this cultural appropriation of a term from the Native Hawaiian language to be a continuation of the colonial project. For more information on this topic, see Mary Bernstein and Marcie De la Cruz, "'What Are You?': Explaining Identity as a Goal of the Multiracial Hapa Movement," *Social Problems* 56, no. 4 (2009):722–745.

61 Yuh, *Beyond the Shadow of Camptown*.

62 Kim Park Nelson, *Invisible Asians: Korean American Adoptees, Asian American Experiences, and Racial Exceptionalism* (New Brunswick, NJ: Rutgers University Press, 2016), 1.

63 For more information about children casualties of the Korean War, see E. Lee, *The Making of Asian America*; Wendy Marie Laybourn, "Korean Transracial Adoptee Identity Formation," *Sociology Compass* 11, no. 1 (2017): 1–9; Mia Tuan and Jiannbin Lee Shiao, *Choosing Ethnicity, Negotiating Race: Korean Adoptees in America* (New York: Russell Sage Foundation, 2011), 20–29.

64 Nelson, *Invisible Asians*, 42–46.

65 Nelson, *Invisible Asians*, 101–103.

Chapter 2   "I Only Knew It in Relation to Its Absence"

1 Jean Phinney, "Ethnic Identity in Adolescents and Adults: Review in Research," *Psychological Bulletin* 108, no. 3 (1990): 503.

2 Urie Bronfenbrenner, *The Ecology of Human Development: Experiments by Nature and Design* (Cambridge, MA: Harvard University Press, 1979), and "Ecology of the Family as a Context for Human Development: Research Perspectives," *Developmental Psychology* 22, no. 6 (1986): 723–742; Cynthia Garcia Coll et al., "An Integrative Model for the Study of Developmental Competencies in Minority Children," *Child Development* 67, no. 5 (1996): 1891–1914; Lisa Kiang and Andrew J. Supple, "Theoretical Perspectives on Asian American Youth and Families in Rural and New Immigrant Destinations," in *Rural Ethnic Minority Youth and Families in the United States: Theory, Research, and Applications*, ed. Lisa J. Crockett and Gustavo Carlo (Cham, Switzerland: Springer International Publishing, 2016): 71–88.

3 Urie Bronfenbrenner. "Ecology of the Family as a Context for Human Development: Research Perspectives"; Garcia Coll et al., "An Integrative Model for the Study of Developmental Competencies in Minority Children."

4 Kiang and Supple, "Theoretical Perspectives on Asian American Youth and Families," 80.

5 Jean S. Phinney, et al, "The Role of Language, Parents, and Peers in Ethnic Identity among Adolescents in Immigrant Families," *Journal of Youth and Adolescence* 30, no. 2 (2001), 136.

6 Henri Taifel and John Turner, eds., *An Integrative Theory of Intergroup Conflict* (Monterey, CA: Brooks/Cole, 1979).

7 Erik Erikson, *Identity: Youth and Crisis* (New York: Norton, 1968).

8 Phinney, "Ethnic Identity in Adolescents and Adults," 503.

9 For example, see Milton M. Gordon, *Assimilation in American Life: The Role of Race, Religion, and National Origins* (New York: Oxford University Press, 1964).

10 For example, see Min Zhou, "Social Capital and the Adaptation of the Second Generation: The Case of Vietnamese Youth in New Orleans," *International Migration Review* 28, no. 4 (1994): 821–845; Margaret A. Gibson, *Accommodation without Assimilation: Sikh Immigrants in American High School* (Ithaca, NY: Cornell University Press, 1988); Alejandro Portes and Rubén G. Rumbaut, *Immigrant America: A Portrait* (Berkeley: University of California Press, 1996), and *Legacies: The Story of the Immigrant Second Generation* (Berkeley: University of California Press, 2001); Mary C. Waters et al., eds., *Coming of Age in America: The Transition to Adulthood in the Twenty-First Century* (Berkeley: University of California Press, 2011); Min Zhou, "Growing Up American: The Challenge Confronting Immigrant Children and Children of Immigrants," *Annual Review of Sociology* 23, no. 1 (1997): 63–95.

11 Zhou, "Social Capital and the Adaptation of the Second Generation," 825.

12 Pawan Dhingra, *Managing Multicultural Lives: Asian American Professionals and the Challenge of Multiple Identities* (Stanford, CA: Stanford University Press, 2007), 2 and 8.

13 See, for example, Mia Tuan, *Forever Foreigners or Honorary Whites? The Asian Ethnic Experience Today* (Piscataway, NJ: Rutgers University Press, 2001); Nazli Kibria, *Becoming Asian American: Second-Generation Chinese and Korean American Identities* (Baltimore, MD: John Hopkins University Press, 2002).

14 Kibria, *Becoming Asian American*, 46.

15 Tuan, *Forever Foreigners or Honorary Whites?*, 76–105.

16 Min Zhou and Carl L. Bankston III, *Growing Up American: How Vietnamese Children Adapt to Life in the United States* (New York: Russell Sage Foundation, 1998), 83 and 100.

17 An extensive discussion of the Vincent Chin murder can be found in chapter 4.

18 George Lipsitz, "Space," in *Keywords for American Cultural Studies*, 2nd ed., ed. Bruce Burgett and Glenn Hendler (New York: New York University Press, 2014), 227–231; Brooke Neely and Michelle Samura, "Social Geographies of Race: Connecting Race and Space," *Ethnic and Racial Studies* 34, no. 11 (2011): 1933–1952.

19 I decided to include participants with an array of experiences in this category so I could account for changes in behavior throughout their lives. For example, some participants shifted from engaging in weekend ethnic activities to engaging in occasional ethnic activities, and this category accounts includes both types of engagement.

20   Kiang and Supple, "Theoretical Perspectives on Asian American Youth and Families," 78.

21   Zhou and Bankston, *Growing Up American*, 71–107.

22   Kiang and Supple, "Theoretical Perspectives on Asian American Youth and Families," 78–81.

23   Yen Le Espiritu, *Asian American Panethnicity: Bridging Institutions and Identities* (Philadelphia: Temple University Press, 1992).

24   Phinney, "Ethnic Identity in Adolescents and Adults: Review in Research," 502.

25   Kiang and Supple, "Theoretical Perspectives on Asian American Youth and Families," 79.

26   Zhou, "Social Capital and the Adaptation of the Second Generation."

27   Kerry Ann Rockquemore and Patricia Arend, "Opting for White: Choice, Fluidity and Racial Identity Construction in Post Civil-Rights America," *Race & Society* 5, no.1 (2002): 59.

28   Kiang and Supple, "Theoretical Perspectives on Asian American Youth and Families," 78–81.

29   Kim Park Nelson, *Invisible Asians: Korean American Adoptees, Asian American Experiences, and Racial Exceptionalism* (New Brunswick, NJ: Rutgers University Press, 2016), 118.

30   Kiang and Supple, "Theoretical Perspectives on Asian American Youth and Families," 78–81; Zhou and Bankston, *Growing Up American*, 71–107.

Chapter 3   "Why Couldn't I Be White?"

1   Jared Olar, "How Did Pekin Get Its Name?," Pekin History, December 2011, https://fromthehistoryroom.wordpress.com/2015/12/12/how-did-pekin-get-its-name.

2   According to James Loewen, sundown towns were prevalent from 1890 through the 1960s and were defined as "any organized jurisdiction that for decades kept African Americans or other [non-White] groups from living in it and was thus 'all-White' on purpose" (*Sundown Towns: A Hidden Dimension of American Racism* [New York: New Press, 2005], 4). These towns maintained their whiteness by passing ordinances that barred Blacks and other nonWhites from being in the town after dark, owning or renting property, working, and so on. The White residents harassed or killed people who they felt violated these ordinances.

3   Loewen, *Sundown Towns*, 340.

4   See Carl V. Hallberg, "'For God, Country, and Home': The Ku Klux Klan in Pekin, 1923–1925," *Journal of the Illinois State Historical Society* 77, no. 2 (1984): 82–90 and 92–93.

5   Hallberg, "'For God, Country, and Home,'" 82.

6   Hallberg, "'For God, Country, and Home,'" 93.

7   Hallberg, "'For God, Country, and Home,'" 82.

8   Loewen, *Sundown Towns*, 304.

9   Loewen, *Sundown Towns*, 303. I choose not to print racial slurs in their entirety in my writings. All of the original content containing racial slurs has been edited to reflect that decision.

10   William Wei, *The Asian American Movement* (Philadelphia: Temple University Press, 1992), 37.

11   "Oriental Discrimination," *Pekinois*, February 17, 1970, 2.

12   "Oriental Discrimination," *Pekinois*, February 17, 1970, 2.

13   "1981: The Pekin Chinks High School Team Becomes the Pekin Dragons,"
      Chinese American Museum of Chicago, accessed September 3, 2021, https://
      ccamuseum.org/1981-the-pekin-chinks-high-school-team-becomes-the-pekin
      -dragons.

14   "1981: The Pekin Chinks High School Team Becomes the Pekin Dragons,"
      Chinese American Museum of Chicago, accessed September 3, 2021, https://
      ccamuseum.org/1981-the-pekin-chinks-high-school-team-becomes-the-pekin
      -dragons.

15   Andy Kravetz, "Pekin Teacher Resigns amid Allegations of Racist, Anti-Semitic
      Internet Posts," *Journal Star*, April 23, 2019, https://www.pjstar.com/story/news
      /education/2019/04/24/pekin-teacher-resigns-amid-allegations/5352852007/.

16   For example, see Frantz Fanon, *The Wretched of the Earth*, trans. Constance
      Farrington. (New York: Grove Press, 1963); Paulo Freire, *Pedagogy of the
      Oppressed*, trans. Myra Berman Ramos (London: Penguin, 1996); Albert Memmi,
      The Colonizer and the Colonized, trans. Howard Greenfeld. (Boston: Beacon
      Press, 1965).

17   E.J.R. David and Annie O. Derthick, "What Is Internalized Oppression, and So
      What?," in *Internalized Oppression: The Psychology of Marginalized Groups*,
      ed. E.J.R. David (New York: Springer, 2013): 1–30.

18   Kevin L. Nadal, "Colonialism: Societal and Psychological Impacts on Asian
      Americans and Pacific Islanders," in *Asian American Psychology: Current
      Perspectives*, ed. .Nita Tewari and Alvin Alvarez (New York: Psychology Press,
      2009): 153–172.

19   Nadal, "Colonialism," 155 and 161.

20   I wish to clarify here that while I am discussing both Asia and the Pacific Islands,
      it should be noted that Asians and Pacific Islanders have had both similar
      experiences (e.g., as subjects of U.S. colonialism) and different ones (e.g., possess-
      ing distinct histories and cultures, and Asian colonialism in Hawai'i). See Paul
      Spickard, "Whither the Asian American Coalition?," *Pacific Historical Review* 76,
      no. 4 (2007): 585–604. My discussion of these two groups together in this chapter
      is based on their shared experiences as colonial subjects and the prevalence of
      internalized racial oppression in both groups.

21   Nadal, "Colonialism"; David, *Internalized Oppression: The Psychology of Marginal-
      ized Groups* (New York: Springer, 2013); James B. Millan and Alvin N. Alvarez,
      "Asian Americans and Internalized Oppression: Do We Deserve This?," in
      Internalized Oppression, 163–190; Noenoe K. Silva, *Aloha Betrayed: Native
      Hawaiian Resistance to American Colonialism* (Durham, NC: Duke University
      Press, 2004).

22   E.J.R. David, "Testing the Validity of the Colonial Mentality Implicit Association
      Test and the Interactive Effects of Covert and Overt Colonial Mentality on Filipino
      American Mental Health," *Asian American Journal of Psychology* 1, no. 1 (2010): 31.

23   David and Derthick, "What Is Internalized Oppression, and So What?," 8.

24   For example, see David and Derthick, "What Is Internalized Oppression, and So
      What?"; Fanon, *The Wretched of the Earth*; Freire, *Pedagogy of the Oppressed*;
      Memmi, *The Colonizer and the Colonized*; Nadal, "Colonialism."

25   Memmi, *The Colonizer and the Colonized*, 121–122.

26   William Edward Burghardt Du Bois, *The Souls of the Black Folk: Essays and
      Sketches* (Chicago: A. C. McClurg, 1903), 3.

27 David and Derthick, "What Is Internalized Oppression, and So What?," 3.

28 Karen Pyke, "What Is Internalized Racial Oppression and Why Don't We Study It? Acknowledging Racism's Hidden Injuries," *Sociological Perspectives* 53, no. 4 (2010): 553; see also Michael Schwalbe et al., "Generic Processes in the Reproduction of Inequality: An Interactionist Analysis," *Social Forces* 79, no. 2 (2000): 419–452.

29 David and Derthick, "What Is Internalized Oppression, and So What?," 4.

30 For example, Evelyn Nakano Glenn, "Yearning for Lightness: Transnational Circuits in the Marketing and Consumption of Skin Lighteners," *Gender & Society* 22, no. 3 (2008): 281–302; Mark E. Hill, "Skin Color and the Perception of Attractiveness among African Americans: Does Gender Make a Difference?," *Social Psychology Quarterly* 65, no. 1 (2002): 77–91; Margaret L. Hunter, "'If You're Light You're Alright': Light Skin Color as Social Capital for Women of Color," *Gender & Society* 16, no. 2 (2002): 175–193; Morgan Maxwell et al., "What's Color Got To Do with It? Skin Color, Skin Color Satisfaction, Racial Identity, and Internalized Racism among African American College Students," *Journal of Black Psychology* 41, no. 5 (2015): 438–461.

31 Signithia Fordham and John U. Ogbu, "Black Students' School Success: Coping with the "Burden of 'Acting White,'" *Urban Review* 18, no. 3 (1986): 176–206; Rita Kohli, "Unpacking Internalized Racism: Teachers of Color Striving for Racially Just Classrooms," *Race Ethnicity and Education* 17, no. 3 (2014): 367–387.

32 Glenn, "Yearning for Lightness," 298.

33 Yen Le Espiritu, "Asian American Panethnicity: Contemporary National and Transnational Possibilities," in *Not Just Black and White: Historical and Contemporary Perspectives on Immigration, Race, and Ethnicity in the United States*, ed. Nancy Foner and George M. Fredrickson (New York: Russell Sage Foundation, 2004), 217–234; Nadia Y. Kim, *Imperial Citizens: Koreans and Race from Seoul to LA* (Stanford, CA: Stanford University Press, 2008); Pyke, "What Is Internalized Racial Oppression and Why Don't We Study It?"

34 N. Kim, *Imperial Citizens*, 7–9.

35 Andrew Young Choi, Tania Israel, and Hotaka Maeda, "Development and Evaluation of the Internalized Racism in Asian Americans Scale (IRAAS)," *Journal of Counseling Psychology* 64, no. 1 (2017): 52–64.

36 Choi, Israel, and Maeda, "Development and Evaluation of the Internalized Racism in Asian Americans Scale," 53.

37 Mia Tuan, *Forever Foreigners or Honorary Whites? The Asian Ethnic Experience Today* (Piscataway, NJ: Rutgers University Press, 2001); Keith Osajima, "Asian Americans as the Model Minority: An Analysis of the Popular Press Image in the 1960s and 1980s," in *Reflections on Shattered Windows*, ed. Gary Okihiro et al. (Pullman: Washington State University Press, 1988), 165–174. See also Yen Le Espiritu, *Asian American Women and Men: Labor, Laws, and Love* (Lanham, MD: Rowman and Littlefield, 2000); Claire Jean Kim, "The Racial Triangulation of Asian Americans," *Politics & Society* 27, no. 1 (1999): 105–138; Luther Spoehr, "Sambo and the Heathen Chinee: Californians' Racial Stereotypes in the Late 1870s," *Pacific Historical Reviews* 43, no. 2 (1973): 185–204; Amy Uyematsu, "The Emergence of Yellow Power in America," *Gidra*, October 1969: 8–11; Ellen D. Wu, *The Color of Success: Asian Americans and the Origins of the Model Minority* (Princeton, NJ: Princeton University Press, 2014); Madeline Y. Hsu, *The Good Immigrants: How the Yellow Peril Became the Model Minority* (Princeton, NJ: Princeton University Press, 2015).

38 Erika Lee, *The Making of Asian America: A History* (New York: Simon and Shuster, 2015); Lisa Lowe, *Immigrant Acts* (Durham, NC: Duke University Press, 1996); Kent A. Ono and Vincent Pham, *Asian Americans and the Media* (Malden, MA: Polity Press, 2009); Nancy Wang Yuen, *Reel Inequality: Hollywood Actors and Racism* (New Brunswick, NJ: Rutgers University Press, 2016).

39 John Mellencamp, "Welcome to Chinatown," track 7 on *John Cougar* (UK, Riva, 1979), compact disc.

40 Espiritu, *Asian American Women and Men*, 16–41; E. Lee, *The Making of Asian America*, 67.

41 E. Lee, *The Making of Asian America*, 67 and 87; Cathy J. Schlund-Vials, K. Scott Wong, and Jason Oliver Chang, eds., *Asian America: A Primary Source Reader* (New Haven, CT: Yale University Press, 2017), 39.

42 Katharine H. S. Moon, "Military Prostitution and the U.S. Military in Asia," *Asia-Pacific Journal* 7, no. 3 (2009): 1–10; Ji-Yeoh Yuh, *Beyond the Shadow of Camptown: Korean Military Brides in America* (New York: New York University Press, 2004).

43 Espiritu, *Asian American Women and Men*, 86–107; Ono and Pham, *Asian Americans and the Media*, 63–79.

44 Espiritu, *Asian American Women and Men*, 94.

45 Patricia Hill Collins, "Learning from the Outsider Within: The Sociological Significance of Black Feminist Thought," *Social Problems* 33, no. 6 (1986): 17.

46 Espiritu, *Asian American Women and Men*, 87; see also Ono and Pham, *Asian Americans and the Media*, 63–79.

47 Espiritu, *Asian American Women and Men*, 98.

48 Quoted in Sam Levin, "'We're the Geeks, the Prostitutes': Asian American Actors on Hollywood's Barriers," *Guardian*, April 11, 2017, https://www.theguardian.com/world/2017/apr/11/asian-american-actors-whitewashing-hollywood.

49 For more information about the impact of racialization on internalized racism, see Memmi, *The Colonizer and the Colonized*; and Osajima, "Asian Americans as the Model Minority."

50 Uyematsu, "The Emergence of Yellow Power in America," 8.

51 The Third World Liberation Front consisted of the following organizations: the Black Students Union, Mexican American Student Confederation, Philippine American Collegiate Endeavor, Intercollegiate Chinese for Social Action, Asian American Political Alliance, Latin American Students Organization, and American Indian Student Organization. For more information about the struggle for ethnic studies, see Russell Jeung et al. eds. *Mountain Movers: Student Activism and the Emergence of Asian American Studies*. Los Angeles: University of California Los Angeles Asian American Studies Center, 2019.

52 For more information about Asian American student activism during this period, see E. Lee, *The Making of Asian America*; Karen Umemoto, "'On Strike!' San Francisco State College Strike, 1968–1969: The Role of Asian American Students," in *Contemporary Asian America: A Multidisciplinary Reader*, ed. Min Zhou and James V. Gatewood (New York: New York University Press, 2000): 49–79.

53 Umemoto, "'On Strike!," 49.

54 E. Lee, *The Making of Asian America*, 306.

55 For a more detailed discussion of the building of Asian American studies, see Sucheng Chan, *In Defense of Asian American Studies: The Politics of Teaching and Program Building* (Champaign: University of Illinois Press, 2005).

56 Gidra Staff, "S.I. Rips Gidra!," *Gidra*, Los Angeles: May 1969 volume 1, no. 2, 1.
    Also in the same issue, the editorial staff of *Gidra* wrote: "It was very appropriate
    that S. I. Hayakawa spoke at Disneyland, for his comments indicate that he lives
    in a fantasyland and is possessed of very little awareness of what is going on"
    (Gidra Staff, editorial, *Gidra*, Los Angeles: May 1969 volume 1, no. 2, 2.)

57 Gidra Staff, "S.I. Rips Gidra!," 4. "Issei" refers to the first generation of Japanese
    Americans, "nisei" to the second generation, and "sansei" to the third generation.

58 Gidra Staff, "S.I. Rips Gidra!," *Gidra*, Los Angeles: May 1969 volume 1, no. 2, 1.

59 Laura Ho, "Pigs, Pickets & a Banana," *Gidra*, May 1969: 1 and 7.

60 For example, see David and Derthick, "What Is Internalized Oppression, and So
    What?"; Glenn, "Yearning for Lightness"; Kohli, "Unpacking Internalized
    Racism"; Millan and Alvarez. "Asian Americans and Internalized Oppression";
    Nadal, "Colonialism"; Pyke, "What Is Internalized Racial Oppression and Why
    Don't We Study It?"; Lindsay Perez Huber, Robin N. Johnson, and Rita Kohli,
    "Naming Racism: A Conceptual Look at Internalized Racism in U.S. Schools,"
    Chicana/o Latina/o Law Review 26, no. 1 (2006): 183–206; N. Kim, *Imperial
    Citizens*.

61 For example, see Choi, Israel, and Maeda, "Development and Evaluation of the
    Internalized Racism in Asian Americans Scale,"; Frances C. Shen, Yu-Wei Wang,
    and Jane L. Swanson, "Development and Initial Validation of the Internalization
    of Asian American Stereotypes Scale," *Cultural Diversity and Ethnic Minority
    Psychology* 17, no. 3 (2011): 283–294; Hyung Chol Yoo, Matthew J. Miller, and
    Pansy Yip, "Validation of the Internalization of the Model Minority Myth
    Measure (IM-4) and Its Link to Academic Performance and Psychological
    Adjustment among Asian American Adolescents," *Cultural Diversity and Ethnic
    Minority Psychology* 21, no. 2 (2015): 237–246.

62 Shen, Wang, and Swanson, "Development and Initial Validation of the Internal-
    ization of Asian American Stereotypes Scale," 283.

63 Choi, Israel, and Maeda, "Development and Evaluation of the Internalized
    Racism in Asian Americans Scale," 52.

64 Choi, Israel, and Maeda, "Development and Evaluation of the Internalized
    Racism in Asian Americans Scale," 60.

65 For example, see Espiritu, *Home Bound: Filipino American Lives across Cultures,
    Communities, and Countries* (Berkeley: University of California Press, 2003);
    Nazli Kibria, *Becoming Asian American: Second-Generation Chinese and Korean
    American Identities* (Baltimore, MD: Johns Hopkins University Press, 2002);
    Karen Pyke and Tran Dang, "'FOB' and 'Whitewashed': Identity and Internal-
    ized Racism among Second Generation Asian Americans," *Qualitative Sociology*
    26, no. 2 (2003): 147–172; Shalini Shankar, "Speaking Like a Model Minority:
    'FOB' Styles, Gender, and Racial Meanings among Desi Teens in Silicon Valley,"
    Journal of Linguistic Anthropology 18, no. 2 (2008): 268–289.

66 Pyke and Dang, "'FOB' and 'Whitewashed,'" 152.

67 Pyke and Dang, "'FOB' and 'Whitewashed,'" 149.

68 For a theoretical discussion of this topic, see Pyke, "What Is Internalized Racial
    Oppression and Why Don't We Study It?"

69 Charlotte Brooks, "In the Twilight Zone between Black and White: Japanese
    American Resettlement and Community in Chicago, 1942–1945," *Journal of
    American History* 86, no. 4 (2000): 1655.

70 Tuan, *Forever Foreigners or Honorary Whites?*

71 For example, see Rosalind S. Chou and Joe R. Feagin, *The Myth of the Model Minority: Asian Americans Facing Racism* (Boulder, CO: Paradigm, 2008); Kibria, *Becoming Asian American*; Pyke and Dang, "'FOB' and 'Whitewashed'"; Tuan, *Forever Foreigners or Honorary Whites?*

72 Chou and Feagin, *The Myth of the Model Minority*, 5.

73 Although I identify various types of exposure that can trigger shifts away from behaviors that perpetuate internalized racism, I acknowledge that not everyone might have such exposures. As Mike's case exemplifies, exposure to ethnic organizations did not alter his perceptions that are associated with internalized racism. However, for the majority of the study participants, these were the dominant recurring themes (critical exposures to ethnic organizations and co-ethnics) that contributed to their emerging critical consciousness—which is a key factor in influencing shifts away from perceptions and behaviors that perpetuate internalized racism.

74 For more information about Japanese Americans and World War II military service, see E, Lee, *The Making of Asian America*. However, as Mire Koikari has argued, the stories of Japanese American World War II veterans were much more complex than simple narratives of blind loyalty and patriotism, ("'Japanese Eyes, American Heart': Politics of Race, Nation, and Masculinity in Japanese American Veterans' WWII Narratives," *Men and Masculinities* 12, no. 5 [2010]: 547–564).

75 Andy, a study participant, describes it as "essentially a government-sponsored thing that the overseas Chinese kids basically—well, young adults from eighteen to like twenty-three . . . go back to Taiwan, for the summer. They teach us cultural stuff." The program is called "the Love Boat" because it is held on a large ship, and parents who send their children hope that they will meet potential future spouses on the trip.

76 Gidra Staff, editorial, 2.

77 William Wei, *The Asian American Movement* (Philadelphia: Temple University Press, 1992), 29–30. Wei quoted from the Rice Paper Collective's publication, Rice Paper. See Rice Paper Collective, Madison Asian Union, "Rice Paper," *Rice Paper* 1, no. 1 (Summer 1974): 3.

78 Freire, *Pedagogy of The Oppressed*, 17. See also Chou and Feagin, *The Myth of the Model Minority*, 194–200; Kohli, "Unpacking Internalized Racism," 384–385.

79 Chou and Feagin, *The Myth of the Model Minority*, 190–214.

Chapter 4   Crafting "Sharp Weapons" in the Heartland

1 In this chapter, I use the term "Asian American cultural productions" in the broadest sense, to include all cultural art forms and productions—both visual and literary.

2 Amy Ling, "Introduction: What's in a Name" in *Yellow Light: The Flowering of Asian American Arts*, ed. Amy Ling (Philadelphia: Temple University Press, 1999), 4.

3 Lisa Lowe, *Immigrant Acts* (Durham, NC: Duke University Press, 1996), x.

4 Lowe, *Immigrant Acts*, 65.

5 Alicia Schmidt Camacho, *Migrant Imaginaries: Latino Cultural Politics in the U.S.-Mexico Borderlands* (New York: New York University Press, 2008), 5.

6 Lowe, *Immigrant Acts*, x.

7 Leslie Bow, *Partly Colored: Asian Americans and Racial Anomaly in the Segregated South* (New York: New York University Press, 2010), 4, 20; See also Homi K.

Bhabha, *The Location of Culture* (London: Routledge, 1994; Elaine Kim, "Interstitial Subjects: Asian American Visual Art as a Site for New Cultural Conversations," in *Fresh Talk/Daring Gazes: Conversations on Asian American Art*, ed. Elaine Kim, Margo Machida, and Sharon Mizota (Berkeley: University of California Press, 2003): 1–50; John Kuo Wei Tchen, "Believing Is Seeing: Transforming Orientalism and the Occidental Gaze," in *Asia/America: Identities in Contemporary Asian American Art*, ed. Margo Machida, Vishakha N. Desai, and John Kuo Wei Tchen (New York: Asia Society Galleries, 1994), 13–25.

8   Bhabha, *The Location of Culture*, 4.

9   Bow, *Partly Colored*; Michael Omi and Howard Winant, *Racial Formation in the United States: From the 1960s to the 1990s*, 2nd ed. (New York, Routledge, 1994).

10 Camacho, *Migrant Imaginaries*, 9.

11 For more information about Asian American art history, see Gordon H. Chang, Mark Dean Johnson, and Paul J. Karlstrom, eds., *Asian American Art: A History, 1850–1970* (Stanford, CA: Stanford University Press, 2008); Shelley Sang-Hee Lee and Sharon Spain, "Chronology of Asian American Art and History, 1850–1965," in *Asian American Art*, 477–512.

12 Kim, "Interstitial Subjects," 13.

13 For more on Noguchi, see Gordon H. Chang, "Emerging from the Shadows: The Visual Arts and Asian American History," in *Asian American Art*, ix–xv; Kim, "Interstitial Subjects." One of Noguchi's best-known cultural contributions is the Noguchi Table, which was a part of Herman Miller's 1947 collection. Noguchi was incarcerated with other Japanese Americans during World War II. However, unlike other Japanese Americans, Noguchi voluntarily went to an internment camp (in Poston, Arizona), where his intention was to assist with the landscape design. He hoped to create a more livable camp life for the internees. After realizing that nobody was interested in his ideas, Noguchi sought to leave the camp but was imprisoned there instead. While in the camp, Noguchi felt like an outsider: other Japanese Americans saw him as a turncoat, and the U.S. military saw him as an enemy of the state, no different from other internees. Noguchi was released after seven months with help from his friend and collaborator, John Collier, head of the Bureau of Indian Affairs. For additional information on Noguchi's life and camp experience, see Roach, Jackson Wiley. "Play Mountain, episode 351." In *99% Invisible*, edited by Avery Trufelman. April 23, 2019. https://99percentinvisible.org/episode/play-mountain/.

14 Bert Winther, "Isamu Noguchi," *Art Journal* 54, no. 3 (1995): 113–115.

15 E. Kim, "Interstitial Subjects," 15.

16 E. Kim, "Interstitial Subjects," 15.

17 Sam Hunter, *Isamu Noguchi* (New York: Abbeville Press, 1978), 56.

18 Paul Bonesteel, dir., *The Mystery of George Masa* (Bonesteel Films, 2002), https://vimeo.com/ondemand/georgemasa. . See also William A. Hart Jr., "George Masa: The Best Mountaineer," in *May We All Remember Well: A Journal of History & Cultures of West North Carolina*, ed. Robert Brunk (Asheville, NC: Robert S. Brunk Auction Services, 1997), 1:249–275.

19 Hart, "George Masa," 252–253. It is important to acknowledge the role of settler colonialism in Masa's work. His mapping and photographs of the area assisted in the development of a national park. The U.S. National Parks are made possible by US government's land theft from the Indigenous Peoples. In this case, theft of land from the Cherokee Indians in the Appalachian Mountain region.

20 Edward W. Said, *Orientalism* (New York: Vintage, 1979), 3.

21 Chang, "Emerging from the Shadows," x.

22 Bonesteel, *The Mystery of George Masa*.

23 Grace Wang, *Soundtracks of Asian America: Navigating Race through Musical Performance* (Durham, NC: Duke University Press, 2015); Said, *Orientalism*.

24 Lowe, *Immigrant Acts*, xxi.

25 For more information about Asian American activism through art during this 1960s and 1970s, see Chris Iijima, "Pontifications on the Distinction between Grains of Sand and Yellow Pearls," in *Asian Americans: The Movement and the Moment*, ed. Steve Louie and Glenn Omatsu (Los Angeles: University of California Los Angeles Asian American Studies Press, 2001): 3–15; Naoko Shibusawa, "'The Artist Belongs to the People': The Odyssey of Taro Yashima," *Journal of Asian American Studies* 8, no. 3 (2005): 257–275; Oliver Wang, "Between the Notes: Finding Asian America in Popular Music," *American Music* 19, no. 4 (2001): 439–465; Daryl J. Maeda, *Chains of Babylon: The Rise of Asian America* (Minneapolis: University of Minnesota Press, 2009); William Wei, *The Asian American Movement* (Philadelphia: Temple University Press, 1992); Deborah Anne Wong, *Speak It Louder: Asian Americans Making Music* (New York: Routledge, 2004).

26 Wei, *The Asian American Movement*, 64.

27 Quoted in Wei, *The Asian American Movement*, 64.

28 Maeda, *Chains of Babylon*, 127–153.

29 Iijima, Chris Kando, Nobuko Miyamoto, and Charlie Chin, "We Are the Children," track 6 on *A Grain of Sand: Music for the Struggle of Asians in America* (Brooklyn, NY: Paredon, 1973), cassette tape.

30 Chris Iijima, "Chris Iijima: Lawyer, Singer, and Songwriter," in *Yellow Light*, 320.

31 Wei, *The Asian American Movement*, 67.

32 Quoted in Maeda, *Chains of Babylon*, 151.

33 Quoted in Maeda, *Chains of Babylon*, 151.

34 Wang, "Between the Notes," 459.

35 Chang, "Emerging from the Shadows," xi.

36 Chang, "Emerging from the Shadows," xi.

37 Yen Le Espiritu, *Asian American Panethnicity: Bridging Institutions and Identities*, (Philadelphia: Temple University Press, 1992), 2; Linda Trinh Võ, *Mobilizing Asian America* (Philadelphia: Temple University Press, 2004), 10–12.

38 Chang, "Emerging from the Shadows," xi.

39 Yen Le Espiritu, "Asian American Panethnicity: Contemporary National and Transnational Possibilities," in *Not Just Black and White: Historical and Contemporary Perspectives on Immigration, Race, and Ethnicity in the United States*, ed. Nancy Foner and George M. Fredrickson (New York: Russell Sage Foundation, 2004), 217–234; Lowe, *Immigrant Acts*; Mae M. Ngai, "Transnationalism and the Transformation of the 'Other': Response to the Presidential Address," *American Quarterly* 57, no. 1 (2005): 59–65; Judy Tzu-Chun Wu, *Radicals on the Road: Internationalism, Orientalism, and Feminism during the Vietnam Era* (Ithaca, NY: Cornell University Press, 2013).

40 Yen Le Espiritu, *Asian American Women and Men: Labor, Laws, and Love* (Lanham, MD: Rowman and Littlefield, 2000), 98.

41 Renee Tajima-Peña, dir. and prod., *My America: Honk if You Love Buddha*. San Francisco: Independent Television Service and Public Broadcasting Service, 1997, DVD.

42 Wei, *The Asian American Movement*, 29–30.

43 William Wei, *The Asian American Movement* (Philadelphia: Temple University Press, 1992), 29–30. Wei quoted from the Rice Paper Collective's publication, Rice Paper. See Rice Paper Collective, Madison Asian Union, "Rice Paper," *Rice Paper* 1, no. 1 (Summer 1974): 3

44 Rice Paper Collective, Madison Asian Union, "Rice Paper," *Rice Paper* 1, no. 2 (Winter 1975): 6.

45 Bill Wu, "University of Michigan-Ann Arbor, MI. East Wind Position Paper," Madison Asian Union, *Rice Paper* 1, no. 2 (Winter 1975): 11–13.

46 Helen Zia, *Asian American Dreams: The Emergence of an American People* (New York: Farrar, Straus and Giroux, 2000), 56–58.

47 Zia, Asian American Dreams, 57.

48 Quoted in Zia, *Asian American Dreams*, 59.

49 Quoted in Zia, *Asian American Dreams*, 60.

50 Tunde Wey, "Soh Suzuki," Detroit Urban Innovation Exchange, September 12, 2012, https://www.uixdetroit.com/people/sohsuzuki.aspx.

51 Frances Kai-Hwa Wang, "Detroit Asian Youth Project Celebrates 10 Years of Mentorship," NBC News, August 22, 2014, https://www.nbcnews.com/news/asian-america/detroit-asian-youth-project-celebrates-10-years-mentorship-n186796. See also S. Mahnke, "Projecting Cultural Space: Vincent Chin Murals," Immigrant Imprints: Filipinx Spaces in Michigan, 2017, http://fil-am-michigan.matrix.msu.edu/mural.html.

52 Wey, "Soh Suzuki."

53 Quoted in F. Wang, "Detroit Asian Youth Project Celebrates 10 Years of Mentorship."

54 Noenoe K. Silva, *Aloha Betrayed: Native Hawaiian Resistance to American Colonialism* (Durham, NC: Duke University Press, 2004), 108–119 and 182.

55 Christine Choy and Renee Tajima-Peña, directors. *Who Killed Vincent Chin?* Film News Now Foundation and Public Broadcasting Service (WTVS), 1987, 89 mins. DVD.

56 James C. Scott, *Domination and the Arts of Resistance: Hidden Transcripts* (New Haven, CT: Yale University Press, 1990), 4, 115; see also pages 108–118.

57 Renee Tajima-Peña, dir. and prod., *My America: Honk if You Love Buddha*. San Francisco: Independent Television Service and Public Broadcasting Service, 1997, DVD.

58 Renee Tajima-Peña, "Renee Tajima-Peña, Filmmaker," in *Yellow Light*, 290–291.

59 Tajima-Peña's work includes *No Más Bebés* (2015), a documentary about Latinx immigrant women who were tricked into being sterilization during labor, and *Asian Americans* (2020), a PBS documentary series on the history of Asian Americans.

60 Lowe, *Immigrant Acts*, x.

61 Tony Lam, dir., *Vincent Who?* (Asian Pacific Americans for Progress and Tony Lam Films, 2009).

62 Jane Hseu, "Teaching Race and Space through Asian American and Latino Performance Poetry: I Was Born with Two Tongues' *Broken Speak* and Sonido Ink(quieto)'s *Chicano, Illnoize*," *Asian American Literature* 4 (2013): 9–10.

63 I Was Born With Two Tongues. "Excuse Me, AmeriKa." Track 15 on *Broken Speak*. Fist of Sound, 1999. Compact disc.

64 Wong, *Speak It Louder*, 3.

65 Bao Phi, "The Measure," in Bao Phi, *Thousand Star Hotel* (Minneapolis, MN: Coffee House Press, 2017), 34–35.

66 Phi, "Vincent Chin: 30 Years Later," *Star Tribune*, June 18, 2012, http://www.startribune.com/vincent-chin-30-years-later/159414685/.

67 To maintain the study participants' anonymity, I do not provide details of their specific cultural productions. However, I refer to general themes that all artist participants explore in their productions.

68 Espiritu, *Asian American Women and Men*, 98.

69 Quoted in Tchen, "Believing Is Seeing," 13.

70 Iijima, "Pontifications on the Distinction between Grains of Sand and Yellow Pearls," 4.

71 A. Ling, "Introduction," 4.

72 Espiritu, *Asian American Women and Men*, 98.

73 Quoted in Maeda, *Chains of Babylon*, 151.

74 Lowe, *Immigrant Acts*, x.

75 Lowe, *Immigrant Acts*, x.

76 Bhabha, *The Location of Culture*, 4.

77 This occurs in Season 7. Frank Darabont, developed by. *The Walking Dead*. U.S.: American Movie Classics (AMC), 2010–2021.

78 For the single exception, see Nina Sharma, "Not Dead," *The Margins*, Asian American Writer's Workshop, July 20, 2017, https://aaww.org/not-dead/.

Conclusion

1 Cathy Park Hong, *Minor Feelings: An Asian American Reckoning* (New York: One World, 2020), 55.

2 William Wei, *The Asian American Movement* (Philadelphia: Temple University Press, 1992), 29–30. Wei quoted from the Rice Paper Collective's publication, Rice Paper. See Rice Paper Collective, Madison Asian Union, "Rice Paper," Rice Paper 1, no. 1 (Summer 1974): 3.

3 Yen Le Espiritu, *Asian American Women and Men: Labor, Laws, and Love* (Lanham, MD: Rowman and Littlefield, 2000), 98.

4 Homi K. Bhabha, *The Location of Culture* (London: Routledge, 1994), 4.

Epilogue

1 Viet Thanh Nguyen, "Asian Americans Are Still Caught in the Trap of the 'Model Minority' Stereotype. And It Creates Inequality for All," *Time*, July 6, 2020, https://time.com/5859206/anti-asian-racism-america/.

2 A 2020 Pew Research Center report, along with numerous news reports, has documented dramatic increases in anti-Asian and anti-Black violence during the period of COVID-19 and Black Lives Matter. See Neil G. Ruiz, Juliana M. Horowitz, and Christine Tamir, "Many Black and Asian Americans Say They Have Experienced Discrimination amid the COVID-19 Outbreak" (Washington: Pew Research Center, 2020) https://www.pewresearch.org/social-trends/2020/07/01/many-black-and-asian-americans-say-they-have-experienced-discrimination-amid-the-covid-19-outbreak/. See also Anh Do, "'You Started the Corona!' As Anti-Asian Hate Incidents Explode, Climbing past 800, Activists Push for Aid," *Los Angeles Times*, July 5, 2020, https://www.latimes.com/california/story/2020

-07-05/anti-asian-hate-newsom-help; Suyin Haynes, "As Coronavirus Spreads, So Does Xenophobia and Anti-Asian Racism," *Time*, March 6, 2020, https://time .com/5797836/coronavirus-racism-stereotypes-attacks.

3   Drishti Pillai, Aggie J. Yellow Horse, and Russell Jeung, "The Rising Tide of Violence and Discrimination against Asian American and Pacific Islander Women and Girls," Stop AAPI Hate coalition and National Asian Pacific American Women's Forum, 2021, https://stopaapihate.org/wp-content/uploads /2021/05/Stop-AAPI-Hate_NAPAWF_Whitepaper.pdf.

4   Quoted in Elisha Fieldstadt, "Suspect in Deadly Atlanta-Area Spa Shootings Charged with 8 Counts of Murder," NBC News, March 17, 2021, https://www .nbcnews.com/news/us-news/suspect-deadly-atlanta-area-spa-shootings-says-he -was-motivated-n1261299.

5   Nancy Wang Yuen, "Atlanta Spa Shooting Suspect's 'Bad Day' Defense, and America's Sexualized Racism Problem," NBC News, March 18, 2021, https://www .nbcnews.com/think/opinion/atlanta-spa-shooting-suspect-s-bad-day-defense -america-s-ncna1261362.

6   Christal Hayes, "Georgia Sheriff Spokesman in Spa Shootings Removed from Case after 'Bad Day' Comment, Controversial Anti-China Shirt," *USA Today*, March 18, 2021, https://www.usatoday.com/story/news/nation/2021/03/18/georgia -sheriffs-spokesman-jay-baker-appeared-promote-racist-shirt/4745028001/.

7   Quoted in Alana Wise, "Biden Announces New Steps to Tackle Anti-Asian Violence and Discrimination," NPR, March 30, 2021, https://www.npr.org/2021 /03/30/982736783/biden-announces-new-steps-to-tackle-anti-asian-violence-and -discrimination.

8   Nicole Chavez, "A Woman's Brutal Attack Exposed a Torrent of Anti-Asian Violence after the Atlanta Shootings," CNN, April 1, 2021, https://www.cnn.com /2021/04/01/us/asian-americans-attacks/index.html; Michael R. Sisak, "NYPD Adding Undercover Patrols to Combat Anti-Asian Attacks," Associated Press, March 25, 2021, https://apnews.com/article/new-york-police-coronavirus -pandemic-crime-hate-crimes-87ea322ab8a4ebbc72748838698efabf.

9   V. Nguyen, "Asian Americans Are Still Caught in the Trap of the 'Model Minority' Stereotype."

10 For example, see V. Nguyen, "Asian Americans Are Still Caught in the Trap of the 'Model Minority' Stereotype."; Cady Lang, "The Asian American Response to Black Lives Matter is Part of a Long Complicated History," *Time*, June 26, 2020, https://time.com/5851792/asian-americans-black-solidarity-history/; Ali Rogin and Amna Nawaz, "'We Have Been through This Before': Why Anti-Asian Hate Crimes Are Rising amid Coronavirus," *PBS News Hour*, June 25, 2020, https:// www.pbs.org/newshour/nation/we-have-been-through-this-before-why-anti-asian -hate-crimes-are-rising-amid-coronavirus.

11 Claire Wang, "Trump's 'Kung Flu' Slur, Pervasive Scapegoating Recall a Brutal Decades-Old Hate Crime, NBC News, June 23, 2020, https://www.nbcnews.com /news/asian-america/anniversary-vincent-chin-death-relevant-era-kung-flu-covid -10-n1231888.

12 William Tong, "AG William Tong: Vincent Chin & Rise of Anti-AAPI Hate Crimes," NowThis News, May 21, 2021, https://www.youtube.com/watch?v =MCSqdAf_Bvo.

13 Other large Midwestern universities established Asian American studies programs later, including the University of Illinois Urbana-Champaign (1997),

Northwestern University (1999), University of Minnesota (2003), Michigan State University (2004), Ohio State University (2006), Purdue University and Indiana University (2007), and University of Illinois Chicago (2010).

14 Asian Americans Advancing Justice, "TEAACH ACT," accessed August 31, 2022, https://www.advancingjustice-chicago.org/teaach/.

15 Illinois General Assembly, "HB 0376," accessed August 31, 2022, https://www.ilga .gov/legislation/102/HB/PDF/10200HB0376.pdf.

16 Abigail Metsch, "Proposed Bill Works to Include Asian American History into Public School Curriculum," WCIA.com, February 26, 2021, https://www.wcia .com/news/proposed-bill-works-to-include-asian-american-history-into-public -school-curriculum/.

17 Quoted in Reuters, "Illinois House Passes Bill Mandating Asian American History in Schools." NBC News, April 15, 2021, https://www.nbcnews.com/news /asian-america/illinois-house-passes-bill-mandating-asian-american-history -schools-rcna690.

18 Grace Hauck, "'A Watershed Moment': Illinois Becomes First State to Mandate Asian American History in Public Schools," *USA Today*, July 9, 2021, https:// www.usatoday.com/story/news/nation/2021/07/09/illinois-mandates-asian -american-history-public-schools-teaach-act/7472690002/.

19 Dorothy Fujita-Rony, "Illuminating Militarized Rupture: Four Asian American Community-Based Archives," *Journal of Asian American Studies* 23, no. 1 (2020), 1.

20 Fujita-Rony, "Illuminating Militarized Rupture," 2.

21 For example, a Vietnamese American businessman in Houston, Texas, received death threats from members of his own Vietnamese American community after putting up a billboard that reads in English and Vietnamese: "Black Lives Matter, Stop Racism." See Brittany Britto, "Black Lives Matter Billboard Sparks Controversy, Death Threats in Houston's Vietnamese Community," *Houston Chronicle*, July 11, 2020, https://www.houstonchronicle.com/news/houston-texas/houston /article/Black-Lives-Matter-billboard-sparks-controversy-15402180.php. See also Wen Liu, "Complicity and Resistance: Asian American Body Politics in Black Lives Matter," *Journal of Asian American Studies* 21, no. 3 (2018): 421–451.

22 Mai Der Vang. "In the Year of Permutations," Academy of American Poets, 2020, Originally published with the Shelter in Poems initiative on poets.org, https:// poets.org/poem/year-permutations.

23 Amy Uyematsu, "The Emergence of Yellow Power in America," *Gidra*, October 1969: 8.

24 Mari Matsuda, *Where Is Your Body? And Other Essays on Race, Gender, and the Law* (Boston: Beacon Press, 1996), 150.

25 Richard Delgado, "Derrick Bell's Toolkit—Fit to Dismantle That Famous House?," *New York University Law Review* 75, no. 2 (2000): 283; see also 290–291.

26 Renee Tajima-Peña, "Renee Tajima-Peña, Filmmaker," in *Yellow Light: The Flowering of Asian American Arts*, ed. Amy Ling (Philadelphia: Temple University Press, 1999), 290.

Bibliography

"1981: The Pekin Chinks High School Team Becomes the Pekin Dragons." Chinese American Museum of Chicago. Accessed September 3, 2021. https://ccamuseum .org/1981-the-pekin-chinks-high-school-team-becomes-the-pekin-dragons/.

Abelmann, Nancy. *The Intimate University: Korean American Students and the Problems of Segregation*. Durham, NC: Duke University Press, 2009.

Almaguer, Tomás. *Racial Fault Lines: The Historical Origins of White Supremacy in California*. Berkeley: University of California Press, 1994.

Aoki, Keith, "No Right to Own?: The Early Twentieth-Century 'Alien Land Laws' as a Prelude to Internment," *Boston College Third World Law Journal* 19, no.1 (1998): 37–72.

Asian Americans Advancing Justice. "TEAACH ACT." Accessed August 31, 2022. https://www.advancingjustice-chicago.org/teaach/.

Badger, Emily, and Kevin Quealy. "Where Is America's Heartland? Pick Your Map." *New York Times*, January 3, 2017. https://www.nytimes.com/interactive/2017/01 /03/upshot/where-is-americas-heartland-pick-your-map.html.

Bean, Frank D., and Gillian Stevens. *America's Newcomers and the Dynamics of Diversity*. New York: Russell Sage Foundation, 2003.

Bernstein, Mary, and Marcie De la Cruz. "'What Are You?': Explaining Identity as a Goal of the Multiracial Hapa Movement." *Social Problems* 56, no. 4 (2009): 722–745.

Bhabha, Homi K. *The Location of Culture*. London: Routledge, 1994.

Binkley, Collin. "Trump Administration Rescinds Rule on Foreign Students." *AP News*, July 14, 2020. https://apnews.com/38b6562b7aaa73ea66fb72b06472e05d.

Blocker, Jack. *A Little More Freedom: African Americans Enter the Urban Midwest, 1860–1930*. Columbus: Ohio State University Press, 2009.

Bloemraad, Irene. *Becoming a Citizen: Incorporating Immigrants and Refugees in the United States and Canada*. Berkeley: University of California Press, 2006.

Bonesteel, Paul, dir. *The Mystery of George Masa*. Asheville, NC: Bonesteel Films, 2002. https://vimeo.com/ondemand/georgemasa.

Bow, Leslie. *Partly Colored: Asian Americans and Racial Anomaly in the Segregated South*. New York: New York University Press, 2010.

Bradley, Mark Philip. *Vietnam at War*. New York: Oxford University Press, 2009.

Britto, Brittany. "Black Lives Matter Billboard Sparks Controversy, Death Threats in Houston's Vietnamese Community." *Houston Chronicle*, July 11, 2020. https://www.houstonchronicle.com/news/houston-texas/houston/article/Black-Lives-Matter-billboard-sparks-controversy-15402180.php.

Bronfenbrenner, Urie. *The Ecology of Human Development: Experiments by Nature and Design*. Cambridge, MA: Harvard University Press, 1979.

Bronfenbrenner, Urie. "Ecology of the Family as a Context for Human Development: Research Perspectives." *Developmental Psychology* 22, no. 6 (1986): 723–742.

Brooks, Charlotte. "In the Twilight Zone between Black and White: Japanese American Resettlement and Community in Chicago, 1942–1945." *Journal of American History* 86, no. 4 (2000): 1655–1687.

Camacho, Alicia Schmidt. *Migrant Imaginaries: Latino Cultural Politics in the U.S.-Mexico Borderlands*. New York: New York University Press, 2008.

Caswell, Michelle. "Seeing Yourself in History: Community Archives and the Fight against Symbolic Annihilation." *Public Historian* 36, no. 4 (2014): 26–37.

Chan, Sucheng. *Asian Americans: An Interpretive History*. New York: Twayne Publishers, 1991.

Chan, Sucheng. "Cambodians in the United States: Refugees, Immigrants, American Ethnic Minority." *Oxford Research Encyclopedia of American History*, September 3, 2015. https://doi.org/10.1093/acrefore/9780199329175.013.317.

Chan, Sucheng. *In Defense of Asian American Studies: The Politics of Teaching and Program Building*. Champaign: University of Illinois Press, 2005.

Chan, Sucheng. *The Vietnamese American 1.5 Generation: Stories of War, Revolution, Flight, and New Beginnings*. Philadelphia: Temple University Press, 2006.

Chang, Gordon H. "Emerging from the Shadows: The Visual Arts and Asian American History." In *Asian American Art: A History, 1850–1970*, edited by Gordon H. Chang, Mark Dean Johnson, and Paul J. Karlstrom, ix–xv. Stanford, CA: Stanford University Press, 2008.

Chang, Gordon H., Mark Dean Johnson, and Paul J. Karlstrom, eds. *Asian American Art: A History, 1850–1970*. Stanford, CA: Stanford University Press, 2008.

Chavez, Nicole. "A Woman's Brutal Attack Exposed a Torrent of Anti-Asian Violence after the Atlanta Shootings." CNN, April 1, 2021. https://www.cnn.com/2021/04/01/us/asian-americans-attacks/index.html.

Chinese Exclusion Act of 1882. Pub. L. No. 47-126, 22 Stat. 58 (1882).

Choi, Andrew Young, Tania Israel, and Hotaka Maeda. "Development and Evaluation of the Internalized Racism in Asian Americans Scale (IRAAS)." *Journal of Counseling Psychology* 64, no. 1 (2017): 52–64.

Chou, Rosalind S., and Joe R. Feagin. *The Myth of the Model Minority: Asian Americans Facing Racism*. Boulder, CO: Paradigm Publishers, 2008.

Choy, Catherine Ceniza. *Empire of Care: Nursing and Migration in Filipino American History*. Durham, NC: Duke University Press, 2003.

Choy, Christine, and Renee Tajima-Peña, directors. *Who Killed Vincent Chin?*. Detroit: Film News Now Foundation and Public Broadcasting Service (WTVS), 1987, 89 mins. DVD.

Collins, Patricia Hill. "Learning from the Outsider Within: The Sociological Significance of Black Feminist Thought." *Social Problems* 33, no. 6 (1986): 14–32.

Corbin, Juliet, and Anselm Strauss. *Basics of Qualitative Research: Techniques and Procedures for Developing Grounded Theory*. 3rd ed. Thousand Oaks, CA: Sage, 2007.

Darabont, Frank, developed by. *The Walking Dead*. U.S.: American Movie Classics (AMC), 2010–2021.

David, E.J.R. "Testing the Validity of the Colonial Mentality Implicit Association Test and the Interactive Effects of Covert and Overt Colonial Mentality on Filipino American Mental Health." *Asian American Journal of Psychology* 1, no. 1 (2010): 31–45.

David, E.J.R., and Annie O. Derthick. "What Is Internalized Oppression, and So What?" In *Internalized Oppression: The Psychology of Marginalized Groups*, ed. E.J.R. David, 1–30. New York: Springer, 2013.

Delgado, Richard. "Derrick Bell's Toolkit—Fit to Dismantle That Famous House?" *New York University Law Review* 75, no. 2 (2000): 283–307.

Delgado, Richard, and Jean Stefancic. "Critical Race Theory and Criminal Justice." *Humanity & Society* 31, no. 1 (2007): 133–145.

Desai, Jigna, and Khyati Y. Joshi. "Introduction: Discrepancies in Dixie: Asian Americans and the South." In *Asian Americans in Dixie: Race and Migration in the South*, edited by Khyati Y. Joshi and Jigna Desai, 1–30. Urbana: University of Illinois Press, 2013.

Dhingra, Pawan. "Introduction to *Journal of Asian American Studies*, Special Issue on the Midwest," in "Special Issue on the Midwest," edited by Pawan Dhingra. Special Issue, *Journal of Asian American Studies* 12, no. 3 (2009): 239–246.

Dhingra, Pawan. *Managing Multicultural Lives: Asian American Professionals and the Challenge of Multiple Identities*. Stanford, CA: Stanford University Press, 2007.

Do, Anh. "'You Started the Corona!' As Anti-Asian Hate Incidents Explode, Climbing past 800, Activists Push for Aid." *Los Angeles Times*, July 5, 2020. https://www.latimes.com/california/story/2020-07-05/anti-asian-hate-newsom -help.

Du Bois, William Edward Burghardt. *The Souls of the Black Folk: Essays and Sketches*. Chicago: A. C. McClurg, 1903.

Duan, Carlina. "Michigan in Color: Our Sacrifice, Our Shame." *Michigan Daily*, February 2, 2014. http://www.michigandaily.com/opinion/michigan-color -american-plus-chinese.

Edmunds, R. David. "Introduction: A People of Persistence." In *Enduring Nations: Native Americans in the Midwest*, edited by R. David Edmunds, 1–14. Champaign: University of Illinois Press, 2008.

Erikson, Erik. *Identity: Youth and Crisis*. New York: Norton, 1968.

Espiritu, Yen Le. *Asian American Panethnicity: Bridging Institutions and Identities*. Philadelphia: Temple University Press, 1992.

Espiritu, Yen Le. "Asian American Panethnicity: Contemporary National and Transnational Possibilities." In *Not Just Black and White: Historical and Contemporary Perspectives on Immigration, Race, and Ethnicity in the United States*, edited by Nancy Foner and George M. Fredrickson, 217–234. New York: Russell Sage Foundation, 2004.

Espiritu, Yen Le. *Asian American Women and Men: Labor, Laws, and Love*. Lanham, MD: Rowman and Littlefield, 2000.

Espiritu, Yen Le. "'Beyond the 'Boat People': Ethnicization of American Life." *Amerasia Journal* 15, no. 2 (1989): 49–67.

Espiritu, Yen Le. "Filipino Navy Stewards and Filipina Health Care Professionals: Immigration, Work and Family Relations." *Asian and Pacific Migration Journal* 11, no. 1 (2002): 47–66.

Espiritu, Yen Le. *Home Bound: Filipino American Lives across Cultures, Communities, and Countries*. Berkeley: University of California Press, 2003.

Fanon, Frantz. *The Wretched of the Earth*. Translated by Constance Farrington. New York: Grove Press, 1963.

Fieldstadt, Elisha. "Suspect in Deadly Atlanta-Area Spa Shootings Charged with 8 Counts of Murder." NBC News, March 17, 2021. https://www.nbcnews.com/news/us-news/suspect-deadly-atlanta-area-spa-shootings-says-he-was-motivated-n11261299.

Fordham, Signithia, and John U. Ogbu. "Black Students' School Success: Coping with the 'Burden of 'Acting White.'" *Urban Review* 18, no. 3 (1986): 176–206.

Freire, Paulo. *Pedagogy of the Oppressed*. Translated by Myra Berman Ramos. London: Penguin, 1996.

"The French Lead the Way: c. 1500–1763." Library of Congress. Accessed August 23, 2022. https://www.loc.gov/collections/pioneering-the-upper-midwest/articles-and-essays/history-of-the-upper-midwest-overview/french-lead-the-way.

Fujita-Rony, Dorothy. "Illuminating Militarized Rupture: Four Asian American Community-Based Archives." *Journal of Asian American Studies* 23, no. 1 (2020): 1–27.

Furiya, Linda. *Bento Box in the Heartland: My Japanese Girlhood in Whitebread America*. Berkeley, CA: Seal Press, 2006.

Garcia, Juan R. Introduction to *Mexicans in the Midwest*, edited by Juan R. Garcia, Ignacio M. Garcia, and Thomas Gelsinon, vii–xvi. Tucson: University of Arizona Press, 1989.

Garcia Coll, Cynthia, Gontran Lamberty, Renee Jenkins, Harriet Pipes McAdoo, Keith Crnic, Barbara Hanna Wasik, and Heidie Vázquez García. "An Integrative Model for the Study of Developmental Competencies in Minority Children." *Child Development* 67, no. 5 (1996): 1891–1914.

Gibson, Margaret A. *Accommodation without Assimilation: Sikh Immigrants in American High School*. Ithaca, NY: Cornell University Press, 1988.

Gidra Staff, editorial, *Gidra*, Los Angeles: May 1969 volume 1, no. 2, 2.

Gidra Staff, "S.I. Rips Gidra!," *Gidra*, Los Angeles: May 1969 volume 1, no. 2, 1 and 4.

Glenn, Evelyn Nakano. "Yearning for Lightness: Transnational Circuits in the Marketing and Consumption of Skin Lighteners." *Gender & Society* 22, no. 3 (2008): 281–302.

Gold, Steven J. *Refugee Communities: A Comparative Field Study*. Newbury Park, CA: Sage, 1992.

Gordon, Milton M. *Assimilation in American Life: The Role of Race, Religion, and National Origins*. New York: Oxford University Press, 1964.

Haddel, Chad C. "Foreign Students in the United States: Policies and Legislation." Washington: Domestic Social Policy Division, Congressional Research Service, 2008.

Hallberg, Carl V. "'For God, Country, and Home': The Ku Klux Klan in Pekin, 1923–1925." *Journal of the Illinois State Historical Society* 77, no. 2 (1984): 82–90 and 92–93.

Hart, William A., Jr. "George Masa: The Best Mountaineer." In *May We All Remember Well: A Journal of History & Cultures of West North Carolina*, edited by Robert Brunk, 1:249–275. Asheville, NC: Robert S. Brunk Auction Services, 1997.

Hauck, Grace. "'A Watershed Moment': Illinois Becomes First State to Mandate Asian American History in Public Schools." *USA Today*, July 9, 2021. https://www

.usatoday.com/story/news/nation/2021/07/09/illinois-mandates-asian-american
-history-public-schools-teaach-act/7472690002.

Hayes, Christal. "Georgia Sheriff Spokesman in Spa Shootings Removed from Case
after 'Bad Day' Comment, Controversial Anti-China Shirt." *USA Today*,
March 18, 2021. https://www.usatoday.com/story/news/nation/2021/03/18/georgia
-sheriffs-spokesman-jay-baker-appeared-promote-racist-shirt/4745028001/.

Haynes, Suyin. "As Coronavirus Spreads, So Does Xenophobia and Anti-Asian
Racism." *Time*, March 6, 2020. https://time.com/5797836/coronavirus-racism
-stereotypes-attacks/.

Hein, Jeremy. *From Vietnam, Laos, and Cambodia: A Refugee Experience in the United
States*. New York: Twayne Publishers, 1995.

Hill, Mark E. "Skin Color and the Perception of Attractiveness among African
Americans: Does Gender Make a Difference?" *Social Psychology Quarterly* 65, no. 1
(2002): 77–91.

Hirschman, Charles, Philip Kasinitz, and Josh DeWind, editors. *The Handbook of
International Migration: The American Experience*. New York: Russell Sage
Foundation, 1999.

Ho, Laura. "Pigs, Pickets & a Banana." *Gidra*, May 1969: 1 and 7.

Hoeffel, Elizabeth M., Sonya Rastogi, Myoung Ouk Kim, and Hasan Shahid. "The
Asian Population: 2010." United States Census Bureau, March 2012. https://www
.census.gov/content/dam/Census/library/publications/2012/dec/c2010br-11.pdf.

Hoganson, Kristin L. *The Heartland: An American History*. New York: Penguin Press,
2019.

Hong, Cathy Park. *Minor Feelings: An Asian American Reckoning*. New York: One
World, 2020.

Hseu, Jane. "Teaching Race and Space through Asian American and Latino Perfor-
mance Poetry: I Was Born with Two Tongues' *Broken Speak* and Sonido
Ink(quieto)'s *Chicano, Illnoize*." *Asian American Literature* 4 (2013): 4–14.Hsu,
Madeline Y. *The Good Immigrants: How the Yellow Peril Became the Model
Minority*. Princeton, NJ: Princeton University Press, 2015.

Huber, Lindsay Perez, Robin N. Johnson, and Rita Kohli. "Naming Racism: A
Conceptual Look at Internalized Racism in U.S. Schools." *Chicana/o Latina/o
Law Review* 26, no. 1 (2006): 183–206.

Hunter, Margaret L. "'If You're Light You're Alright': Light Skin Color as Social
Capital for Women of Color." *Gender & Society* 16, no. 2 (2002): 175–193.

Hunter, Sam. *Isamu Noguchi*. New York: Abbeville Press, 1978.

I Was Born With Two Tongues. "Excuse Me, AmeriKa." Track 15 on *Broken Speak*.
Fist of Sound, 1999. Compact disc.

Iijima, Chris. "Chris Iijima, Lawyer, Singer, and Songwriter." In *Yellow Light: The
Flowering of Asian American Arts*, edited by Amy Ling, 319–323. Philadelphia:
Temple University Press, 1999.

Iijima, Chris. "Pontifications on the Distinction between Grains of Sand and Yellow
Pearls." In *Asian Americans: The Movement and the Moment*, edited by Steve Louie
and Glenn Omatsu, 3–15. Los Angeles: University of California Los Angeles Asian
American Studies Press, 2001.

Iijima, Chris Kando, Nobuko Miyamoto, and Charlie Chin. "We Are the Children."
Track 6 on *A Grain of Sand: Music for the Struggle of Asians in America*. Brooklyn,
NY: Paredon, 1973. Cassette tape.

Illinois General Assembly. "HB 0376." Accessed August 31, 2022. https://www.ilga
.gov/legislation/102/HB/PDF/10200HB0376.pdf.

Integrated Public Use Microdata Sample-Current Population Survey Data.
IPUMS-CPS University of Minnesota, 2008–2018. www.ipums.org.

Jeung, Russell, Karen Umemoto, Harvey Dong, Eric Mar, Lisa Hirai Tsuchitani,
and Arnold Pan, eds. *Mountain Movers: Student Activism and the Emergence of
Asian American Studies.* Los Angeles: University of California Los Angeles Asian
American Studies Center, 2019.

Keil, Janine. 2006. "Voices of Hope, Voices of Frustration: Deciphering U.S. Admis-
sion and Visa Policies for International Students." Washington: Institute for the
Study of Diplomacy, Edmund A. Walsh School of Foreign Service, Georgetown
University, 2006.

Kiang, Lisa, and Andrew J. Supple. "Theoretical Perspectives on Asian American
Youth and Families in Rural and New Immigrant Destinations." In *Rural Ethnic
Minority Youth and Families in the United States: Theory, Research, and Applica-
tions,* edited by Lisa J. Crockett and Gustavo Carlo, 71–88. Cham, Switzerland:
Springer International Publishing, 2016.

Kibria, Nazli. *Becoming Asian American: Second-Generation Chinese and Korean
American Identities.* Baltimore, MD: Johns Hopkins University Press, 2002.

Kim, Claire Jean. "Are Asians the New Blacks? Affirmative Action, Anti-Blackness,
and the 'Sociometry' of Race." *Du Bois Review* 15, no. 2 (2018): 1–28.

Kim, Claire Jean. "The Racial Triangulation of Asian Americans." *Politics & Society*
27, no. 1 (1999): 105–138.

Kim, Claire Jean. "Unyielding Positions: A Critique of the 'Race' Debate." *Ethnicities*
4, no. 3 (2004): 337–355.

Kim, Elaine. "Interstitial Subjects: Asian American Visual Art as a Site for New
Cultural Conversations." In *Fresh Talk/Daring Gazes: Conversations on Asian
American Art,* edited by Elaine Kim, Margo Machida, and Sharon Mizota, 1–50.
Berkeley: University of California Press, 2003.

Kim, Elaine. Preface to *Charlie Chan Is Dead: An Anthology of Contemporary Asian
American Fiction,* edited by Jessica Hagedorn, vii–xiv. New York: Penguin Press, 1993.

Kim, Nadia Y. *Imperial Citizens: Koreans and Race from Seoul to LA.* Stanford, CA:
Stanford University Press, 2008.

Kohli, Rita. "Unpacking Internalized Racism: Teachers of Color Striving for Racially
Just Classrooms." *Race Ethnicity and Education* 17, no. 3 (2014): 367–387.

Koikari, Mire. "'Japanese Eyes, American Heart': Politics of Race, Nation, and
Masculinity in Japanese American Veterans' WWII Narratives." *Men and
Masculinities* 12, no. 5 (2010): 547–564.

Kravetz, Andy. "Pekin Teacher Resigns amid Allegations of Racist, Anti–Semitic
Internet Posts." *Journal Star,* April 23, 2019. https://www.pjstar.com/story/news
/education/2019/04/24/pekin-teacher-resigns-amid-allegations/5352852007/.

Kwon, Yaejoon. "Transcolonial Racial Formation: Constructing the 'Irish of the
Orient' in U.S.-Occupied Korea." *Sociology of Race and Ethnicity* 3, no. 2 (2017):
268–281.

Lam, Tony, dir. *Vincent Who?* Asian Pacific Americans for Progress and Tony Lam
Films, 2009.

Lang, Cady. "The Asian American Response to Black Lives Matter Is Part of a Long
Complicated History." *Time,* June 26, 2020. https://time.com/5851792/asian
-americans-black-solidarity-history/.

Laybourn, Wendy Marie. "Korean Transracial Adoptee Identity Formation." *Sociology Compass* 11, no.1 (2017): 1–9.

Lee, Erika. "Asian American Studies in the Midwest," in "Special Issue on the Midwest," edited by Pawan Dhingra. Special Issue, *Journal of Asian American Studies* 12, no. 3 (2009): 247–273.

Lee, Erika. *The Making of Asian America: A History.* New York: Simon and Schuster, 2015.

Lee, Jennifer, and Frank D. Bean. *The Diversity Paradox: Immigration and the Color Line in Twenty-First Century America.* New York: Russell Sage Foundation, 2010.

Lee, Robert G. *Orientals: Asian Americans in Popular Culture.* Philadelphia: Temple University Press, 1999.

Lee, Shelley Sang-Hee, and Sharon Spain. "Chronology of Asian American Art and History, 1850–1965." In *Asian American Art: A History, 1850–1970,* edited by Gordon H. Chang, Mark Dean Johnson, and Paul J. Karlstrom, 477–512. Stanford, CA: Stanford University Press, 2008.

Lee, Stacey J. *Up against Whiteness: Race, School, and Immigrant Youth.* New York: Teachers College Press, 2005.

Levin, Sam. "'We're the Geeks, the Prostitutes': Asian American Actors on Hollywood's Barriers." *Guardian,* April 11, 2017. https://www.theguardian.com/world/2017/apr/11/llin-american-actors-whitewashing-hollywood.

Levitt, Peggy, and Mary C. Waters, eds. 2002. *The Changing Face of Home: The Transnational Lives of the Second Generation.* New York: Russell Sage Foundation, 2002.

Ling, Amy, "Introduction: What's in a Name," in *Yellow Light: The Flowering of Asian American Arts,* ed. Amy Ling. Philadelphia: Temple University Press, 1999, 4.

Ling, Huping. *Chinese Chicago: Race, Transnational Migration, and Community since 1870.* Stanford, CA: Stanford University Press, 2012.

Ling, Huping. *Chinese St. Louis: From Enclave to Cultural Community.* Philadelphia: Temple University Press, 2004.

Ling, Huping. "Reconceptualizing Chinese American Community in St. Louis: From Chinatown to Cultural Community." *Journal of American Ethnic History* 24, no. 2 (2005): 65–101.

Lipsitz, George. "The Racialization of Space and the Spatialization of Race: Theorizing the Hidden Architecture of Landscape." *Landscape Journal* 26, no. 1 (2007): 10–23.

Lipsitz, George. "Space." In *Keywords for American Cultural Studies,* 2nd ed., edited by Bruce Burgett and Glenn Hendler, 227–231. New York: New York University Press, 2014. http://search.credoreference.com/content/entry/nyupacs/space/0.

Liu, Wen. "Complicity and Resistance: Asian American Body Politics in Black Lives Matter." *Journal of Asian American Studies* 21, no. 3 (2018): 421–451.

Loewen, James. *Sundown Towns: A Hidden Dimension of American Racism.* New York: New Press, 2005.

Lofland, John, David Snow, Leon Anderson, and Lyn Lofland. *Analyzing Social Settings: A Guide to Qualitative Observation and Analysis.* Belmont, CA: Wadsworth Publishing, 2006.

Lowe, Lisa. *Immigrant Acts.* Durham, NC: Duke University Press, 1996.

Lynch, James P., and Rita J. Simon. *Immigration the World Over: Statutes, Policies, and Practices.* Lanham, MD: Rowman and Littlefield, 2003.

Maeda, Daryl J. *Chains of Babylon: The Rise of Asian America.* Minneapolis: University of Minnesota Press, 2009.

Mahnke, S. "Projecting Cultural Space: Vincent Chin Murals." Immigrant Imprints: Filipinx Spaces in Michigan, 2017. http://fil-am-michigan.matrix.msu.edu/mural.html.

Maira, Sunaina Marr. *Desis in the House: Indian American Youth Culture in New York City*. Philadelphia: Temple University Press, 2002.

Marrow, Helen B., "Assimilation in New Destinations," *Daedalus* 142, no. 3 (2013): 107–122.

Massey, Dorsey. *Space, Place, and Gender*. Minneapolis: University of Minnesota Press, 1994.

Matsuda, Mari. "We Will Not Be Used." *University of California Los Angeles Asian American Pacific Islands Law Journal* 1, no.1 (1993): 79–84.

Matsuda, Mari. *Where Is Your Body? : and Other Essays on Race, Gender, and the Law*. Boston: Beacon Press, 1996.

Maxwell, Morgan, Joshua Brevard, Jasmine Abrams, and Faye Belgrave. "What's Color Got to Do with It? Skin Color, Skin Color Satisfaction, Racial Identity, and Internalized Racism among African American College Students." *Journal of Black Psychology* 41, no. 5 (2015): 438–461.

McFadden, Robert D. "Grace Lee Boggs, Human Rights Advocate for 7 Decades, Dies at 100." *New York Times*, October 5, 2015. https://www.nytimes.com/2015/10/06/us/grace-lee-boggs-detroit-activist-dies-at-100.html.

McKee, Kimberly D. *Disrupting Kinship: Transnational Politics of Korean Adoption in the United States*. Urbana: University of Illinois Press, 2019.

Mellencamp, John. "The Great Midwest." Track 4 on *John Cougar*. UK: Riva, 1979. Compact disc.

Mellencamp, John. "Welcome to Chinatown." Track 7 on *John Cougar*. UK: Riva, 1979. Compact disc.

Memmi, Albert. *The Colonizer and the Colonized*. Translated by Howard Greenfeld. Boston: Beacon Press, 1965.

Metsch, Abigail. "Proposed Bill Works to Include Asian American History into Public School Curriculum." WCIA.com, February 26, 2011. https://www.wcia.com/news/proposed-bill-works-to-include-asian-american-history-into-public-school-curriculum/.

Millan, James B., and Alvin N. Alvarez. "Asian Americans and Internalized Oppression: Do We Deserve This?" In *Internalized Oppression: The Psychology of Marginalized Groups*, edited by E.J.-R. David, 163–190. New York: Springer, 2013.

Moon, Katharine H. S. "Military Prostitution and the U.S. Military in Asia." *Asia-Pacific Journal* 7, no. 3 (2009): 1–10.

Nadal, Kevin L. "Colonialism: Societal and Psychological Impacts on Asian Americans and Pacific Islanders." In *Asian American Psychology: Current Perspectives*, edited by Nita Tewari and Alvin Alvarez, 153–172. New York: Psychology Press, 2009.

Neely, Brooke, and Michelle Samura. "Social Geographies of Race: Connecting Race and Space." *Ethnic and Racial Studies* 34, no. 11 (2011): 1933–1952.

Nelson, Kim Park. *Invisible Asians: Korean American Adoptees, Asian American Experiences, and Racial Exceptionalism*. New Brunswick, NJ: Rutgers University Press, 2016.

Ngai, Mae M. "The Architecture of Race in American Immigration Law: A Reexamination of the Immigrant Act of 1924." *Journal of American History* 86, no. 1 (1999): 67–92.

Ngai, Mae M. "Transnationalism and the Transformation of the 'Other': Response to the Presidential Address." *American Quarterly* 57, no. 1 (2005): 59–65.

Nguyen, Bich Minh. *Stealing Buddha's Dinner: A Memoir*. New York: Penguin Press, 2007.

Nguyen, Viet Thanh. "Asian Americans Are Still Caught in the Trap of the 'Model Minority' Stereotype. And It Creates Inequality for All." *Time*, July 6, 2020. https://time.com/5859206/anti-asian-racism-america/.

Olar, Jared. "How Did Pekin Get Its Name?" Pekin History, December 2011. https://fromthehistoryroom.wordpress.com/2015/12/12/how-did-pekin-get-its-name/, accessed July 18, 2020.

Omi, Michael, and Howard Winant. *Racial Formation in the United States: From the 1960s to the 1990s*. 2nd ed. New York, Routledge, 1994.

Ong, Paul, and Tania Azores. "The Migration and Incorporation of Filipino Nurses." In *The New Asian Immigration in Los Angeles and Global Restructuring*, edited by Paul Ong, Edna Bonacich, and Lucie Cheng, 164–195. Philadelphia: Temple University Press, 1994.

Ono, Kent A., and Vincent Pham. *Asian Americans and the Media*. Malden, MA: Polity Press, 2009.

"Oriental Discrimination." *Pekinois*, February 17, 1970. 2.

Osajima, Keith. "Asian Americans as the Model Minority: An Analysis of the Popular Press Image in the 1960s and 1980s." In *Reflections on Shattered Windows*, edited by Gary Okihiro, Shirley Hune, Arthur A. Hansen, and John M. Liu, 165–174. Pullman: Washington State University Press, 1988.

Park, Sharon. "Indochinese Refugee Resettlement Office, 1975–1986." *MNOPEDIA*, November 6, 2017. http://www.mnopedia.org/group/llinoisse-refugee-resettlement-office-1975-1986.

Peterson, William. "Success Story of One Minority Group in the U.S." *U.S. News and World Report*, December 26, 1966, 73–78.

Pew Research Center. "The Rise of Asian Americans." April 4, 2013. https://www.pewresearch.org/social-trends/2012/06/19/the-rise-of-asian-americans/.

Phi, Bao. "The Measure." In Bao Phi, *Thousand Star Hotel*, 34–35. Minneapolis, MN: Coffee House Press, 2017.

Phi, Bao. "Vincent Chin: 30 Years Later." *Star Tribune*, June 18, 2012. http://www.startribune.com/llinoi-chin-30-years-later/159414685/.

Phinney, Jean. "Ethnic Identity in Adolescents and Adults: Review in Research." *Psychological Bulletin* 108, no. 3 (1990): 499–514.

Phinney, Jean. "Stages of Ethnic Identity in Minority Group Adolescents." *Journal of Early Adolescence* 9, no. 1–2 (1989): 34–49.

Phinney, Jean, Irma Romero, Monica Nava, and Dan Huang. "The Role of Language, Parents, and Peers in Ethnic Identity among Adolescents in Immigrant Families." *Journal of Youth and Adolescence* 30, no. 2 (2001): 135–153.

Pillai, Drishti, Aggie J. Yellow Horse, and Russell Jeung. "The Rising Tide of Violence and Discrimination against Asian American and Pacific Islander Women and Girls." Stop AAPI Hate coalition and National Asian Pacific American Women's Forum, 2021. https://stopaapihate.org/wp-content/uploads/2021/05/Stop-AAPI-Hate_NAPAWF_Whitepaper.pdf.

Portes, Alejandro, and Rubén G. Rumbaut. *Immigrant America: A Portrait*. Berkeley: University of California Press, 1996.

Portes, Alejandro, and Rubén G. Rumbaut. *Legacies: The Story of the Immigrant Second Generation*. Berkeley: University of California Press, 2001.

Posadas, Barbara M. "Teaching about Chicago's Filipino Americans." *Organization of American Historians Magazine of History* 10, no. 4 (1996): 38–45.

Poston, Dudley L., Jr., and Hua Luo. "Chinese Student and Labor Migration to the United States: Trends and Policies since the 1980s." *Asian and Pacific Migration Journal* 16, no. 3 (2007): 323–355.

Pulido, Laura. *Black, Brown, Yellow, and Left: Radical Activism in Los Angeles*. Berkeley: University of California Press, 2006.

Pyke, Karen. "What Is Internalized Racial Oppression and Why Don't We Study It? Acknowledging Racism's Hidden Injuries." *Sociological Perspectives* 53, no. 4 (2010): 551–572.

Pyke, Karen and Tran Dang. "'FOB' and 'Whitewashed': Identity and Internalized Racism among Second Generation Asian Americans." *Qualitative Sociology* 26, no. 2, (2003): 147–172.

Rana, Junaid. *Terrifying Muslims: Race and Labor in the South Asian Diaspora*. Durham, NC: Duke University Press, 2011.

Ray, Robert D., Irena Kirkland, Gale W. McGee, Jonathan Moore, and Edward C. Schmults. "Report of the Indochinese Refugee Panel." Washington: Department of State, 1986.

Redden, Elizabeth. "Government Rescinds International Student Policy." *Inside Higher Education*, July 15, 2020. https://www.insidehighered.com/news/2020/07 /15/trump-administration-drops-directive-international-students-and-online -courses.

Reeves, Mary Helen. "A Descriptive Case Study of the Impact of 9/11 on International Student Visa Policy in the 20 Months Following the Attacks." PhD diss., University of Oklahoma, 2005.

Reuters. "Illinois House Passes Bill Mandating Asian American History in Schools." NBC News, April 15, 2021. https://www.nbcnews.com/news/llin-america/llinois -house-passes-bill-mandating-asian-american-history-schools-rcna690.

Rice Paper Collective, Madison Asian Union, *Rice Paper* 1, no. 2 (Winter 1975): 1–89.

Roach, Jackson Wiley. "Play Mountain, episode 351." In *99% Invisible*, edited by Avery Trufelman. April 23, 2019. https://99percentinvisible.org/episode/play-mountain/.

Rockquemore, Kerry Ann, and Patricia Arend. "Opting for White: Choice, Fluidity and Racial Identity Construction in Post Civil-Rights America." *Race & Society* 5, no. 1 (2002): 49–64.

Rodríguez, Noreen Naseem. "'This Is Why Nobody Knows Who You Are': (Counter) Stories of Southeast Asian Americans in the Midwest." *Review of Education, Pedagogy, and Cultural Studies* 42, no. 2 (2020): 157–174.

Rogin, Ali, and Amna Nawaz. "'We Have Been through This Before.' Why Anti-Asian Hate Crimes Are Rising amid Coronavirus." *PBS News Hour*, June 25, 2020. https://www.pbs.org/newshour/nation/we-have-been-through-this-before-why -anti-asian-hate-crimes-are-rising-amid-coronavirus.

Ruiz, Neil G. "Key Facts about the U.S. H-1B Visa Program." Pew Research Center, April 27, 2017. http://www.pewresearch.org/fact-tank/2017/04/27/key-facts-about -the-u-s-h-1b-visa-program/.

Ruiz, Neil G., Juliana M. Horowitz, and Christine Tamir. "Many Black and Asian Americans Say They Have Experienced Discrimination amid the COVID-19 Outbreak." Washington: Pew Research Center, 2020. https://www.pewresearch

.org/social-trends/2020/07/01/many-black-and-asian-americans-say-they-have
-experienced-discrimination-amid-the-covid-19-outbreak/.

Ruiz, Neil G., and Jynnah Radford. "New Foreign Student Enrollment at U.S. Colleges and Universities Doubled since Great Recession." Pew Research Center, November 20, 2017. http://pewrsr.ch/2hFbZCf.

Rumbaut, Rubén G. "Ages, Life Stages, and Generational Cohorts: Decomposing the Immigrant First and Second Generations in the United States." *International Migration Review* 38, no. 3 (2004): 1160–1205.

Rumbaut, Rubén G. "A Legacy of War: Refugees from Vietnam, Laos, and Cambodia." In *Origins and Destinies: Immigration, Race, and Ethnicity in Contemporary America*, edited by Silvia Pedraza and Rubén G. Rumbaut, 315–333. Belmont, CA: Wadsworth, 1996.

Rumbaut, Rubén G. "Vietnamese, Laotian, and Cambodian Americans." In *Asian Americans: Contemporary Trends and Issues*, edited by Pyong Gap Min, 262–289. Thousand Oaks, CA: Sage, 2005.Said, Edward W. *Orientalism*. New York: Vintage, 1979.

Sakamoto, Arthur, ChangHwan Kim, and Isao Takei. "Moving out of the Margins and into the Mainstream: The Demographics of Asian Americans in the New South." In *Asian Americans in Dixie: Race and Migration in the South*, edited by Khyati Y. Joshi and Jigna Desai, 131–164. Urbana: University of Illinois Press, 2013.

Schlund-Vials, Cathy J., K. Scott Wong, and Jason Oliver Chang, eds. *Asian America: A Primary Source Reader*. New Haven. CT: Yale University Press, 2017.

Schwalbe, Michael, Sandra Godwin, Daphne Holden, Douglas Schrock, Shealy Thompson, and Michele Wolkomir. "Generic Processes in the Reproduction of Inequality: An Interactionist Analysis." *Social Forces* 79, no. 2 (2000): 419–452.

Schwalm, Leslie. *Emancipation's Diaspora: Race and Reconstruction in the Upper Midwest*. Chapel Hill: University of North Carolina Press, 2009.

Scott, James C. *Domination and the Arts of Resistance: Hidden Transcripts*. New Haven, CT: Yale University Press, 1990.

Shankar, Shalini. "Speaking Like a Model Minority: 'FOB' Styles, Gender, and Racial Meanings among Desi Teens in Silicon Valley." *Journal of Linguistic Anthropology* 18, no. 2 (2008): 268–289.

Sharma, Nina. "Not Dead." *The Margins*. Asian American Writer's Workshop, July 20, 2017. https://aaww.org/not-dead/.

Shen, Frances C., Yu-Wei Wang, and Jane L. Swanson. "Development and Initial Validation of the Internalization of Asian American Stereotypes Scale." *Cultural Diversity and Ethnic Minority Psychology* 17, no. 3 (2011): 283–294.

Shibusawa, Naoko. "'The Artist Belongs to the People': The Odyssey of Taro Yashima." *Journal of Asian American Studies* 8, no. 3 (2005): 257–275.

Silva, Noenoe K. *Aloha Betrayed: Native Hawaiian Resistance to American Colonialism*. Durham, NC: Duke University Press, 2004.

Silverman, Edwin B. "Indochina Legacy: The Refugee Act of 1980." *Publius* 10, no. 1 (1980): 27–41.

Sisak, Michael R. "NYPD Adding Undercover Patrols to Combat Anti-Asian Attacks." Associated Press, March 25, 2021. https://apnews.com/article/new-york-police
-coronavirus-pandemic-crime-hate-crimes-87ea322ab8a4ebbc72748838698efabf.

Smith, James P., and Barry Edmonston, eds. *The New Americans: Economic, Demographic, and Fiscal Effects of Immigration*. Washington: National Academy Press, 1997.

Smithsonian Hirshhorn Museum. "Isamu Noguchi's 'Lunar Landscape' (1943–44)." Accessed September 17, 2022. https://hirshhorn.tumblr.com/post/153302672774 /we-are-a-landscape-of-all-we-have-seen.

Spickard, Paul. "Whither the Asian American Coalition?" *Pacific Historical Review* 76, no. 4 (2007): 585–604.

Spoehr, Luther. "Sambo and the Heathen Chinee: Californians' Racial Stereotypes in the Late 1870s." *Pacific Historical Reviews* 43, no. 2 (1973): 185–204.

Sukrungruang, Ira. *Talk Thai: The Adventures of Buddhist Boy.* Columbia: University of Missouri Press, 2010.

Taifel, Henri, and John Turner, eds. *An Integrative Theory of Intergroup Conflict.* Monterey, CA: Brooks/Cole, 1979.

Tajima-Peña, Renee, dir. and prod. *My America: Honk if You Love Buddha.* (San Francisco: Independent Television Service and Public Broadcasting Service, 1997), DVD.

Tajima-Peña, Renee. "Renee Tajima-Peña, Filmmaker." In *Yellow Light: The Flowering of Asian American Arts*, edited by Amy Ling, 287–294. Philadelphia: Temple University Press, 1999.

Tchen, John Kuo Wei. "Believing Is Seeing: Transforming Orientalism and the Occidental Gaze." In *Asia/America: Identities in Contemporary Asian American Art*, edited by Margo Machida, Vishakha N. Desai, and John Kuo Wei Tchen, 13–25. New York: Asia Society Galleries, 1994.

Telemaque, Eleanor Wong. *It's Crazy to Stay Chinese in Minnesota.* Bloomington, IN: Xlibris, 2000.

Tong, William. "AG William Tong: Vincent Chin & Rise of Anti-AAPI Hate Crimes." NowThis News, May 21, 2021. https://www.youtube.com/watch?v =MCSqdAf_BVo.

Trieu, Monica M. *Identity Construction among Chinese-Vietnamese Americans: Being, Becoming, and Belonging.* El Paso, TX: LFB Scholarly Publishing, 2009.

Tuan, Mia. *Forever Foreigners or Honorary Whites? The Asian Ethnic Experience Today.* Piscataway, NJ: Rutgers University Press, 2001.

Tuan, Mia, and Jiannbin Lee Shiao. *Choosing Ethnicity, Negotiating Race: Korean Adoptees in America.* New York, NY: Russell Sage Foundation, 2011.

Uchida, Yoshiko. *Desert Exile: The Uprooting of a Japanese American Family.* Seattle: University of Washington Press, 1982.

Umemoto, Karen. "'On Strike!' San Francisco State College Strike, 1968–1969: The Role of Asian American Students." In *Contemporary Asian America: A Multidisciplinary Reader*, edited by Min Zhou and James V. Gatewood, 49–79. New York: New York University Press, 2000.

University of Colorado Boulder. "National Interest Exceptions for Certain Travelers from the Schengen Area, United Kingdom, and Ireland," Accessed September 17, 2022, https://www.colorado.edu/isss/2020/07/20/national-interest-exceptions -certain-travelers-schengen-area-united-kingdom-and-ireland.

Urias, David, and Carol Camp Yeakey. "Analysis of the U.S. Student Visa System: Misperceptions, Barriers, and Consequences." *Journal of Studies in International Students* 13, no. 1 (2009): 72–109.

U.S. Census Bureau, American Community Survey 2019. "American Community Survey 1-Year Estimates Selected Population Profiles." https://www.census.gov/acs /www/data/data-tables-and-tools/data-profiles/2019/.

U.S. Census Bureau. "Census Regions and Divisions of the United States," https://www2.census.gov/geo/pdfs/maps-data/maps/reference/us_regdiv.pdf.

U.S. Citizenship and Immigration Services. "H-1B Specialty Occupation, DOD Cooperative Research and Development Project Workers, and Fashion Models." Accessed May 1, 2020. https://www.uscis.gov/working-united-states/temporary-workers/h-1b-specialty-occupations-dod-cooperative-research-and-development-project-workers-and-fashion-models.

U.S. Citizen and Immigration Services. "Legislation from 1981–1996." Accessed August 25, 2022. https://ilw.com/resources/Immigration_Legal_History_Legislation_1981–1996.pdf.

U.S. Immigration and Customs Enforcement. "SVEP Modifies Temporary Exemptions for Nonimmigrant Students Taking Online Courses during Fall 2020 Semester." July 6, 2020. https://www.ice.gov/news/releases/sevp-modifies-temporary-exemptions-nonimmigrant-students-taking-online-courses-during.

Uyeki, Eugene Shigemi. "Process and Patterns of Nisei Adjustment to Chicago, 1953." PhD diss., University of Chicago, 1953.

Uyematsu, Amy. "The Emergence of Yellow Power in America." *Gidra*, October 1969, 8–11.

Vang, Chia Youyee. *Hmong America: Reconstructing Community in Diaspora*. Champaign: University of Illinois Press, 2010.

Vang, Mai Der. "In the Year of Permutations," Academy of American Poets, 2020, Originally published with the Shelter in Poems initiative on poets.org, https://poets.org/poem/year-permutations.

Võ, Linda Trinh. *Mobilizing Asian America*. Philadelphia: Temple University Press, 2004.

Vue, Pao Lee. *Assimilation and the Gendered Color Line: Hmong Case Studies of Hip-Hop and Import Racing*. El Paso, TX: LFB Scholarly Publishing, 2012.

Wang, Claire. "Trump's 'Kung Flu' Slur, Pervasive Scapegoating Recall a Brutal Decades-Old Hate Crime." NBC News, June 23, 2020. https://www.nbcnews.com/news/asian-america/anniversary-vincent-chin-death-relevant-era-kung-flu-covid-10-n1231888.

Wang, Frances Kai-Hwa. "Detroit Asian Youth Project Celebrates 10 Years of Mentorship." NBC News, August 22, 2014. https://www.nbcnews.com/news/asian-america/detroit-asian-youth-project-celebrates-10-years-mentorship-n186796.

Wang, Grace. *Soundtracks of Asian America: Navigating Race through Musical Performance*. Durham, NC: Duke University Press, 2015.

Wang, Oliver. "Between the Notes: Finding Asian America in Popular Music." *American Music* 19, no. 4 (2001): 439–465.

Waters, Mary C., Patrick J. Carr, Maria J. Kefalas, and Jennifer Holdaway, eds. *Coming of Age in America: The Transition to Adulthood in the Twenty-First Century*. Berkeley: University of California Press, 2011.

Wei, William. *The Asian American Movement*. Philadelphia: Temple University Press, 1992.

Wey, Tunde. "Soh Suzuki." Detroit Urban Innovation Exchange, September 12, 2012. https://www.uixdetroit.com/people/sohsuzuki.aspx.

Wilkinson, Sook, and Victor Jew, eds. *Asian Americans in Michigan: Voices from the Midwest*. Detroit, MI: Wayne State University Press, 2015.

Winther, Bert. "Isamu Noguchi." *Art Journal* 54, no. 3 (1995): 113–115.

Wise, Alana. "Biden Announces New Steps to Tackle Anti-Asian Violence and Discrimination." NPR, March 30, 2021. https://www.npr.org/2021/03/30/982736783/biden-announces-new-steps-to-tackle-anti-asian-violence-and-discrimination.

Wong, Deborah Anne. *Speak It Louder: Asian Americans Making Music.* New York: Routledge, 2004.

World Health Organization. "Coronavirus disease (COVID-19): Situation Report—193." Accessed September 17, 2022, https://www.who.int/docs/default-source/coronaviruse/situation-reports/20200731-covid-19-sitrep-193.pdf.

Wu, Bill. "University of Michigan-Ann Arbor, MI. East Wind Position Paper." Madison Asian Union, *Rice Paper* 1, no. 2 (Winter 1975): 11–13.

Wu, Ellen D. *The Color of Success: Asian Americans and the Origins of the Model Minority.* Princeton, NJ: Princeton University Press, 2014.

Wu, Judy Tzu-Chun. *Radicals on the Road: Internationalism, Orientalism, and Feminism during the Vietnam Era.* Ithaca, NY: Cornell University Press, 2013.

Wu, Yu-Wei. "Transnational Teacher Mobility: Patterns, Qualities, Institutional Actors and Policy Implication." PhD diss., The Pennsylvania State University, 2012.

Yeun, Steven. "*Minari* post event Q&A." Accessed on December 15, 2020. https://watch.eventive.org/minari/play/600b3e847d9e040045241bbd.

Yoo, Hyung Chol, Matthew J. Miller, and Pansy Yip. "Validation of the Internalization of the Model Minority Myth Measure (IM-4) and Its Link to Academic Performance and Psychological Adjustment among Asian American Adolescents." *Cultural Diversity and Ethnic Minority Psychology* 21, no. 2 (2015): 237–246.

Yuen, Nancy Wang. "Atlanta Spa Shooting Suspect's 'Bad Day' Defense, and America's Sexualized Racism Problem." NBC News, March 18, 2021. https://www.nbcnews.com/think/opinion/atlanta-spa-shooting-suspect-s-bad-day-defense-america-s-ncna1261362.

Yuen, Nancy Wang. *Reel Inequality: Hollywood Actors and Racism.* New Brunswick, NJ: Rutgers University Press, 2016.

Yuh, Ji-Yeoh. *Beyond the Shadow of Camptown: Korean Military Brides in America.* New York: New York University Press, 2004.

Yuh, Ji-Yeoh. "Moved by War: Migration, Diaspora, and the Korean War." *Journal of Asian American Studies* 8, no. 3 (2005): 277–291.

Zhou, Min. "Growing Up American: The Challenge Confronting Immigrant Children and Children of Immigrants." *Annual Review of Sociology* 23, no. 1 (1997): 63–95.

Zhou, Min. "Social Capital and the Adaptation of the Second Generation: The Case of Vietnamese Youth in New Orleans." *International Migration Review* 28, no. 4 (1994): 821–845.

Zhou, Min, and Carl L. Bankston III. *Growing Up American: How Vietnamese Children Adapt to Life in the United States.* New York: Russell Sage Foundation, 1998.

Zia, Helen. *Asian American Dreams: The Emergence of an American People.* New York: Farrar, Straus and Giroux, 2000.

Index

Note: Page numbers in *italics* refer to illustrative matter.

About the Author

MONICA MONG TRIEU is an associate professor of American studies and Asian American studies at Purdue University. She received her PhD in sociology from the University of California, Irvine. Her research focuses on children of Asian immigrants and refugees, racialization, identity, and Asian American history. She is the author of *Identity Construction among Chinese-Vietnamese Americans: Being, Becoming, and Belonging,* and her work has also appeared in the *Journal of Asian American Studies, Sociology of Race and Ethnicity, Race Ethnicity and Education, Ethnicities,* and the *Journal of Ethnic and Migration Studies.*